The Human Person ~
Dignity Beyond Compare

Fourth Edition

Sister Terese Auer, O.P.
Dominican Sisters of St. Cecilia Congregation
Nashville, Tennessee

Nihil obstat: Reverend John Rock, S.J.
 Diocese of Nashville
 July 22, 2008

 Brother Ignatius Perkins, O.P., Ph.D., R.N., F.A.A.N.
 Diocese of Nashville
 July 23, 2012

Imprimatur: Most Reverend David R. Choby, S.T.B., J.C.L.
 Bishop, Diocese of Nashville
 July 22, 2008; July 23, 2012

Copyright © 2008 and 2021 by St. Cecilia Congregation, LBP Communications.
 All rights reserved. Revised in 2020.

Published by St. Cecilia Congregation
 801 Dominican Drive, Nashville, TN, 37228
 615-256-5486
 615-726-1333 (fax)
 www.nashvilledominican.org

Cover design: Sister Mary Justin Haltom, O.P., and Sister Cecilia Joseph Dulik, O.P.
Printed in the United States of America

ISBN 978-0-578-89341-9

*Dedicated to
Pope Saint John Paul the Great, whose memory we cherish,
and to the Young People of the world
whom he loved so much.
May they respond with courage
to the challenge he left them:*

**"... Be vigilant and alert 'sentinels,'
in order to be genuine protagonists of a new humanity."**

CONTENTS

Prologue 1

Part I: The Human Person

Chapter I: Introduction 7

Chapter II: Foundational Philosophical Principles 23

Chapter III: The Human Soul and Body 41

Chapter IV: Vegetative & Sensitive Powers (Part I) 51

Chapter V: Vegetative & Sensitive Powers (Part II) 69

Chapter VI: The Rational Powers of the Soul 85

Chapter VII: The Rational Soul 103

Conclusion: The Human Person ~ Dignity Beyond Compare 117

Part II: The Embodied Person

Chapter I: Human Love 129

Chapter II: Language of the Body 165

Chapter III: Love Worthy of the Human Person: Living Within the Truth...................175

Conclusion 211

Appendices

    A. Award Winning Essay 213

    B. Pope Saint John Paul to the People of the USA 215

    C. Key Thinkers Referred to in the Text 217

Glossary 219

Resources Cited 229

Prologue

You are about to begin the study of your wonderful **dignity** as a human person. Of all the topics you will investigate during your high school education, this is one of the most important - *and* exciting! In fact, this course will provide you with a foundation on which you will continue to grow, not only during these high school years but throughout your adult life.

Pope Saint John Paul the Great was a witness to the horrors of Nazism and Communism. He saw first-hand man's inhumane treatment of his fellowman. His response was to spend his life and his pontificate in defense of the worth and dignity of every human person. In his 1979 Apostolic Visit to our country, he told us:

*"I come to the United States of America as Successor of Peter
and as a pilgrim of faith.
It gives me great joy to be able to make this visit.
And so my esteem and affection go out
to all the people of this land.
I greet all Americans without distinction;
I want to meet you and tell you all --
men and women of all creeds and ethnic origins,
children and youth,
fathers and mothers, the sick and the elderly --
that God loves you,
that he has given you a dignity as human beings
that is beyond compare.
I want to tell everyone that the Pope is your friend
and a servant of your humanity."*

With his gift to the Church of the *Theology of the Body*, Saint John Paul II[1] deepened our understanding of the human person, bringing together the Church's traditional view of the person with new insights he had acquired in response to some of the problems we face in modern times.

Our study here will focus on that "traditional view" of the human person which serves as the basis for understanding not only Saint John Paul's teachings but also the teachings of the Catholic Church in general. This traditional view of the human person has been best expressed and explained by Saint Thomas Aquinas, a **Doctor of the Church** who lived in the 13th century. Saint John Paul was a stu-

---
[1] Throughout this text, we will refer to St. John Paul II as simply St. John Paul.

NOTES

Dignity - from the Latin *dignitas*, "worthiness," of high rank or worth.

Doctor of the Church - "Doctor" comes from the Latin *docere*, "to teach." In order to be called a Doctor of the Church, a person must:
1. possess a high degree of sanctity;
2. be very learned; and,
3. be declared a Doctor by the Church.

While this title is given to certain people on account of the great advantage the Church has gained from their doctrine, it does not mean that the Church is saying this person's teaching is completely free of error. The persons most recently declared Doctors of the Church are St. Teresa of Avila, St. Catherine of Siena and St. Thérèse of Lisieux.

dent of the **Thomist tradition**: he studied at the **Pontifical** University of St. Thomas Aquinas in Rome (commonly called the **Angelicum**), and he completed his final paper under the direction of one of the greatest Thomists of the 20th century, a Dominican priest named Father Reginald Garrigou-Lagrange.

St. Thomas (1225-1274) was a brilliant and holy man whose contributions to the Church are vast and enduring. He was a renowned philosopher and a theologian, a Dominican priest and a scholar, but most of all he was a devout Christian who spent long hours in prayer and possessed an extraordinary love for the Eucharist.

St. Thomas' keen intellect drew on the wisdom of both his contemporaries and his instructors in university (St. Albert the Great was his mentor), as well as the saints who had come before him, notably St. Augustine of Hippo. His search for the truth drove him to explore even the contributions of the pre-Christian philosophers, among them Plato and Aristotle.

If you are unfamiliar with St. Thomas Aquinas, you might wonder how the writings of a Dominican preacher from the Middle Ages can matter to young people of the 21st century. For anyone who has studied St. Thomas, however, the answer to that question is clear:

- ❖ St. Thomas believed that there is such a thing as "truth" and that the human person has the ability to come to know it.

- ❖ St. Thomas believed that the truth we can come to know about the real world is the same for all of us because reality is the same for all of us.

- ❖ St. Thomas believed that what we know by faith and what we know by using our reason alone can never be in contradiction if the faith is true and our reasoning is correct.

- ❖ St. Thomas believed that truth, at its source, is Jesus Christ.

For young people, who are especially interested in discovering the truth about themselves as human beings, St. Thomas Aquinas will be a superior teacher. For those who follow the lead of many in our modern society and think that truth is different for everyone, St. Thomas will be a formidable opponent. For those who question whether it is possible to be both a person who believes and a person who thinks, St.

NOTES

Thomist tradition - all that we have inherited from St. Thomas Aquinas' teaching in philosophy and theology. One who accepts Thomas' philosophical outlook is called a "Thomist."

Pontifical - the adjectival form of the word "Pontiff" (from the Latin *pontem facere*, "to build a bridge"). The title "Pontiff" or "Supreme Pontiff" is used in reference to the Pope, the person who is the chief "bridge-builder" on earth between God and man. A Pontifical University is one of eighteen universities and theological faculties in Rome affiliated with the Pope. These institutes of higher learning offer courses in philosophy, theology, Canon Law, and Church history.

Angelicum - from a title by which Saint Thomas Aquinas is often known: *Angelic Doctor*. Among the reasons given for this title are that St. Thomas wrote a great deal about angels, explaining their unique nature. Another reason for the title has to do with St. Thomas' personal life of virtue and holiness.

"Truth is the light of the human intellect. If the intellect seeks, from youth onwards, to know reality in its different dimensions, it does so in order to possess the truth: *in order to live the truth.* Such is the structure of the human spirit. Hunger for truth is its fundamental aspiration and expression."

Saint John Paul II,
Apostolic Letter to the Youth of the World

Thomas will be a model. For those who want to know and love God better, St. Thomas will be a sure guide.

Today, more than ever, there is a need for the truth to be known, especially the truth about the dignity of the human person. We need the light of that truth to shine into the murky waters of moral confusion. Harsh and noisy voices in our society cry out proclaiming a woman's "so-called right" to destroy the life within her womb. They demand scientific experimentation that threatens human dignity. They demean human sexuality and marriage. They threaten the weakest and most vulnerable members of our human family. In these all-important battles of our day, victory will not go to the loudest; victory will always be on the side of Truth.

During his 26 years as the Vicar of Christ on this earth, Pope Saint John Paul the Great never ceased to highlight the immense value and dignity of every human being. He challenged us all to do our part in building a civilization of love. To the Youth of the World in 2002, he said the following:

"The aspiration that humanity nurtures,
amid countless injustices and sufferings,
is the hope of a new civilization marked by freedom and peace.
But for such an undertaking, a new generation of builders is needed.
Moved not by fear or violence but by the urgency of genuine love,
they must learn to build, brick by brick,
the city of God within the city of man.
Allow me, dear young people, to consign this hope of mine to you:
you must be those "builders!"
You are the men and women of tomorrow.
The future is in your hearts and in your hands.
God is entrusting to you the task,
at once difficult and uplifting,
of working with him in the building of the civilization of love."

Let us reflect on Saint John Paul's challenging words and let them spur us on in our present study.

Part I:

The Human Person

Chapter I

THOMAS AQUINAS & TRUTH

Let us begin our study of the dignity of the human person by taking a close look at the man responsible for expressing the traditional teaching of the nature of the human person. In doing so, we will be following in the footsteps of Saint John Paul. He was well grounded in Thomism. In fact, he drew much of his understanding of the human person from the work of St. Thomas.

> **Vocabulary**
>
> *Dominican*   *subjective*   *philosophy*
> *truth*   *objective*   *revelation*

WHO IS ST. THOMAS AQUINAS?

Saint Thomas Aquinas was born in 1224 or 1225 at Roccasecca, the castle of his father, Count Landulf of Aquino, in Italy. He was the youngest son in a family of nine children. After spending his first five years at home under the care of his mother and nurse, Thomas was sent to study at the **Benedictine** monastery of Monte Cassino. His parents hoped he would one day become abbot there. Thomas was known to have a sharp intelligence and a remarkable memory. He memorized the Psalms, the Gospels, and the Epistles of Paul, and translated the **Fathers of the Church**, the sermons of St. Gregory, the letters of St. Jerome, and excerpts from the writings of St. Augustine - all by the age of 13!

At the age of 15, Thomas was sent to the University of Naples to continue his studies. It was during his studies at Naples that he was introduced to the writings of the ancient Greek philosopher, Aristotle. Thomas also came into contact with the newly established religious order, the **Dominicans**. Because he understood that God was calling him to join them, he abandoned the plans his family had for him. Despite the objections of his mother (his father had already died), Thomas offered himself at the **priory** of St. Dominic in Naples and received the Dominican habit at the age of 19.

NOTES

Benedictine - The religious order of both men and women following the Rule of St. Benedict of Nursia, which began in the first half of the sixth century. Their Rule of life emphasizes obedience to superiors, the importance of the balance between liturgical prayer and manual labor, and the value of community life. The Benedictine Rule is the foundation for monasticism in the Western Church.

Fathers of the Church - Title given to writers of the early Church who were notable for their correct teaching, and who by their writing, preaching, and holy lives defended the Faith.

Dominicans - Members of the Order founded by St. Dominic de Guzman in the 13th Century for the special purpose of preaching and teaching. It is formally known as the Order of Preachers.

Priory - The houses of monastic orders that are governed by religious superiors who are called "priors" or "prioresses."

NOTES

Novitiate - the period of formation and testing of those desiring to enter a religious community.

Doctor of Theology - an accomplished teacher of theology.

"You call him a Dumb Ox; I tell you that the Dumb Ox will bellow so loud that his bellowing will fill the world." St. Albert the Great (commenting on the nickname given to Thomas by some of his classmates because of his size and his quiet disposition)
-- G.K. Chesterton, *St. Thomas Aquinas*

Summa Theologiae - This Latin title means a "Summary of Theology." This best known work of St. Thomas was intended as a manual for those beginning to study theology in St. Thomas' day.

Holy See - Term for the central government of the Catholic Church. The word "see" comes from the Latin *sedes*, "chair." The chair was an ancient symbol of authority.

The Dominicans, aware of the possibility of encountering trouble with the Aquino family, attempted to rush Thomas to Rome and then on to Bologna. Thomas' mother, however, had her other sons capture Thomas on the way and force him to return home. A year later, realizing that it was impossible to change Thomas' mind, she relented and set him free.

Upon Thomas' release, the Dominicans sent him to Paris for his **novitiate** and further studies. From the ages of 23-27, Thomas studied in Cologne, Germany, under the Dominican scholar, St. Albert the Great. At the age of 26, he was ordained a priest. After completing his studies in Cologne, Thomas returned to Paris to complete his theological education, becoming a **Doctor of Theology** at the age of 31. During these years of study at Paris, Thomas composed his first major work: a commentary on the texts of the Fathers of the Church compiled by Peter the Lombard.

Thomas remained at the University of Paris three more years. As a professor of theology, he lectured on the Bible and held public debates on theological topics. He was known for entering into discussion in a charitable and humble manner with people who disagreed with him. In fact, Thomas was often able to present his opponents' arguments more clearly and convincingly than they themselves could do. He was able to do this because he loved the truth and was willing to embrace it wherever he found it. Presenting his opponents' positions as clearly as possible aided him in determining to what extent their views were true.

When he was 34-years-old, Thomas returned to Italy as professor of theology in the Dominican houses of study. Six years later he was asked to open a new house of study for Dominicans in Rome, and he taught there for two years. It was during this time that Thomas began to write his most important work, a new textbook of theology, entitled the ***Summa Theologiae***.

After serving as professor for a year at the court of Pope Clement IV, Thomas returned to the University of Paris for another three years of teaching. In addition to his academic responsibilities of lecturing on the Bible and conducting public debates, Thomas continued writing his *Summa Theologiae*. He also began to compose commentaries on many of Aristotle's works. Throughout the last 15 years of his life, Thomas was in constant contact with cardinals and popes, serving as a theologian for the **Holy See**.

At the age of 47, Thomas returned to Naples, Italy, and continued his work at the Dominican house of studies. The two small rooms in which he worked and slept are there today, adjoining the Dominican church in which Thomas is reported to have spent most of the nights in prayer.

On December 6, 1273, at the age of 49, Thomas had an extraordinary spiritual experience, after which he ceased his theological writing. When his friend and secretary asked him why he had given up his work, Thomas replied, "I cannot go on…. All that I have written seems to me like so much straw compared to what I have seen and what has been revealed to me."[1] The following year when he was on his way to attend the Ecumenical Council at Lyon, in France, he was injured in an accident. He died shortly afterwards on March 7, 1274. The room in which he died is preserved today as a place of prayer.

Thomas, the Philosopher

Philosophers are "lovers of wisdom" (Latin *philo*, love, and *sophia*, wisdom). Philosophical wisdom is the highest kind of natural knowledge a person can have, because it enables one to know an object in relation to its Creator. In other words, the wise person is the one who knows not only *what* a thing is but also *why* it is. The great philosophers are the ones who wrestle with the big questions: Who am I? Why am I here? What is the purpose of my life? Throughout history, philosophers have discussed these questions. They hold them up to the light of human reason (our ability to think), examine the evidence of human experience and draw conclusions that help to shape human civilization.

A Thinker with a God-Centered View of the World

The diagram below shows how St. Thomas viewed the world in relation to its Creator. He understood that we come from God and that we are to live in such a way that one day we can return to Him. The explanation that follows will help us understand what this means:

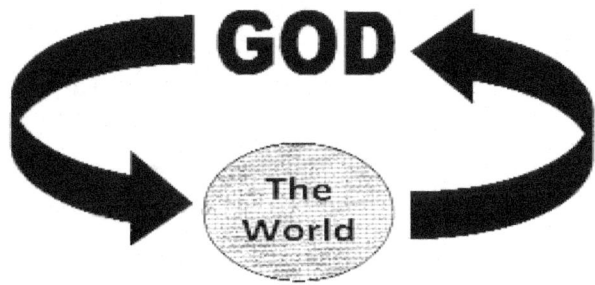

God is the Creator of the world and the universe as a whole. Within the world, He created human beings with minds able to understand much about the world. From that understanding we can come to

---

[1] William of Tocco, *Vita*, 47; *Fontes* 4:376377.

know that He exists.[2] This knowledge, acquired by reason without any added input from God, was meant to prepare us to receive faith (supernatural input) whereby we could know God more intimately. *The Catechism of the Catholic Church* expresses this beautifully:

> Man's faculties *[mental powers]* make him capable of coming to a knowledge of the existence of a personal God. But for man to be able to enter into real intimacy with him, God willed both to reveal himself to man and to give him the grace of being able to welcome this revelation in faith.[3]

It is possible for us to come to know *something* of God through the light of human reason. But this knowledge will never be "enough." Why not?

For one thing, because our minds are darkened by original sin, our reason often makes mistakes. Because of this, it is quite possible for people to reach incorrect conclusions in their thinking about God. For example, some have looked upon powerful forces of nature as being "gods," or have thought that there must be many gods. You can probably think of many other mistaken notions of God throughout history. Human reason can make mistakes.

In addition to this, there are truths about God and our relationship with Him that are far beyond human reason's ability to grasp by itself. This is because we are creatures with a limited nature, but God is divine, unlimited. We can never know all there is to know about Him.

Still, our human minds are such that we want to know Him, with a desire that is like an intellectual hunger and thirst. We need divine **revelation** if we are to know God more fully.

The wonderful thing is that God also wants us to know Him! He has revealed Himself. God has gradually made Himself known to us throughout human history through such people as Abraham, Moses, and the Prophets. This revelation of God reached its fullness in the coming of Jesus Christ, the Son of God. In Him, God took on our human nature so that we could become certain of God and know Him as a personal friend -- and not as a *distant* first cause of the world.[4] God reveals these truths to us through both Sacred Scripture and **Sacred Tradition**, which He entrusts to His Church to faithfully preserve and spread abroad. In our response of faith in God's revelation, our human reason receives divine assistance. In this way, our knowledge of God and the things of God can be certain.

---

[2] We will learn a few philosophical arguments for God's existence in the next chapter, after we have understood some basic philosophical parincples.

[3] *The Catechism of the Catholic Church*, #35.

[4] Pope Benedict XVI, *Spe Salvi*, #26.

NOTES

Revelation - In a religious sense, revelation refers to the manifestation of the hidden by God, as a result of the personal word and witness of God Himself.

Sacred Tradition - from the Latin meaning "handing over." The teachings and practices handed down, whether in oral or written form, separately from but not independent of Sacred Scripture.

Chapter I
THOMAS AQUINAS & TRUTH

A Believer in Objective Reality

One of the "things of God" is the world He created. Thomas understood that in creating the world, God established an order in it, an order which can be known. For example, the sun and the planets do not act *randomly*. There is a regularity or a pattern to their activity (an order) which we can come to know. This order is **objective**: it is *in the things* that exist. It is there whether we know it or not, whether we think about it or not. In addition, this order is in *all* of creation, from the tiniest cell in our bodies to the planets in our galaxy. This order in the whole of creation is what we mean by the term "objective reality." For example, the temperature is freezing at the North Pole whether or not *I* know it. Objective reality doesn't depend on *my* thinking; it depends on the will of the One who created things to be the way they are.

Objective - (related to object) whatever is determined by the object or based on the object. The term is often used in contrast to the "subjective," i.e., to what is based on the subject.

A Lover of Truth

St. Thomas understood that there is an objective reality. He also realized that the human mind was made precisely in order to know this reality. In fact, human beings are the only creatures on this earth who are able to know the world and *to **know** that we know it*. When we are able to know in our minds the order that exists in reality outside of our minds, then we say that our thinking is *true*.

Truth, according to St. Thomas, refers to this agreement between a person's thinking and reality. Truth is based on objective reality. For example, if I think that the sun revolves around the earth, when in fact it does not, then my thinking about it is false. I am in error. If I think that Jeff is sitting to my right, and he **is** sitting there, then my thinking is true.

Truth, then, is itself something *objective* (based on the *objects* outside of us). It is not something *subjective* (based on us, the *subjects*)

"St. Thomas is an authentic model for all who seek the truth. In his thinking, the demands of reason and the power of faith found the most elevated synthesis (blend) ever attained by human thought...."

Saint John Paul II,
Fides et Ratio

11.

which we *invent*. Rather, it is something already there in the world in which we live, waiting for us to *discover* it. We do not "make our own truth."

St. Thomas believed that truth is something that more than one person can know because we all are surrounded by the same real world. The modern claim, "You have your truth, and I have mine," would make no sense to St. Thomas. For example, if the lights are on in this room, and there are five people here capable of knowing that they are on, all five of us should agree that the lights are, in fact, on. If one of the five disagrees, thinking that the lights are off, then we would rightly wonder if he is blind. It might be true that *in his experience* (subjective) the lights are off, but his experience of objective reality is faulty because of his blindness.

St. Thomas did not limit his search for the truth just to what our senses can perceive in the physical world. In fact, Thomas would say that to fully understand the physical world, we need to understand its relationship to its Creator. St. Thomas offers convincing reasons explaining why this Creator would have to be spiritual and not physical. Here, too, he searches for the truth, trying to line up his thinking with that spiritual reality.

For St. Thomas, truth is all-important. As he explained, "Philosophy is not studied in order to find out what people may have thought but in order to discover what is true."[5] Philosophers are those people who try to know the truth in as complete a manner as is possible while using only their own natural powers of reason. They may believe in supernatural reality, but they do not use any supernatural aid in their reasoning. We human beings need to know the truth about reality so that we will be able to move ourselves toward what will, in reality, be *truly* good for us. This is what Jesus was talking about when He told us, "… you will know the truth, and the truth will set you free."[6]

What can we know by using our intellect enlightened by *faith in God's revelation*? We are able both to come to know God as the source of all truth and to know the order He has established in all creation. And once we know this, we can then choose to direct our actions in accordance with that order. We have the dignity, as human beings, of being able to choose to act (or not to act) in accord with God's ordering. All the other creatures of our world follow God's order because they *have to*, either because they are compelled by the laws of physics (e.g., unsupported rocks have to fall down) or by their own instincts (e.g., squirrels have to gather nuts in the fall -- they can't help it!). In making our choices daily, however, we are free. We can move ourselves either *back to* God for whom we were made, or *away from* Him into everlasting separation from Him.

---

[5] St. Thomas Aquinas, *De Caelo et Mundo,* I, d. 22, n. 228.
[6] John 8:32.

NOTES

"If anyone wishes to write against this, I will welcome it. For true and false will in no better way be revealed and uncovered than in resistance to a contradiction, according to the saying: 'Iron is sharpened by iron' *(Prov. 27:17)*. And between us and them may God judge, Who is blessed in eternity. Amen."

St. Thomas Aquinas,
On the Perfection of the Spiritual Life

Complementarity of Reason and Faith

As we saw in looking at St. Thomas' God-centered worldview, Thomas was open to both reason and faith as he tried to know reality. He recognized that God is the source of all truth because He is the Creator of all things. The visible world is the way it is, Thomas thought, because it is the way God wants it to be. Thomas recognized, then, that we can know God's mind about things by looking in two places:

1) at the order of creation (objective reality), and
2) at God's revelation communicated to us in both Sacred Scripture and Sacred Tradition, which Jesus entrusted to His Church.

Thomas had a total, life-long acceptance of the teaching authority of the Catholic Church, the **Magisterium**. He believed that the Catholic Church, established by Jesus Christ, is guided by the Holy Spirit in her teaching on faith and morals.

Since both the order of creation and the teachings of the Catholic Church express the mind of God, St. Thomas knew that, if they are understood properly, they can never contradict one another. God doesn't contradict Himself. Thomas knew the following about matters where the Church has pronounced a teaching:

♦ If a person *correctly* uses his own natural powers of reasoning (philosophy) to examine reality, then he will never disagree with what the Church teaches about it.

♦ He might not *fully* understand with his reason alone, because faith can know more than our reason can know, but correct reasoning will never contradict true faith.

True faith and correct human reasoning will always be compatible with one another. So, for example, the Church teaches that all human beings have a fundamental dignity which ought not to be vio-

---

Magisterium - from the Latin *magister*, "teacher;" the teaching authority of the Catholic Church regarding all matters pertaining to salvation. The Church's bishops in union with the Pope, as successors to the apostles, are charged with the sacred duty of passing on the truth and interpreting faithfully those teachings that come from Sacred Scripture and Sacred Tradition.

"Faith and reason are like two wings on which the human spirit rises to the contemplation of truth; and God has placed in the human heart a desire to know the truth -- in a word, to know himself -- so that, by knowing and loving God, men and women may also come to the fullness of truth about themselves."

St. John Paul II,
Fides et Ratio

NOTES

"Just when Saint Thomas distinguishes perfectly between faith and reason, he unites them in bonds of mutual friendship, conceding to each its specific rights and to each its specific dignity."

Pope Leo XIII,
Aeterni Patris, #109

"Though faith is above reason, there can never be any real discrepancy between faith and reason. Since the same God who reveals mysteries and infuses faith has bestowed the light of reason on the human mind, God cannot deny himself, nor can truth ever contradict truth."

CCC, #159

---

lated. Human beings can use their reason to think about human nature. But if someone concludes that some people are "inferior" and ought to be enslaved by "superior" people, then we know that their reasoning is wrong. Even if we can't say exactly what their mistake is, we know that they've made a mistake.

This explains why St. Thomas was not afraid of hearing his opponents' arguments. He knew that if they were reasoning correctly about objective reality, then they could not be in opposition to the faith or the moral teaching of the Catholic Church. If they were in opposition to that teaching, then he knew that there must be some error in their reasoning.

St. Thomas understood that there are some truths we can know simply by using reason alone, without faith. For example, Orville Wright did not need to check his calculations with the Church to see if his plane would fly safely. On the other hand, there are other truths that we can know only through faith. For example, that Jesus is *both* God and man can only be known by faith. And there are still other truths that can be known by both faith and reason. The chart below depicts the various truths that can be known in these different ways.

Known by reason alone and not by faith	Known by reason and faith	Known by faith alone and not by reason
What a planet is made of	Why the universe is so well ordered	God's plan to save us
That Jupiter exists	The historical existence of Jesus	How much God loves us
The Law of Gravity	That the human soul will not die	God is a Trinity of persons

St. Thomas went a step further than merely saying that faith and reason are compatible, however. He claimed that although faith and reason are distinct and independent ways of knowing the truth, nevertheless, they were meant to work as *partners*. This is what we mean when we say they are "complementary:" faith and reason "complete" each other. They work together to aid us in understanding ourselves and the world.

Chapter I
THOMAS AQUINAS & TRUTH

On the one hand, faith acts as a guide. It guides us in determining whether our reasoning is correct. It provides our limited reason with an external reference mark or a hand rail, better enabling us to stay on the path toward the truth. On the other hand, reason works to express truths. It is an indispensible tool that faith needs in order for it both to develop in the human mind and to be readily passed on to others. Because it is such an indispensible tool, philosophy (the fruit of reason) is referred to as the "handmaid of faith."

In modern times, many people think that faith and reason are on two completely different tracks. They think not only that faith and reason have nothing to do with each other, but also that they contradict each other on numerous points. For example, people often speak of science and religion as enemies. John Paul II wanted so strongly to correct this mistaken understanding that he wrote an entire **encyclical**, *Fides et Ratio (Faith and Reason)*, dedicated to the subject. In it, he teaches us the following:

> [This] truth, which God reveals to us in Jesus Christ, is not opposed to the truths which philosophy perceives. On the contrary, the two modes [ways] of knowledge lead to truth in all its fullness. ... It is the one and the same God who establishes and guarantees the intelligibility and reasonableness of the natural order of things upon which scientists confidently depend, and who reveals himself as the Father of our Lord Jesus Christ. This unity of truth, natural and revealed, is embodied in a living and personal way in Christ, as the Apostle reminds us: "Truth is in Jesus" (cf. Eph. 4:21; Col. 1:15-20).[7]

Encyclical - an official letter from the Pope to Catholics all over the world. It is one of the chief ways by which he teaches us.

Study Guide Questions:

1. *How would a person's attitude toward the truth be different if he thought he were the inventor and not merely the discoverer of the truth?*

2. *What is the difference between natural (human reason) and supernatural knowledge (faith)?*

3. *Why do we say that truth is primarily based on objective reality?*

4. *Why must faith and reason be compatible?*

5. *How does faith come to the aid of human reason? How does reason serve faith?*

---

[7] Saint John Paul, *Fides et Ratio*, #34.

The Human Person ~ Dignity Beyond Compare

NOTES

>
> # CASE IN POINT
>
> We have probably all heard people say something like, *"That may be true for you but not for me."* Maybe we've heard it from people of a different culture or religious belief. Some people might use this expression because they want to show "openness" to those with different opinions about certain moral issues. This idea of *"your truth and my truth"* is so widespread today that some in our society think of it as a central "moral principle."
>
> - What does the phrase imply about the meaning of the word "truth"?
>
> - Why would St. Thomas Aquinas not agree, in most cases, with the use of the phrase *"true for you but not for me"*?
>
> - Are there ever situations when it might be correct to say that *what is true for you is not true for me*?

Thomas, the Theologian

Studying about God with information we have acquired through revelation is called **theology,** and the one who does this is called a theologian. To do theology is to use our natural reason to reflect on what God reveals to us in supernatural ways, through both Scripture and the Church. That is why theology is often referred to as "faith seeking understanding." In order to do a fruitful study of theology, we must have faith that God is, in fact, the source of the teaching of Sacred Scripture and of the Church and its teachings. Faith itself is a supernatural gift to our intellect, whereby it is able to accept knowledge because God reveals it rather than because of evidence given.

When we do philosophy, we keep to what we can know about the world without the aid of supernatural revelation. We use only human reason, which any human being has available for use. When we do theology, we use *both* human reason and divine revelation. In other words, a theologian approaches the study of God using both the natural and the supernatural knowledge available to him. Unlike the philosopher who uses only human reason, the theologian can draw from the Bible and from Church teaching in his attempt to discover and explain the truth about reality.

Theology - the study of God and things pertaining to the divine. Often spoken of as "faith seeking understanding," the study of theology generally pre-supposes a faith in the existence of God.

"Whatever its source, truth is of the Holy Spirit."
St. Thomas Aquinas,
ST I-II, 109, 1 ad. 1

"Being aware of this, young people of today and adults of the new millennium, let yourselves be 'formed' in the school of Jesus."
Saint John Paul II,
Message for the 14th World Youth Day

St. Thomas was a theologian as well as a philosopher. When he argued his point by appealing to truths that could be known by faith, he was acting as a theologian. When he argued his point by appealing to truths that could be known by human reason, he was acting as a philosopher. Thomas was careful to distinguish between the two ways of knowing and to use them as partners in his search for and explanation of the truth.

As a theologian who spent his life in the search for truth, St. Thomas realized that the source of all truth is a divine Person: Jesus Christ. All things were created through Him and find their source and meaning only in Him. Jesus Himself told us, "I am the way, the truth and the life."[8]

Jesus is **Incarnate** Truth Itself. He is the Source of the order in the world. So, when our thinking lines up with objective reality, we actually come closer to Jesus Himself. Thomas knew that if we want to possess the fullness of truth, then we must seek Jesus. If we want to give the fullness of truth to others, we must give them Jesus.

Thomas, the Writer

Thomas was an extremely productive writer. His works include:

- 15 philosophical or theological works (of which the *Summa Theologiae* is most well known),
- 11 commentaries on books of the Bible,
- 12 commentaries on works of Aristotle,
- 4 other commentaries on works of other major writers,
- 5 treatises addressing particular controversies of his day,
- 18 letters (including responses to requests for expert opinion),
- 23 sermons and liturgical compositions (includes the Office of Corpus Christi).

Given the fact that St. Thomas lived only to the age of 49, this level of productivity is astonishing.

There is a reliable story about Thomas that clearly illustrates both his professional accomplishments and his single-minded focus. Dominic of Caserta, the sacristan of the chapel of St. Nicholas in Naples, reported that on one morning during the last year of Thomas' life, before the rest of the community had risen and entered the chapel, he saw Thomas alone, praying in front of the crucifix. This did not surprise Dominic because Thomas frequently came very early to pray.

---
[8] John 14:5

NOTES

"Jesus Christ is the answer to the question posed by every human life, and the love of Christ compels us to share that great good news with everyone."
Saint John Paul II,
Baltimore, Maryland, 1995

Incarnate - from the Latin *incarnare*, "to make into flesh;" to be embodied in flesh or to be given a body.

The Human Person ~ Dignity Beyond Compare

NOTES

"We are all called to be saints. Every one of us has heard, and still hears, ringing in his conscience, the command: 'Climb higher;' higher, ever higher, until while we are on this earth we can reach up and grasp the heavens, until we can join our saints, whether they be the venerable saints of old or the wonderful saints of modern times, who were our own contemporaries, and in whom our Mother the Church already rejoices."
Pope St. John XXIII,
Writings and Addresses while Patriarch of Venice

Viaticum - From Latin, meaning "provisions for a journey." The Church uses this term for giving the Holy Eucharist to those who are about to die. She sees Viaticum as Food for the passage through death to eternal life.

But suddenly Dominic realized that Thomas was kneeling two feet above the floor, levitating before the crucifix! Dominic reported that while he stood staring in shock, he heard a voice coming from the crucifix say, "You have spoken well of Me, Thomas. What would you have as your reward?" To which Thomas answered, "Nothing but You, Lord."

Thomas, the Saint

Thomas Aquinas is "Saint" Thomas for one reason only: his personal holiness. His deep love of God completely affected every aspect of his life, but especially his work as a thinker, teacher and writer. For Thomas, his life of faith and his life of work were one and the same life. When he would lecture, write, study or debate, he would always begin with prayer. It is said that when he ran into difficulty in his work, he would kneel before the tabernacle with his head pressed upon it and, in tears, beg for God's inspiration.

St. Thomas recognized that human beings long for a happiness only God can satisfy. We are creatures wounded by sin who are unable to reunite ourselves with God by our own efforts. Only through Jesus Christ, Who redeemed and saved us, can we be brought into the fullness of what it means to be made in God's image and likeness. Only through Him are we able to reach the unending happiness we all desire. The key to understanding Thomas the Saint, then, is to recognize his intense desire to be a disciple of Jesus Christ and to share Him with others. Although St. Thomas' work was academic, he didn't write to impress scholars. His primary concern was the glory of God and the salvation of souls.

Shortly before he died, upon receiving Sacred **Viaticum**, Thomas expressed an act of faith which reveals the mind and heart of the Saint:

*"I firmly believe and know as certain
that Jesus Christ,
true God and true Man,
Son of God and Son of the Virgin Mary,
is in this Sacrament."*

Then he added:

*"I receive Thee, the price of my redemption,
for Whose love I have watched, studied, and labored.
Thee have I preached; Thee have I taught.
Never have I said anything against Thee:
if anything was not well said, that is to be attributed to my ignorance.*

*Neither do I wish to be obstinate in my opinions,
but if I have written anything erroneous concerning this sacrament
or other matters,
I submit all to the judgment and correction
of the Holy Roman Church,
in whose obedience I now pass from this life."*

Thomas: His Lasting Influence

Thomas' personal holiness and the importance of his scholarly work were well recognized following his death in 1274. Fifty-one years after his death, he was canonized a saint by Pope John XXII. In the 15th and 16th centuries, Thomas' *Summa Theologiae* became the chief "text book" for theological education. In 1567, Pope Pius V declared Thomas a Doctor of the Church. In his 1879 encyclical entitled *On the Restoration of Christian Philosophy*, Pope Leo XIII called for a renewed reliance on Aquinas in theological work. In 1914, Pope Pius X required that the *Summa Theologiae* should be the basis for teaching in all universities affiliated to the Holy See. In 1917, Benedict XV required all religious to "devote themselves for two years at least to philosophy and for four years to theology, following the teaching of St. Thomas."[9] He also directed that all professors in seminaries and pontifical universities teach "according to the arguments, doctrine, and principles of St. Thomas."[10] In the second half of the 20th century, St. Thomas was singled out as an exemplary teacher for Catholics by Pope Paul VI. St. Thomas' work is referenced throughout the documents of Vatican Council II, in the **Code of Canon Law**, and he is among the most frequently cited writers in the *Catechism of the Catholic Church*.

Conclusion

Thomas used reason, enlightened by faith, to understand more clearly all kinds of truths concerning the human person:

- The dignity of our nature, created in the image and likeness of God;

- Our dignity, worthy of respect from the first moment of conception;

- Our supernatural destiny, to live with God forever in heaven;

- Our ability to discover (not invent) truth, and to choose to be guided in our actions by this truth.

---

[9] 1917 *Code of Canon Law,* Canon 589.
[10] 1917 *Code of Canon Law,* Canon 1366, #2.

NOTES

"Young people, do not be afraid to be holy! Fly high, be among those whose goals are worthy of sons and daughters of God. Glorify God in your lives!"
Saint John Paul II, *Message for the VI World Youth Day*

Code of Canon Law - The book containing the universal and fundamental laws of the Roman Catholic Church.

NOTES

This is not all, though. Thomas knew that through revelation, God has shed even greater light on the truth our reason is able to know. God shows us the truth most fully in Jesus Christ and in His Church.

So it is to this great Doctor of the Church and lover of Truth that we now turn as we begin our investigation into the nature and dignity of the human person -- a dignity beyond compare!

Study Guide Questions:

1. What was it about St. Thomas' life that earned him the title of "Saint"?

2. How does man differ from God in his relationship to truth?

3. List three things not mentioned in the chapter that can be known (a) by faith alone,
    (b) by reason alone, and
    (c) by both faith and reason.   (3 each)

4. What does it mean to say that Jesus Christ is the source of truth?

Point to Consider:

*"Young people of every continent,
do not be afraid to be the saints of the new millennium!
Be contemplative, love prayer;
be coherent with your faith
and generous in the service of your brothers and sisters,
be active members of the Church and builders of peace....
The Lord wants you to be intrepid apostles of his Gospel
and builders of a new humanity."*

Saint John Paul II,
Message to the Youth of the World, 2000, #3

Chapter 1
THOMAS AQUINAS & TRUTH

NOTES

 **CASE IN POINT**

In March, 2008, an article was published about Guiliano Ferrara, an atheist journalist who proposed that the United Nations should pass "a moratorium" on abortions world-wide. When asked in an interview why he had made this proposal, Mr. Ferrara replied:

"...I proposed a moratorium on abortion just to draw attention to the fact that abortion is an evil and to mobilize people against this evil. When they ask me in what capacity I did this, I replied that I made this decision because I am a rational human being. The fact that I was a Communist ... that I was born into a Communist and atheistic family ... the fact that I ironically refer to myself as a 'devout atheist,' is not of any importance. What matters is that I am a rational human being like anybody else. ... [A]s a rational human being, I think abortion is an evil and must be opposed."*

- What advantage does a person have if he is able to explain why abortion is wrong using natural reason rather than only appealing to the Bible or to the Church's teachings for his explanation?

- How convincing do you think people will find Mr. Ferrera? Why?

* "'Let No One Touch the Unborn Child,' Non-Believer Says," interview with Giuliano Ferrara by Wlodzimierz Redzioch, *Inside the Vatican*, March, 2008, p. 18.

21.

Chapter II

FOUNDATIONAL PHILOSOPHICAL PRINCIPLES

Introduction

With St. Thomas Aquinas as our guide, let us begin our study of the human person by getting acquainted with some foundational philosophical principles. Working hard to understand these principles is worth our effort, for they are foundational to a correct understanding of all reality. Understanding them will enable us to discover basic truths about the human person, especially about the relationship of his soul to his body.

> **Vocabulary**
>
> *potency   substance   principle*
> *actuality   accident   intrinsic*

POTENCY AND ACTUALITY

St. Thomas agreed with the ancient Greek philosopher Aristotle (384-322 B.C.) in the way he viewed the things of our world. Aristotle had taught that the change we see happening in the world around us can be explained if we appeal to a distinction between act and potency. It is important for us to understand what these terms mean.

To say that something is in "**potency**" or has "potential" means that it *does not yet exist, but it could.* It has *"the power"* or potency to be. To say that something is "in act" or has "**actuality**," on the other hand, is to say that it is *real*, that it truly exists. For example, to say that the dough is *potentially* pizza means that the pizza is not yet there, but the dough has the capacity to become pizza. To say that pizza coming out of the oven piping hot exists "in actuality" is to say that it really is there.

You might be thinking, "Then why speak about 'potency' at all if potency does not imply real existence?" "Potency" is telling you something real about a thing; it is telling you about the thing's possibilities. Dough has the potency for becoming pizza; a block of wood does not have that potentiality. Wood cannot become pizza! This shows us that although we might be able to conceive in our imagination of

NOTES

Potency - the capacity or ability of a thing to be actualized; the opposite of actuality.

Actuality - having real existence; the opposite of the merely possible.

The Human Person ~ Dignity Beyond Compare

NOTES

Nature - the essence of a thing which it has from its beginning; what a thing is.

Change - a movement from potency to act.

wood becoming pizza, the potentiality that Aristotle and Aquinas have in mind is one which is rooted in a thing's **nature** as it actually exists. In other words, there is nothing in the nature of wood that indicates that it has any potentiality for becoming pizza, while there is something in the nature of dough that indicates this potentiality.

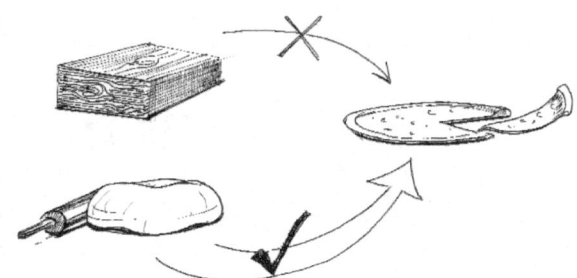

So, how do these terms "act" and "potency" help to explain the change we see in the world around us? Well, something is able to change only if it has potency for the change. Once the change occurs, we say that the *potency* the thing had has now been *actualized*. **Change**, then, involves *a movement from potency to act*. In change, potency is replaced by actuality. As I sit here at my desk, I am in potency to standing. When I stand up, I actualize my potency to stand. The change from dough to pizza occurs when the potency of the dough is actualized and pizza actually exists.

POTENCY ⟶ ACT = CHANGE

The *actual* substance of dough has the *potency* to become pizza.

When the dough's *potency* to become pizza is *actualized*, pizza comes into existence.

While these terms *potency* and *act* are essential for helping us understand change, they are not enough. We need something more; we need something external to the change in order to bring it about. For example, dough does not become pizza on its own; it requires an external agent (a person) to actualize the dough's potentiality. If it could actualize itself, then why didn't it do so long before now?

Aquinas explains, then, that potency must be raised to act by something that is in act. *"Whatever is moved is moved by another."*[1] Now you might argue against this by pointing out that a dog can move itself to act, for example, when it barks. But what is really happening here is that one part of the dog is being changed or moved by another part. In the case of a dog barking, the vocal cords of the dog are in poten-

[1] St. Thomas Aquinas, *In Phys.* VI.2.891.

cy to vibrating rapidly and thus making sound when air from the lungs is forced between them. Air is moved out of the lungs and through the vocal cords due to the coordinated action of the diaphragm, abdominal muscles, chest muscles, and rib cage. This coordinated action occurs due to motor neurons firing, and these are actualized by other neurons, and so on.

Did you notice that actuality always comes before potentiality? This is because potentiality cannot exist on its own but must always be in combination with actuality. Thus, the potential for pizza is present *only if* there is actual dough. The potential for the dog barking exists *only if* there is an actual dog with vocal chords.

Thus, it is not possible for potentiality to exist on its own, without something actual. But it is possible for something to be purely actual, with no potentiality whatsoever. We'll talk about this later in the chapter when we talk about the First Cause of objective reality.

FORM AND MATTER

From what we have said so far, we see that both Aristotle and Aquinas think that in everything which is moved, there must be a composition of act and potency. These two philosophers also hold that every physical thing is made up of two principles: form and matter. Now do not let that word "**principle**" trip you up. It is simply a term philosophers use to mean "basic source." So, for example, chocolate and sugar are two *principles* of brownies; focused study is usually a *principle* of good grades.

Principle - from the Latin *principium*, "beginning;" the source or origin of something; that from which a thing comes into being.

Thomas and Aristotle are saying that all physical things are the result of a union of two principles: *form and matter*.[2] The **form** of a thing is *what makes it to be the kind of thing that it is.* It is what gives a thing its basic identity, revealing to us its innermost being. For example, "tableness" is the *form* of this table before me, and "doggie-ness is the *form* of my dog Snarles. Now, it is true that we do not usually think of "doggie-ness" or "table-ness," so it may sound strange, but the *idea* of what makes this furniture a table and not a chair or a door -- its flat, elevated, sturdy surface -- is not at all new.

Form - the essence of a thing, the determining principle of a physical thing that makes it to be the kind of thing that it is.

What makes a dog a dog rather than a cat is what we mean by "doggie-ness." Neither "table-ness" nor "doggie-ness" exists in reality by themselves; only *individual* tables and *individual* dogs exist. More is needed, therefore, than form alone to explain physical things.

---

[2] This Aristotelian doctrine is known as *hylemorphism* (also spelled hylomorphism) after the Greek words *hyle* (matter) and *morphe* (form).

The Human Person ~ Dignity Beyond Compare

NOTES

Matter - the receptive principle of a physical thing; that out of which a physical being is made.

"Since the form is not for the matter, but rather the matter for the form, we must gather from the form the reason why the matter is such as it is; and not conversely."
St. Thomas Aquinas, *Summa Theologiae* I, 76, 5

The other principle involved in physical things must be something which limits form, "tying it down" so to speak to one particular thing. It will be what makes the thing to be individual instead of general, to have a certain size, color and shape. This second principle in physical things is called **matter**. Philosophers define "matter" as *that out of which a thing comes to be*. The matter of the table would be the wood or steel out of which it is made, and the matter of Snarles would be the various cells of his body.

Form, then, is the more general term. It accounts for our being able to know what a thing is. Once we grasp the form of a thing, we know whether there is a table or a dog in front of us. But forms do not just float around by themselves. Outside of our minds, out in the real world, forms exist only united with matter. For example, in reality "doggie-ness" is united with the physical matter of a particular dog.

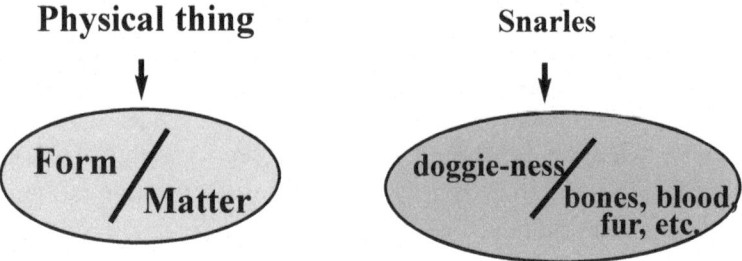

In fact, St. Thomas says that the form is not for the matter; rather, the *matter is for the form*.³ So if we want to know why a certain matter is the way that it is, we must look to its form for the reason. For example, the reason why the matter of desks is always smooth is because a desk's form requires that it have a writing surface. And the reason why the matter of a window is always transparent is because a window is the kind of thing through which one sees.

Matter, as a principle of a physical thing, is in potency to a form which makes it actual or real. The two principles form and matter are in relation to each other, then, *as act is to potency*. Another way to express this is to say that **form actualizes matter**.

POTENCY	ACTUALITY
Matter	**Form**
dough	*pizza-ness*
flour, salt, etc.	*dough-ness*
brass	*candlestick-ness*
molecules	*brass-ness*

---

³ St. Thomas Aquinas, *Summa Theologiae* I, 76, 5.

Chapter II
FOUNDATIONAL PHILOSOPHICAL PRINCIPLES

Take the example of a brass candlestick. Brass is used to make the candlestick because brass has the potency to hold a candle and not be melted when the candle burns low. We could not make a candlestick out of ice cream, because ice cream does not have the right potency. The form of a thing *actualizes* one (or more) of the potencies of the matter. In the case of the candlestick, the form candlestick-ness *actualizes* the brass's potency to hold a candle. A different form would actualize the potency of the brass to be a statue or a paper weight.

Applying these terms to physical beings, St. Thomas says that the form of a thing is the thing's *first* act. When the form unites with matter, it makes the thing really exist. Any other activity a thing might do once it exists, he calls its *second* act. For example, the form of a rose is its *first* act because it makes the rose exist. The fact that the rose takes in nourishment from the soil or grows is called its *second* act. We will see in Chapter Seven why these terms are important, especially as we talk about the human person.

One more point about form and matter: they are both **intrinsic** principles of physical things. That word "intrinsic" means "*from within.*" These principles are from within a thing. Matter is the "stuff" out of which the thing is made, and form is the arrangement of that stuff. Be careful not to confuse the form with merely the external shape of a thing. The external shape "announces" the form to us. It is bound up with the form, but the form is not simply the *outside* shape of a thing. Rather, form is part and parcel of what a thing is.

For example, the external shape of a table announces the form "table-ness," but "tableness" is more than the external shape. If something had the external shape of a table but was merely a cardboard cutout of a table, we would not call it a table. We would call it a model of a table or an attempt at a table. The form "table-ness" influences every aspect of the thing we call a table. It makes the table to be very sturdy and able to hold weight. In a wooden table, the form "table-ness" and the matter (wood) are intimately united in making up the table.

Now, those who know science might be wondering, "What about the atoms and molecules that make up the wood which makes up the table?" Atoms and molecules -- matter in its very simplest way of existing -- do not change the point philosophers are making regarding matter and form. For matter to exist at all, it must be united with a form. Thus, an atom is an atom because it has the form of atom-ness, and an atom of hydrogen is actually hydrogen, but potentially dihydrogen monoxide, otherwise known as water (a molecule).

NOTES

Intrinsic - from the Latin *intrinsecus*, "inward;" in and of itself, or essentially. It is the opposite of extrinsic, meaning external or unessential.

The Human Person ~ Dignity Beyond Compare

NOTES

Substance - that which is able to exist in and for itself and not in another.

Substantial form - that which makes a thing exist on its own, as a substance.

Accident - that which is able to exist only in another; it requires a substance in which to inhere.

Accidental form - that which makes a substance exist in a particular manner.

SUBSTANCE AND ACCIDENTS

In speaking of form, Aristotle and St. Thomas distinguish between two kinds, based on the two fundamentally different ways a thing can exist. If the thing is able to exist in and for itself and not in another, in a relatively independent way, it is a **substance**. The form of a substance is called its **substantial form**. Examples of substances would be such things as a human person, a tree, a block of gold. A key trait of a substance is its unity; it is <u>one</u> thing. Strictly speaking, then, a machine like a car would be a collection of substances (nuts, bolts, wires, etc.) and not a substance itself.

In addition to substance which is able to exist on its own, there is also a kind of being which can exist only *in another*. A being such as this is called an **accident**. The form of an accident is called an **accidental form**. Examples of accidents would be such things as the *speed* of a racing horse, the *shape* of a maple leaf, or the *cheerfulness* of a human being. Speed, shape, and cheerfulness cannot exist on their own. They can only be present in substances, such as horses, leaves, or human beings.

A physical thing can have only <u>one</u> substantial form because the substantial form makes the thing to be the kind of thing that it is. If it had more than one substantial form, the thing would be more than one thing. Usually physical beings have numerous accidental forms, accounting for qualities such as size, shape, or color. For example, the substance "this lemon" has only one substantial form: lemon-ness. However, in addition to the substantial form (lemon-ness) and the matter (that out of which this lemon comes to be), the lemon may have numerous accidental forms accounting for the fact that it is a rather big, tart lemon which is discolored by age.

Substantial form: Lemon-ness

Accidental forms:

- Yellow-ness
- Rough-ness
- Tart-ness
- Large-ness

Notice that both the substantial and accidental forms are non-material. They are united with matter, but they are not matter itself.

Before going on, let us stop to check our understanding.

Study Guide Questions:

1. *Give five examples of things that are both in potency and in act. For example, dough is actually dough, but it is potentially pizza.*

2. *What do you think we will mean later when we say that the soul is the "first act" of a living body?*

3. *What is the difference between a substantial form and an accidental form? Give an example of each.*

CASES IN POINT

#1 -- The practice of unjust discrimination against people means that one sees qualities or "differences" in certain people, and then treats them less favorably because of this. We often hear of such unjust discrimination based on race, sex, religion, social status, national origin, etc.

- How might an understanding of *substance* and *accident* help us to avoid unjust discrimination? On the other hand, how would it help us to discriminate ***rightly***?

* * * * *

#2 -- "Embryos are human individuals at an early stage of their development, just as adolescents, toddlers, infants, and fetuses are human individuals at various developmental stages. So to say ... that embryos and human beings are different *kinds* of things is true only if one focuses exclusively on the accidental characteristics -- size, degree of development, and so on. But the central question is, precisely, should we focus only on the accidental characteristics by which embryonic human beings differ from mature human beings, or should we recognize their essential nature (that is, *what they are*)?"*

- How would you express the point this author is making here?

- Why should knowing the correct answer to the question raised by these authors be crucial to each one of us as citizens of this country? Explain.

* Patrick Lee and Robert P. George, "Acorns and Embryos," *The New Atlantis*, Winter, 2005, pp. 90-100.

The Human Person ~ Dignity Beyond Compare

NOTES

Prime matter - the "matter" which substantial form actualizes; pure potentiality; the principle of receptivity in every physical thing.

Secondary matter - matter which exists because it has already received a substantial form.

Now we are ready to go on to some more difficult concepts. With what we have learned so far in this chapter, though, we are ready to tackle them.

PRIMARY AND SECONDARY MATTER

We have seen that a substance and an accident each has its own kind of form because they are different kinds of being. In the same way, we speak of two types of matter. Aristotle and St. Thomas used the term "**prime matter**" in referring to the "matter" which the substantial form actualizes (makes to exist). Using these terms, they said that every physical substance is made up of substantial form and prime matter.

$$\text{Physical Substance} = \boxed{\frac{\text{Substantial Form}}{\text{Prime Matter}}} = \text{Secondary Matter}$$

Remember we said earlier that *form actualizes the potency of matter*. It is important to understand that when we use the term "prime matter," we are speaking of *pure potentiality*. Prime matter is a principle of receptivity. Prime matter is what receives substantial form; therefore, it has the potential to make up a thing. If it is not united with a substantial form, then prime matter does not make up anything. Together, these two principles make up a physical thing we call a substance. So, for example, the physical substance, this lemon, is made up of the *substantial form* "lemon-ness" and the *prime matter* which received this form and which together with it make this particular thing we call a lemon.

We cannot actually draw a picture of prime matter. If we could draw a picture of it, then it would not be prime matter any more. It would be **secondary matter**. Secondary matter is any physical substance, like the lemon, whose prime matter has been actualized by a substantial form. Secondary matter is a substance that can receive and lose accidental forms.

An accidental form makes a substance to be *in a particular manner.* For example, the substance we call the human person is able to gain weight or blush or get older or become ill. Weight, a flushed face, aging and ill-health are all accidental forms that reside in the substance, the person.

30.

SUBSTANTIAL AND ACCIDENTAL CHANGE

If you found the previous discussion about prime matter puzzling, then you are like most people when they begin to study philosophy. When they first hear of it, they ask, "Why must we learn about something that does not actually exist, something that is *pure potency*?" It is true that prime matter does not have substantial existence yet (because it needs a substantial form to give it that). Still, prime matter is a *real principle of being*. It is what enables us to understand how some things in our world change.

Any change requires something constant (which does not change) that endures throughout the change. Whether it is a candle burning or a piece of clay being molded, something constant endures throughout the changes. Without this "constant," there would be a gap in being. We would not be able to talk about *change* at all. Rather, we would have to say that one thing stopped existing and another began to exist, and between these two things there is a "gap." Having an underlying constant which is the same in both things before and after the change fills in the gap. It lets us explain what we really mean when we say that a thing "changes."

Do you remember what we said it means for a thing to change? We said that something is able to change only if it has potency for the change. Once the change occurs, we say that the *potency* the thing had has now been *actualized*. **Change**, then, involves *a movement from potency to act*. In change, potency is replaced by actuality.

Change can be *accidental* or *substantial*. An example of an accidental change would be Sally using dye on her blond hair. The change from Sally with blond hair to Sally with brown hair occurs when her potency for becoming a brunette is actualized by hair dye. To speak even more precisely, we could say that when her hair is dyed, Sally undergoes an accidental change of hair color. That is, Sally remains **essentially** the same, i.e., Sally remains Sally, but something non-essential about her changes. In undergoing this change, her substance loses the accidental form of "blond hair-ness" and acquires the accidental form of "brown hair-ness." Throughout this accidental change, Sally remains constant. This underlying constant (Sally) is the thing (substance) that changes accidentally (hair color).

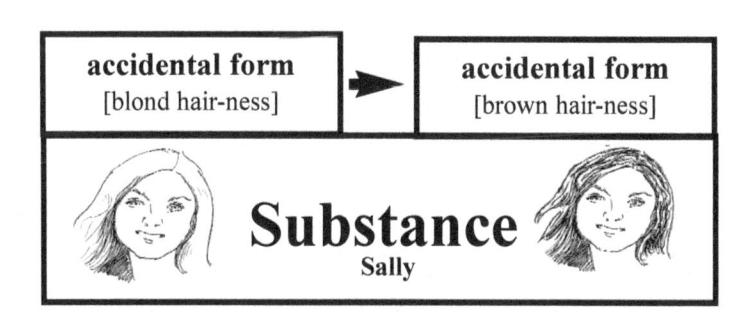

Change - a movement from potency to act.

Essential - the adjectival form of the word "essence." Essence is the underlying identity or nature of a thing throughout the process of change.

NOTES

Accidental change - change in accidental form only; non-essential change because the substance remains the same; change in the manner in which a substance exists.

Substantial change - change in substantial form; change in the essence of a thing whereby the substance itself changes.

So in **accidental change**, the thing that changes is still essentially the same thing after the change that it was *before* the change. We see these changes daily: gaining or losing weight, getting a hair cut, dressing up, becoming happy or sad. In every case, the substance that changes accidentally always remains the very same substance.

Substantial change also involves a movement from potency to act. Since the substance itself changes, the constant in a substantial change is *prime matter*. Prime matter loses one substantial form and receives another. In other words, the substance changes *essentially* as a result of this change.

For example, take a piece of wood. We could change it accidentally by giving it a coat of paint or sawing it in half. Or we could change it substantially by placing it in a fireplace to burn. As the fire consumes the wood, a number of accidental changes occur (changes in size, texture, and color) which prepare the way for the substantial change that happens *instantaneously*, without our being able to observe it. In this instantaneous substantial change, the substance *wood* becomes the substance *ashes*. It is no longer wood. It is a completely different substance with a different substantial form.

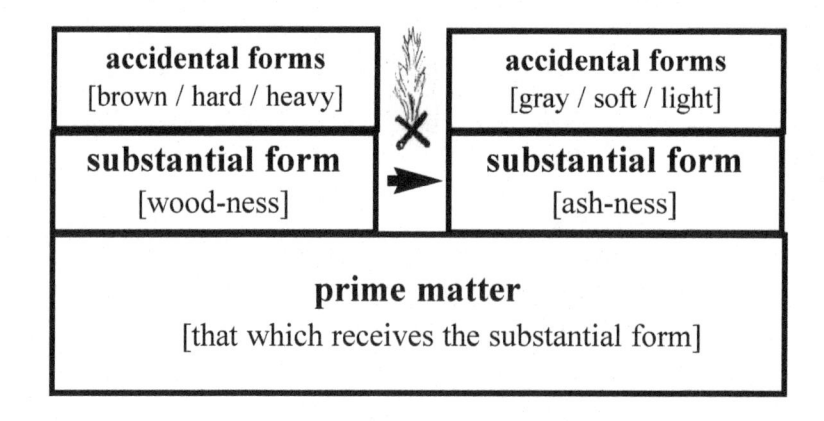

accidental forms [brown / hard / heavy]	**accidental forms** [gray / soft / light]
substantial form [wood-ness]	**substantial form** [ash-ness]
prime matter [that which receives the substantial form]	

Study Guide Questions:

1. *How does secondary matter differ from primary matter?*

2. *Give five examples each of accidental and substantial changes. Identify the constant in each of these changes.*

3. *Why is it so important that there be something that is constant whenever there is a change?*

Chapter II
FOUNDATIONAL PHILOSOPHICAL PRINCIPLES

NOTES

CASES IN POINT

#1 -- Identify the *kind of change* that takes place in each of the following scenarios:

- The change which takes place in each student who increases his knowledge through studying this chapter.

- The change which takes place in the food that we ate at breakfast.

- The change which takes place in us because of the food that we ate at breakfast.

- The change which takes place in a person who has plastic surgery to repair a badly injured face.

- The change which takes place in a baptized person who chooses to commit a mortal sin.

- The change which takes place in your bedroom when you decide to clean it.

- The change which takes place in the spider you step on and kill.

* * * * *

#2 -- The *Catechism of the Catholic Church* uses St. Thomas Aquinas' term **transubstantiation** to explain the Catholic Church's teaching regarding the Real Presence of Jesus in the Sacrament of the Eucharist: "...[B]y the consecration of the bread and wine there takes place a change of the whole substance of the bread into the substance of the body of Christ our Lord and of the whole substance of the wine into the substance of his blood." *#1376*

- How does understanding the terms *substance* and *accident* help us to explain what we believe as Catholics regarding the Real Presence of Christ in the Eucharist?

The Human Person ~ Dignity Beyond Compare

THE FOUR CAUSES

In order to offer a full explanation of a thing, Aristotle and Aquinas teach the importance of the four causes: material, formal, efficient, and final. Two of these causes we have already somewhat discussed, but let's take a look at them again in view of the other two we haven't yet talked about.

- The **material cause** of a thing is the underlying stuff out of which a thing is made, such as bones, skin, blood, flesh are the material cause of a human person. In other words, the material cause of a thing is the matter out of which it comes to exist.

- The **formal cause** of a thing is the form, pattern, or structure that it exhibits. It is what makes the thing to be the kind of thing that it is, such as desk-ness or human-ness.

- The **efficient cause** of a thing is that which actualizes its potency to exist. The efficient cause is the agent or machine that brings about the thing's existence through its activity. The efficient cause of a cake is the one who gathers its ingredients, puts them together and bakes them.

- The **final cause** of a thing is the end, goal, or purpose of a thing. It answers the question "why?" the thing exists and why the agent (efficient cause) acted. It is the goal the agent seeks through his activity. The final cause of a cake is to provide good tasting celebratory nourishment.

Final causes go hand-in-hand with efficient causes, just like material and formal causes go together. As Aquinas says, *"Every agent acts for an end."*[4] Agents are not merely thinking beings, however; anything that brings about an effect is an agent. Thus, the final cause of an acorn is the oak tree. The acorn regularly brings about an oak tree and not a cactus or a sunflower. Ice causes things around it to be cold, never does it cause them to boil or to smell like roses. The moon's "goal" is movement around the earth. This *causal regularity* that we observe everywhere in nature is evidence of final causality.

Acorn becomes an oak tree.

NOTES

"A thing's formal cause is, at the deepest level, its substantial form or essence; its material cause entails that it has certain potentialities and lacks others; its formal cause, being its substantial form or essence, is shared by other things and known by the intellect via abstraction from experience...."

Edward Feser,
*The Last Superstition,
A Refutation of the New Atheism,*
p. 64

"Just as material and formal causation are deeply intertwined on Aristotle's account, so too are efficient causes and final causes. You simply cannot properly understand the one apart from the other; indeed, there *cannot* be efficient causes without final ones."

Edward Feser,
The Last Superstition,
p. 64

---

[4] St. Thomas Aquinas, *Summa Theologiae* I, 44.4.

Chapter II
FOUNDATIONAL PHILOSOPHICAL PRINCIPLES

All together, these four causes provide a full or complete explanation of a thing. For example, if we wanted to know fully about this book you are now using, we would seek to know its four causes: Its *material cause* is the paper, ink, and glue out of which the book was made. The book's *formal cause* would be its "book-ness," that is, it is what makes this paper, ink, and glue a book rather than a sign or a paper plane. The *efficient cause* of the book would be the writer herself as well as all of the people and the machines used to print and publish the book. The *final cause* of the book would be to communicate information about the dignity of the human person.

These four causes apply to all things in our world, not just to human artifacts. Thus, if you wanted to know about the human heart, you would seek to find its *material cause:* muscle tissue. Since there are many muscles in the human body, however, we would need to be able to distinguish it from other muscles. Thus we would need to know that heart tissue is a certain sort of muscle because it is organized into ventricles, atria, etc. The *formal cause* gives us this information, telling us what makes the heart to be the kind of muscle tissue that it is. Then we would need to know the *efficient cause* of the heart: the biological processes that determined that some embryonic cells would form a heart rather than a liver or a brain. Finally, the heart's *final cause:* to pump blood throughout the body.[5]

ARGUMENTS FOR THE EXISTENCE OF GOD

With this understanding of the four causes, we are in a good position now to do what we promised earlier we would do: take a look at a few arguments for the existence of God. The first is one which Aquinas considered to be the most evident of arguments for God's existence: the Argument from Motion.[6]

Argument from Motion (Change)

1. Some things are in motion.
2. Nothing can be reduced[7] from potency to actuality except by something in a state of actuality.
3. Whatever is in motion must be put in motion by another.[8]

NOTES

"Aquinas refers to the final cause as 'the cause of causes,' .... The material cause of a thing underlies its potential for change; but potentialities are always potentialities *for*, or directed *toward*, some actuality. Hence final causality underlies all potentiality and thus all materiality. The final cause of a thing is also the central aspect of its formal cause; indeed, it determines its formal cause. For it is only because a thing has a certain end or final cause that it has the form it has. ... Efficient causality cannot be made sense of apart from final causality. Indeed, *nothing* makes sense -- not the world as a whole, not morality or human action in general, not the thoughts you're thinking or the words you're using, not *anything at all* -- without final causes."
Edward Feser,
The Last Superstition,
p. 70

"The moment I knew that God existed, I realized that I could do nothing but live for him alone."
Charles de Foucauld

Motion - the reduction of potency to actuality.

---

[5] Edward Feser, *Aquinas, A Beginner's Guide*, London: OneWorld Publications, 2009, pp. 16-23.

[6] Both Aristotle and Aquinas had a version of this argument.

[7] This is Aquinas' way of saying that when a thing moves, its potentiality is actualized.

[8] This is true because it is impossible for anything to be at the same time and in the same respect both that which is moved and that which does the moving.

NOTES

Subsequent - occurring or coming later or after; following in order.

"The sort of 'first' cause we are talking about is one which can actualize the potential for other things to exist without having to have its own existence actualized by anything.

"What this entails is that this cause doesn't have any *potential* for existence that needs to be actualized in the first place. It just *is* actual, always and already actual, as it were. Indeed, you might say that it doesn't merely *have* actuality, the way the things it actualizes do, but that it just *is pure actuality* itself."

Edward Feser,
Five Proofs of the Existence of God, p. 27

"To live is to be desired and loved by God, moment after moment."
Congregation for Institutes of Consecrated Life

Infinite - from the Latin *infinire*, "not to limit," unlimited; inexhaustible; endless.

An **accidentally ordered** causal series - a series of causes that are able to act independently of one another.

---

4. If that which puts something else in motion is itself moving, then there must be yet something further moving it, and so on.

5. This series of moved movers cannot be infinite because without a first mover, there would be no **subsequent** movers.

6. Therefore, there must be a First Mover, put in motion by no other -- the Unmoved Mover -- a Purely Actual Being!

The second argument is another of Aquinas' arguments: the Argument from Causality.

Argument from Causality

1. Something exists.

2. This something either:
   a. Caused itself to exist,
   b. Was caused to exist by another,
   c. Or has always existed.

3. But nothing can cause itself to exist, so *if it was caused*, it was caused by something else.

4. There cannot be an infinite series of *essential* causes, because without a first cause there would be no subsequent causes.

5. Therefore, there is a First Cause that is Uncaused -- the Uncaused Cause!

This argument is very similar to the previous one, especially if you consider that the existence of everything we experience on this earth is potential until it is actualized. So if there is something whose existence has been actualized by another, then we can reason to the fact that there must exist a being whose very nature or essence is existence itself, one whose existence requires no actualization because the being is Pure Act.

Both of these first two arguments are also similar in that the series of moved movers or caused causes cannot be **infinite** because both series of causes are ordered *per se* or *essentially* rather than being *accidentally* ordered. It is very important to understand the difference between these two types of series; the truth of both arguments depends on it.

Causes which are **accidentally ordered** to one another have the ability to cause *independently* of the cause that precedes them. For example, Tom is the son of Peter who is the son of Robert. Once Robert generates Peter, Peter is later able to generate Tom without the assistance of Robert. Robert, in fact, could be dead, and still Peter would be able to generate Tom. In other words, causes that are accidentally ordered typi-

Accidentally Ordered Series of Causes
In Time

cally extend backward in time, in what we might think of as a *linear* fashion. Each of these causes has its own ability to cause the next in the series without depending on the cause that brought it into existence. St. Thomas thinks that it cannot be proven that such an accidentally ordered series of causes must have a beginning; that is, he thinks that created beings could be an *eternal effect* of the First Cause.[9] Thus, if the causal series in the two previous arguments are merely *accidentally ordered*, i.e., extending back in time, then it does not necessarily follow that there is a First Mover or an Uncaused Cause that exists *here and now*.

An **essentially ordered** series of causes is different because such a series would demonstrate that there must be a First Mover or an Uncaused Cause existing *here and now*. So let's see if we can understand what such a series of causes is like.

In order to understand such a series, think about a single moment in time. For example, imagine that *at this moment* a lamp is hanging five feet above the floor in your living room. The lamp *of itself* does not have the ability to keep itself in the air. In order to do so, it depends *completely* on the chain link that is holding it there. But that one chain link has no ability *on its own* to keep the lamp in the air; it depends completely on the chain link that is attached to it. The entire chain holding up the lamp depends on the hook on the ceiling to which it is connected; the hook depends on the ceiling; the ceiling depends on the walls supporting it; the walls depend on the floor; the floor depends on the ground; the ground depends on materials below it. This series doesn't stop with the earth itself, since the earth cannot explain its own existence. It, too, depends on another cause.

Even if these dependent causes should go on infinitely, that would not adequately explain why the lamp is able to be suspended in air because none of these causes in this *essentially ordered* series has the power *of itself* to bring about the lamp hanging in the air; they are

---

An **essentially ordered** causal series - a series of causes in which each cause is completely dependent on the others for its ability to act (cause).

"What makes these series hierarchical in the relevant sense is not that they are simultaneous, but that there is a certain sort of *dependence* of the later members on the earlier ones."

Edward Feser,
Five Proofs of the Existence of God,
p. 22

---

[9] St. Thomas Aquinas, *De Aeternitate Mundi*.

NOTES

"The sort of 'first' cause that a hierarchical series must have is a cause that has the power to produce its effects in a *non*-derivative and *non*-instrumental way."

Edward Feser,
Five Proofs of the Existence of God,
p. 23

"God is not a faraway 'ultimate cause,' God is not the 'great architect' of deism, who created the machine of the world and is no longer part of it. On the contrary: God is the most present and decisive reality in each and every act of my life, in each and every moment of history."

Joseph Cardinal Ratzinger,
The Way to True Happiness

Inherent - existing in someone or something as a permanent and inseparable element, quality, or attribute.

---

all merely *instruments* being used by a cause which is not dependent on any other cause.

In this *hierarchical* series, then, where the causing occurs *simultaneously*, there must be a first cause which does not derive its causal ability from any other. It is this type of essentially ordered series which Aquinas is referring to in these arguments for God's existence. *Here and now*, there must be a First Cause, a First Mover that accounts for the existence of a thing, for the movement we see. This explains why a series of *essentially ordered* causes cannot be infinite.

The last argument that we will consider is Aquinas' argument based on the final causality that we see everywhere present in our world.

Argument from Final Causality

1. Things that lack intelligence act for an end. This is evident from their acting always, or nearly always, in the same way, so as to obtain the best result.

2. This acting for an end cannot be by chance, but by design.

3. But that which lacks intelligence can only act for an end if it is directed by something which has intelligence.

4. Therefore, there must exist some intelligent being by whom all natural things are directed to their ends.

This argument assumes an understanding of final causality. A final cause is only able to bring about an effect *if the final cause actually exists*. For instance, a person who wants to enjoy a batch of brownies will not even begin to gather the necessary ingredients until he has the idea of brownies in his mind. This "idea in his mind" is the final cause that *begins* the process of bringing the brownies into existence.

Thus, the final causality that we see everywhere present in our world indicates that a final cause must have existed *from the very beginning* **in the mind of the First Efficient Cause**. This is the only way final causality can work. So the final causality that we observe **inherent** in the natural world around us is due to the First Efficient Cause of that world who made the natures of the things to act in certain ways so as to attain their ends.

This Unmoved Mover, Uncaused Cause or First Efficient Cause we identify as God because this being is the ultimate cause of the existence of all things, in the sense of being that which keeps them in existence at any moment at which they exist at all. It will take more argument, however, to show that this Uncaused Cause is *one, omnipotent, perfect,* and *fully good*. We'll not take the time here, however, to go into those arguments.[10]

Study Guide Questions:

1. *Identify the four causes of a podium which sits in the front of a classroom.*

2. *Give an example of a series of accidentally ordered causes.*

3. *Give an example of a series of essentially ordered causes.*

4. *Which of the arguments for the existence of God do you find most convincing? Why?*

* * * * *

Point to Consider:

> *"Knowing and loving God*
> *is the vocation of every human person,*
> *the key to happiness,*
> *the answer to every question.*
> *Its greatest nourishment is prayer,*
> *and its greatest fruit is love."*
>
> Archbishop J. Peter Sartain

NOTES

"If there was a controlling power outside the universe, it could not show itself to us as one of the facts inside the universe -- no more than the architect of a house could actually be a wall or staircase or fireplace in that house. The only way in which we could expect it to show itself would be inside ourselves as an influence or a command trying to get us to behave in a certain way. And that is just what we do find inside ourselves.

C.S. Lewis
Mere Christianity

---

[10] For those interested in going further into these arguments, see Edward Feser's *Five Proofs of the Existence of God,* Ignatius Press, 2017, pp. 74-82.

CASES IN POINT

#1 -- "The wrath of God is indeed being revealed from heaven against every impiety and wickedness of those who suppress the truth by their wickedness. For what can be known about God is evident to them, because God made it evident to them. Ever since the creation of the world, his invisible attributes of eternal power and divinity have been able to be understood and perceived in what he has made. As a result, they have no excuse; for although they knew God they did not accord him glory as God or give him thanks. Instead, they became vain in their reasoning, and their senseless minds were darkened." *(Romans 1:18-21)*

Joseph Ratzinger notes that St. Paul is telling the Romans that truth was available to them "but they did not want it nor the claim it would make on them. ... Human beings oppose the truth that would demand submission of them -- submission in the form of honoring God and giving God thanks." Ratzinger points out that St. Paul thinks that human beings "are not condemned to ignorance with regard to God. We can 'see' God if we hearken to the voice of our essential nature, to the voice of creation, and let ourselves be led by this."

Joseph Ratzinger, *The Yes of Jesus Christ*, pp. 22-24.

- Do you agree with St. Paul? Do you think that a person's not seeing the evidence of God's existence is a matter of personal choice rather than a real lack of evidence? Explain.

*****

#2 -- "They (contemporary secularists) think that God's a being. They think God is one big being among many. It's what I call the yeti theory of God. (The yeti is a legendary creature in the folklore of Nepal, basically their version of Bigfoot.) There's supposed to be this thing out there. Some say he's there, some say he's not; so let's go see if we can find him out there. The question then becomes, "Is there evidence for a yeti? Is there evidence for God?"

"It's precisely the wrong way to think about God. God's not an item in the universe. ... I always go back to Thomas Aquinas, who said that God isn't a being, he's *ipsum esse subsistens*, 'subsistent being itself.' God's not in the genus of being; God is the ground of all being. ... God is not a thing in the world but rather the reason why there's something rather than nothing."

Bishop Robert Barron, *To Light a Fire on the Earth*, New York, pp. 193-194.

- *What is Bishop Barron's point? Why does this really matter?*
- *Do the arguments for God's existence presented in this chapter argue for a zeti type of God? Explain.*

Chapter III

THE HUMAN SOUL AND BODY

NOTES

Introduction

Now that we have struggled through trying to understand the philosophical principles, let us now turn to the more exciting work. Let's apply them to the human person.

According to St. Thomas, the central fact of human nature is that the human person is made up of a soul and a body. Understanding the soul and the body as well as their relationship to each other will be the basis for appreciating numerous truths regarding the human person:

- the goodness of the human body,
- the immortality of the human soul,
- the supreme value of the human person at every stage of his life.

Grasping the relationship between the soul and body will also enable us to see concretely how natural and supernatural knowledge (reason and faith) work together.

> **Vocabulary**
>
> nature   soul   zygote
> intrinsic   ensoulment   immortal

THE HUMAN SOUL

In applying some of the philosophical principles we have learned, we quickly realize that we, too, like all physical beings, are a union of form and matter. Aristotle had a special name for the form of a living physical being. He called this form a **soul** (in Latin *anima*, living). The soul is the substantial form of a body which has the potency to be alive.

Remember in the previous chapter when we talked about how form is more than just the external shape of something? We saw the example that if something had the external shape of a table but was not

Soul - in Latin *anima*, "living;" the first principle of life; the substantial form of a body which has the potency to be alive; the form of a living physical being.

engineered to have adequate stability and collapsed as soon as we set something on it, then we would not call it a table. There is a lot more to table-ness than just external shape. Well, when it comes to living beings, it is even clearer that form - soul - accounts for much more than the external shape of the being. It is the engineering and organizing principle of the body. It adjusts the molecules to their cells, the cells to their organs, the organs to their functions, arranging them all in a whole which is *its* body.

Did you notice that possessive pronoun "its" in the previous sentence? The body belongs to the soul and vice versa. They are not two separate things. Together they form <u>one</u> being: the human person. The soul is the source of the body's life. That's what we mean when we say that the soul is the *principle* of life. It is what makes the whole body to be alive. It makes the body's organs develop and function, making the body be a perfectly structured whole.

It is true that we speak of several "principles of life" in a human body, such as its brain, heart and lungs. These other principles of life are *secondary* principles. St. Thomas says they are simply signs of a more basic or ultimate principle of life: the <u>*first* principle of life</u>, the soul.

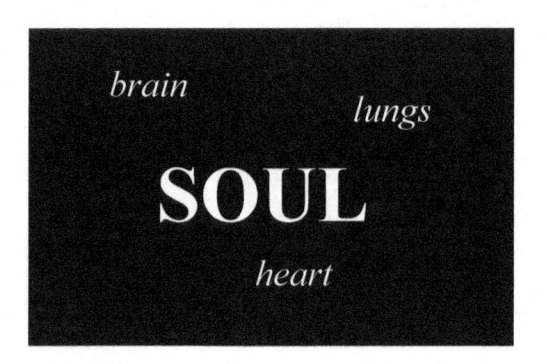

brain *lungs*
SOUL
heart

As the first principle of life, the soul is the "source" of life in a body. It makes possible the *first act* of any human being. This "first act" is its simple existence as a living being. Anything else that we do is "built on" this fundamental act of existence. This is important because it shows us that a person does not have to <u>do</u> anything to count as a human being. A person who is mentally disabled, physically handicapped, in a coma, or in some other way unable to do "normal" human activities is not any less human than the rest of us, no matter what his limitations are on the level of "second act."

So, then, any physical being that is alive should have a soul, according to this way of thinking, right? Yes, that is exactly right. Human persons are not the only beings with souls. Plants and animals have souls, too. But there are big differences among the souls of plants, animals, and human beings.

Just think about it a little. Remember what the form of a thing does for it. It makes the thing be the kind of thing that it is. This means that the human soul accounts for our *human* **nature**, just as the plant soul accounts for its plant nature, and the animal soul accounts for its animal nature. Now since these three natures are very different from each other, it seems reasonable to think that the souls must be very different, too.

We will look much more closely at the human soul and how it differs from the souls of plants and animals later in our study. For now, let us turn our attention to the body which the human soul animates.

Nature - the essence of a thing which it has from its origin; what a thing is.

THE HUMAN BODY

If we continue to apply our principles to the human person, we see easily where the body fits in. The human soul *informs* the matter of the human body. In other words, the human soul gives form to the body (the matter), making it to be a *human* body. This means that the human soul -- its essence and capabilities -- bring about the structure and physical attributes of the body. Thus, we have a larynx because our souls have something to say.[1]

"The body, in fact, and only the body, is capable of making visible what is invisible: the spiritual and the divine."
  Saint John Paul II
  Theology of the Body

As Aristotle himself said, "The whole body exists for the soul."[2] Now, since the soul is not material, it needs the body in order to express itself visibly. You could call us "body-persons" or "incarnate spirits."

"The body is the work of the soul. It is its expression …."
  Paul Claudel

Sometimes we joke about a person being unable to talk if his hands were tied behind his back; or we might observe that someone is "all-smiles;" or that one's "body-language" shows desire or anger or agreement. It really is true that we do come to know the person himself through his body. The body expresses the person. This is one reason why we claim that the human body is good and that what we do to a person's body we do to the person himself.

"A fine way to know the soul is to regard the body."
  Paul Claudel

The *Catechism of the Catholic Church* affirms this same truth. It teaches that the human body, sometimes called "the flesh," is **intrinsically** good. The *Catechism* says:

Intrinsic - from the Latin *intrinsecus*, "inward;" in and of itself, or essentially. It is the opposite of extrinsic, meaning external or unessential.

> … [M]an may not despise his bodily life. Rather he is obliged to regard his body as good and to hold it in honor since God has created it and will raise it up on the last day.[3]

---

[1] Cf. Msgr. Charles Pope, "The body God gave us doesn't lie: a meditation on the sexual confusion of our day," Lifesitenews.com.
[2] Aristotle, *The Parts of Animals*, 64b.13.
[3] The *Catechism of the Catholic Church*, 364.

The Human Person ~ Dignity Beyond Compare

NOTES

In fact, the Church teaches:

> 'The flesh is the hinge of salvation.' We believe in God who is Creator of the flesh; we believe in the Word made flesh in order to redeem the flesh; we believe in the resurrection of the flesh, the fulfillment of both the creation and the redemption of the flesh.[4]

By now you should be getting the picture that our bodies are really important! Saint John Paul worked very hard to help us realize this. In fact, this truth is at the heart of his *Theology of the Body*, where he says:

> The fact that theology also includes the body should not astonish or surprise anyone who is conscious of the mystery and reality of the Incarnation. Through the fact that the Word of God became flesh, the body entered theology … through the main door.[5]

With our bodies we not only express our souls; we also have something to say about who God is, for He made us in His image -- *soul* and *body*. There is way too much in that last statement to explain right now, but we will come back to it before we finish our study of the human person.

> **My soul is in my finger tip as much as it is in my head.**

THE UNION OF SOUL AND BODY

So, how does it work that the soul and body make up the person? Well, because the soul makes the whole body to be alive and human, it must be present *everywhere* in the body. This is not as wild an idea as it might seem at first, if you remember that the soul is not material. Because it is not material, it does not have to be located in a particular "place." This is, in fact, what St. Thomas means when he says that the soul is united to the body *as form is united to matter*. The form permeates the matter.

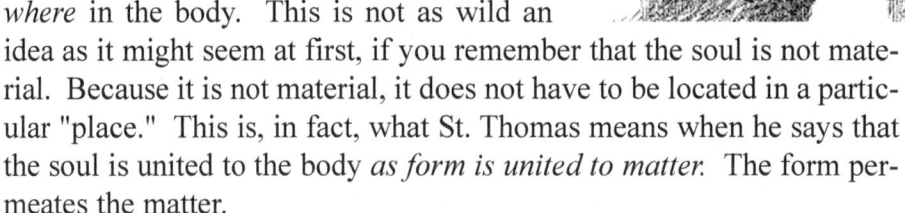

Remember, the substantial form is what gives a thing its *unity*. Because the substantial form of a thing is everywhere in it, the thing is organized into one coherent whole. In the same way, the soul must be everywhere in the body so that the body will be *one* body. It must be in the whole body and in each part of it -- with nothing excluded! We can easily check this out experimentally. Notice that we experience the

---

"The unity of soul and body is so profound that one has to consider the soul to be the 'form' of the body: … spirit and matter, in man, are not two natures united, but rather their union forms a single nature."

CCC, #365

"The soul acts upon every part of the body, and its action is to vivify, to make it alive (indeed, according to St. Thomas, the soul not only makes the body alive, it makes it a body). In some ways the presence of the soul in every part of the body is comparable to the presence of God in every part of the universe."

Frank Sheed,
Theology and Sanity

---

[4] *The Catechism of the Catholic Church*, #1015.
[5] Saint John Paul II, *Theology of the Body*, 23:4.

sense of touch in our hands and our feet *at the same time*. The soul is aware of both simultaneously: it doesn't have to "move" from one to the other but is equally present to both.

To say that the soul is present everywhere in the body is not to say that the soul does *all that it can do* in each part of the body. It acts in each part according to the purpose of the bodily part. For instance, the soul can see only with the eye, and it can hear only with the ear. The soul does what is proper to each particular part of the body, organizing them all to work as one united whole.

Let us sum this up. It is incorrect, Thomas says, to say the human person is either a soul *or* a body. Human persons are not just their bodies or just their souls. Rather, the human being is a body-soul unity.

The Beginning of the Union

When does it all begin, this body-soul union? That is kind of an easy question to answer, at least at the philosophical level. Since the soul is the first life principle of the body, the philosopher knows that it must be present to the body (one with the body) at the very beginning of the life of the person. Sometimes we use the word "**ensoulment**" to refer to this beginning point of the body-soul union.

Well, then, when does ensoulment occur? Doesn't the Catholic Church teach us this? No, the Church doesn't teach us about when ensoulment occurs, probably because determining this is not within her authority. It is a question philosophers must answer once the scientists have provided them with data indicating when there is a new, unique, and living human organism present. You see, it is science that determines when human life begins. The philosopher merely steps in to explain what it means to say that a thing is living. So let us turn first to the data the scientists have to offer us on this question.

Any high school biology text will point out that a human being is a whole, living member of the species *homo sapiens*. Clearly, human

---

Chapter III
THE HUMAN SOUL AND BODY

NOTES

"As a being at once body and spirit, man expresses and perceives spiritual realities through physical signs and symbols."
CCC, #1146

"Soul and body are not thus casually brought together; they are united to form one complete individual reality; they would not come into existence without each other; if they are separated they suffer loss -- the body ceases to be a body, and the spirit, although it survives, survives with a large part of its powers idle within it for lack of a body to use them on. You must never think of your soul simply as a more powerful thing which dominates your body: soul and body are partners in the business of being you."
Frank Sheed,
Theology and Sanity

Ensoulment - the beginning point of the body-soul union.

45.

The Human Person ~ Dignity Beyond Compare

NOTES

Fertilization - the procession of events that begins when a sperm penetrates an ovum and ends with the intermingling of maternal and paternal chromosomes in the zygote.

Zygote - the single cell phase of a new human being that is formed through the process of fertilization.

sperm cells and ova are not human beings. These sex cells are parts of male or female human beings. The ova and sperm lack the necessary human genetic matter (46 chromosomes). They also lack the ability to direct from within themselves their own organic functioning and development throughout all the various stages of life. The sex cells have only 23 chromosomes each: half of what is needed for human life. On its own, each ovum and each sperm will just maintain its identity as an ovum or sperm and will never develop into a human being.

Once a human ovum and sperm unite, however, there is present in that new single cell the full 46 chromosomes which identify it as being human. This is why we say that human life begins with **fertilization**, a process of events which begins when a sperm penetrates an ovum.[6] At the end of the fertilization process, usually 12-24 hours after the process has begun, a **zygote** is produced. When the zygote divides; it becomes an embryo.

Scientists have observed that once the union of ovum and sperm begins, the new single human cell directs its own organic functioning and development, an internal ordering which the new human being then has throughout all the stages of his or her life: fetal, infant, child, adolescent, and adult. (Note that the gender of the person is also determined at the moment of fertilization!)

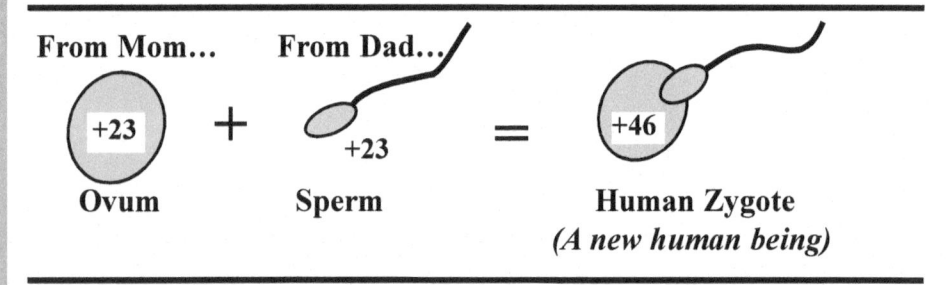

From Mom... **From Dad...**

$\text{Ovum } (+23) \;+\; \text{Sperm } (+23) \;=\; \text{Human Zygote } (+46)$
(A new human being)

Biologists have observed that at the single cell stage, the human embryo already has what we could call "a body plan." The embryo uses the point at which the sperm entered and penetrated the ovum's surface to determine what is top, bottom, left, and right.[7] So, that very first cell which was already you had what it needed to determine where your head and feet would go.

To sum up, then, science shows us that the first cell formed by the union of human ovum and sperm has its own 46 chromosomes and is operating under the direction of its own organizing principle. It is

---

[6] Since 1942 the internationally grounded Carnegie Stages of Early Human Embryonic Development -- the "gold standard" of human embryology -- makes it perfectly clear that in sexual human reproduction the new human being begins to exist at first contact of the sperm and oocyte.

[7] Rev. Nicanor Austriaco, O.P. "The Respondents," *Providence Magazine,* Spring, 2003, pp. 26-27.

already determined that this person will have green eyes, not blue eyes like her mother. To put it simply, science shows that from that very first cell, the embryo is an alive human being distinct from his mother and father.

Once science tells us this, the Thomistic philosopher knows that the human embryo must have a human soul, because the soul is the source of life and the cause of our being the kind of beings we are. In other words, at the moment of fertilization (conception), both a human body (the single first 46 chromosome cell) and a human soul (the life principle) are present, intimately united to form this new human being.

In light of all this, we would be wrong to speak about a human embryo as *potential* life, just as we would be wrong to speak about a two year old child as *potentially* living. Both are fully, actually living, though at different stages of their lives. The tiniest embryo is an <u>actual</u> human being, although he or she is a potential *child*, a potential *adolescent*, and a potential *adult*. He has the *potential* to be at these various stages of life, but he is not there yet.

Various Stages in the Life of a Human Being

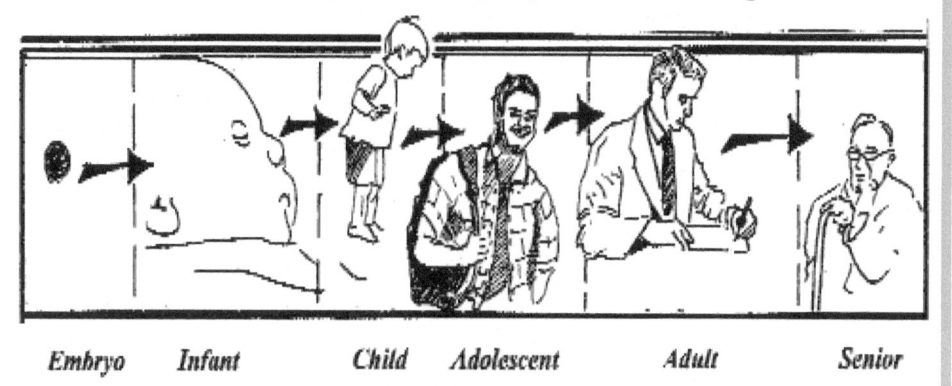

Embryo　　Infant　　Child　　Adolescent　　Adult　　Senior

One other point is worth making before we end this section: the body-soul union begins by means of a *substantial change*. The ovum from the mother and the sperm from the father change *substantially*. They each become a different kind of substance. The two cells that were a part of the parents' substances become a new, *unique* human substance -- this tiny little person has his own DNA! Even though he will continue to live within his mother's body for nine months, the new human person is *substantially* different from her. He is his own person, with his own body and soul. All of the later changes that this new human being will endure throughout his life will be simply accidental changes until the moment of death comes when his soul separates from his body (a change of substantial forms).

NOTES

On January 22, 1973, the United States Supreme Court handed down its Roe v. Wade decision legalizing abortion throughout all nine months of a woman's pregnancy. In that decision, the court mistakenly referred to the human life in its mother's womb as "potential life."

The Human Person ~ Dignity Beyond Compare

NOTES

The End of the Union

The only substantial changes that occur in a human person's life happen at its beginning and at its end, i.e., at his conception and death.[8] All of the other changes we experience in our lives are accidental, non-essential changes. This is important to remember when you see your grandmother who has suffered a stroke or a friend so severely burned that he is unrecognizable. These accidental changes do not alter the essence or the dignity of the people who endure them, nor do they remove our obligation to love and care for them.

When the soul-body union does come apart, the human person experiences a substantial change. This means that the human person stops being a human being. He or she dies. **Death**, then, is defined philosophically as the separation of the soul from the body.

Death - the separation of the soul from the body.

Just as wood will stop being wood if we burn it (because the wood loses the substantial form "wood-ness" and acquires the substantial form "ash-ness"), so the human being stops being a human being when his soul no longer informs his body. What happens at this point is that the substantial form "human-ness" (the human soul) leaves the body. The matter of the body which remains takes on a variety of new substantial forms as it decays. There is no *one* substantial form uniting this matter that was once the body. This is why after death the body begins to decompose. (This is true except in miraculous instances of incorrupt bodies or where science is able to keep the corpse artificially together.) The soul is no longer there to act as the unifying principle. This means that a human being and a human corpse are very different substances. What accounts for the difference is the presence or absence of the human soul. (We still treat a human corpse with respect, however, because it is the matter that once was united to a human soul.)

When the human soul separates from its body at death, however, the soul goes on existing. St. Thomas understood that this happens because of the kind of soul that it is. That is what we mean when we say the human soul is "**immortal**:" it cannot die. Once it is created, the human soul will never stop existing. (We will leave the discussion about precisely *why* St. Thomas thought this to a later chapter.)

Immortal - From the Latin *immortalis*, "not subject to death;" the unending continued existence of life.

Plants and animals are different. When they die, their souls also die. This is because their souls and bodies cannot exist without one another. So, when the animal or plant body and soul separate, *both* the body and soul cease to exist. Their souls are **mortal**, i.e., subject to death.

Mortal - From the Latin *mortalis*, "subject to death."

Because the human soul continues to exist after it is separated from its body, we can say that it exists *in an unnatural condition*. Body and soul are not two separate things; souls are forms of bodies; together

---

[8] Our faith tells us that the human corpse undergoes another substantial change when it reunites with its human soul at the resurrection of the dead.

they form a substantial whole, a living being. Human souls without their bodies, therefore, are existing in an unnatural condition.

Some people mistakenly think that a deceased human becomes an angel. But angels are not souls, because a soul is a form of a body, and angels do not have bodies. Angels are pure spirits. They are completely different creatures from human beings.

Separated human souls are no longer human beings because a human being is a body-soul union. The human soul separated from its body is in an *unnatural* condition. This is why St. Thomas says that the human soul in this condition will long to be reunited with its body. And our Christian faith tells us that this reuniting of soul and body will occur at the "resurrection of the body" at the end of the world, when the human person will once again experience a substantial change as his soul reunites with his resurrected and glorified body. What a happy day that will be, if we have lived our lives in keeping with our God-given dignity!

Conclusion:

As you have probably realized by now, even though it is difficult at first, the material studied in this chapter is of great significance both to each of us personally and to the well being of our world. Some of the most important and controversial positions the Catholic Church has taken in the 20th and 21st centuries are based in the correct understanding of the intimate relationship between the human soul and body. So intimate is this relationship that we rightly speak of the soul and *its* body, for it is the soul that constructs the body, organizing it and giving it life. It is to this organizing and life-giving principle of the human person that we turn our attention again in the next chapter as we look more in detail at all that the human soul can do.

Study Guide Questions:

1. *How ought the teaching that each person is both body and soul affect the way you regard yourself?*

2. *Why does it matter when ensoulment occurs?*

3. *Does it bother you to think that plants and animals no longer exist once they die? Why or why not?*

4. *What is imprecise about referring to a corpse as a human body? Why do we often do this very thing?*

The Human Person ~ Dignity Beyond Compare

CASES IN POINT

#1 -- In view of what we have studied in this chapter, how might you respond to the following opinions of one writer regarding abortion and the rights of the human embryo?

♦ "Abortion is not murder, because a fetus is not an actual human being -- it is a potential human being, i.e., it is a part of the woman. The concept murder only applies to the initiation of physical force used to destroy an actual human being."

♦ "An embryo has no rights. Rights do not pertain to a potential, only to an actual being. A child cannot acquire any rights until it is born. The living take precedence over the not-yet-living (or the unborn)."
- Ayn Rand

*****

#2 -- Anencephaly (*an*, "lacking;" *encephalo*, "brain") is a congenital birth defect which results in the failure in the devcopment of a person's brain. Babies born with this disorder of the brain lack the largest part of their brain, consisting mainly in the cerebral hemispheres, which are responsible for their ability to think. Because the brain stem is present, these babies are able to breathe, blink their eyes, and carry on other normal bodily functions.

Today, 95% of the babies with anencephaly are aborted while they are still in their mother's wombs. The remaining 5% are either still born or die within a few hours or days after birth. There is no cure or treatment for anencephaly.

♦ How do you think we should treat these little babies when they are born? Why?

♦ Would there be anything wrong with taking vital organs from their bodies which other babies might need in order to live? (In order to get these organs, we would have to kill the baby.)

*****

#3 -- "Sexuality is more than skin-deep. When it comes to sexuality in the human person, our sex is not just a coin toss. Our soul is either male or female and our body reflects that fact. I don't just "happen" to be male; I *am* male. My soul is male; my spirit is male; hence, my body is male.... *[Nothing we do to our bodies can]* change the truth of what the soul is. You can adapt the body, but you cannot adapt the soul. The soul simply says, 'Sum quod sum' (I am what I am)."
- Msgr. Charles Pope

♦ How does St. Thomas' understanding of form and matter explain the fact that our sexuality must be "more than skin-deep"?

Point to Consider:

"What the soul is to the human body,
the Holy Spirit is to the Body of Christ, which is the Church."
Catechism of the Catholic Church, #797

Chapter IV

VEGETATIVE & SENSITIVE POWERS
(Part I)

Introduction

In the last chapter we looked at the soul as being the first principle of a living body. In other words, the soul is what makes a thing to be *alive*. We also said that the soul is the *substantial form* of the body. As a substantial form, the soul makes a living thing to be the *kind of thing* that it is. This means that it is the plant soul that makes my flower a plant; the animal soul that makes Snarles an animal; and the human soul that makes you a human being.

What we would like to do in this chapter is to begin focusing in more detail on the human soul, looking specifically at what it can *do*. The human soul can do a great many things, though. So we will focus in this chapter and the next on what we have in common with lower forms of life -- with the plants and animals.

> **Vocabulary**
>
> vegetative   rational   phantasm
> sensitive   internal senses percept

POWERS OF THE SOUL

When St. Thomas speaks about *what a thing can do*, he uses the term "power" or "**faculty**." Thus, he refers to the *powers* or *faculties* of the human soul when he is speaking about the soul's *ability to do something*.

How do we know what powers a soul has, since we cannot *see* souls, let alone their powers? Remember what we learned in the last chapter: the soul expresses itself through its body. So, the first way

NOTES

Faculty - from the Latin *facere*, "to make;" a power of the soul that produces certain operations.

51.

The Human Person ~ Dignity Beyond Compare

NOTES

we know what faculties a soul has is to look at what we see its body doing. For example, if we know that a body can digest food, then we conclude that its soul has the *power* to nourish itself. Once we know the faculties of a soul, then we know something about what kind of a being it is, its *nature*. The following diagram might help to clarify this:

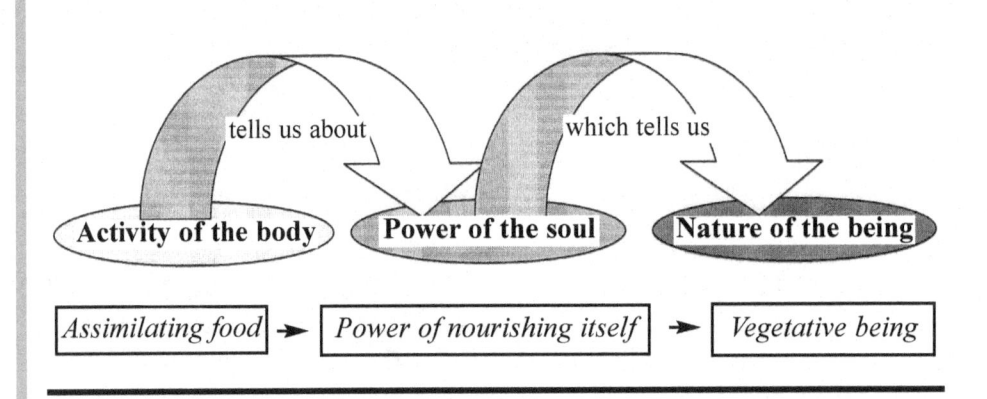

Activity of the body	tells us about	Power of the soul	which tells us	Nature of the being
Assimilating food	→	Power of nourishing itself	→	Vegetative being

The second way we can know the faculties of the human soul is by *looking within* ourselves, through a process called **introspection**. Through introspection, the human soul can actually "see" itself at work.

Using these two methods:
- looking at the activities of the body and
- the process of introspection,

St. Thomas identifies the human soul as the source for three main kinds of activities: **vegetative**, **sensitive** and **rational**. This is why he speaks of the soul's vegetative powers, its sensitive powers and its rational powers. These powers account for the soul's many and varied activities, as we'll soon see.

Before we look at the powers themselves, however, it is important to clarify one other thing. We call the souls of plants "vegetative souls" because they have only the vegetative powers. The souls of non-human animals have *both* vegetative and sensitive powers. We refer to their souls as "sensitive souls" because the sensitive powers are the highest ones they possess. This term "sensitive" comes from the fact that the soul of an animal has one or more of the fives senses. Plants can't sense anything. A tree does not wince in pain or even say, "Ouch!" when we tear off a leaf. But animals can feel pain.

The soul of a human being possesses both the vegetative and sensitive powers. But it has two more powers in addition to these.

Introspection - from the Latin *intro*, "inwardly, within, into," and *specere*, "to look." It refers to the practice of looking into -- giving mental attention to -- one's mental states and functions in an attempt to describe, study, or enjoy them.

52.

Chapter IV
VEGETATIVE & SENSITIVE POWERS -- Part I

Kind of Being	Kind of Soul	Powers of the Soul		
		Vegetative	*Sensitive*	*Rational*
Human	Rational	✓	✓	✓
Non-human Animal	Sensitive	✓	✓	
Plant	Vegetative	✓		

Every human soul has an intellect and a free will. It is because of these two rational powers that we call the soul of a human being a "rational soul."

Be careful not to make the mistake of thinking the human being has *three* souls because it has these three kinds of powers. If it had three souls, then it would be three *kinds of beings*. It would lack the unity required to be the *one being* which it is. The human person has only one soul, but his one rational soul has a greater variety of powers than do plant or animal souls. Animal souls have more powers than plant souls. This is precisely why we speak about *higher* or *lower* life forms. The more powers a soul has, the higher is its form of life.

The chart on the next page gives you the "big picture" regarding the soul and its powers. Having a look at "the big picture" now will be a help as we progress in considering the powers of the human soul.

NOTES

Vegetative - refers to the powers of the soul which enable it to grow, nourish itself, and reproduce. The souls of plants have only these powers.

Sensitive - refers to the powers of the soul which enable it to receive and react to sensations. All animals have the sensitive powers of the soul as well as the vegetative powers.

Rational - from the Latin *ratio*, "reason." It refers to the human way of thinking because our minds move in a step-by-step fashion from understanding one idea to understanding another one, to understanding a third. It is as if we come to knowledge in "piecemeal" fashion. Sometimes the word "rational" is used interchangeably with "intellectual," but strictly speaking they have different meanings.

The Human Person ~ Dignity Beyond Compare

POWERS OF THE SOUL

Rational Powers →	**Intellect** -- the ability to think (and come to know the truth) **Will** -- the ability to choose freely (to do right or wrong)
Sensitive Powers →	**Sensation** -- the ability to "take in" the environment in an immaterial way *External senses*: *Internal senses*: - Touch - Common sense - Taste - Imagination - Smell - Memory - Hearing - Estimative / Cogitative sense - Sight **Appetition** -- the ability to respond *internally* to what is sensed *Concupiscible Appetite*: *Irascible Appetite*: - Love - Hope - Desire - Despair - Pleasure / Joy - Courage - Hate - Fear - Aversion - Anger - Pain / Sorrow **Locomotion** - the ability to move oneself from place to place
Vegetative Powers →	**Nutrition** -- the ability to take in nutrients and assimilate them **Growth** -- the ability to progress in quantity and in overall life **Reproduction** -- the ability to pass on life to another being of the same species

Vegetative Powers

The lowest powers of the human soul -- the vegetative -- are those which it has in common with all living beings -- that is, with plants and animals, too. The vegetative powers govern the *most basic* processes a being needs in order to maintain its life. These are the activities of nourishing, growing, and reproducing. The vegetative powers of nutrition, growth, and reproduction account for these activities.

With the vegetative power of nutrition, a soul is able to take in the necessary nourishment it needs from its environment. In doing this, it relates with the world around it in a purely *material* way. For example, the soul of a plant literally draws the nutrients from the soil and the air physically into itself, transforming them into itself. In animals and human beings, the process is similar. The nutrients are taken in physically and changed into the substance of the one being nourished. With this nourishment, the being is able to grow. The vegetative power of reproduction enables the soul/body union to generate a new member of its species.

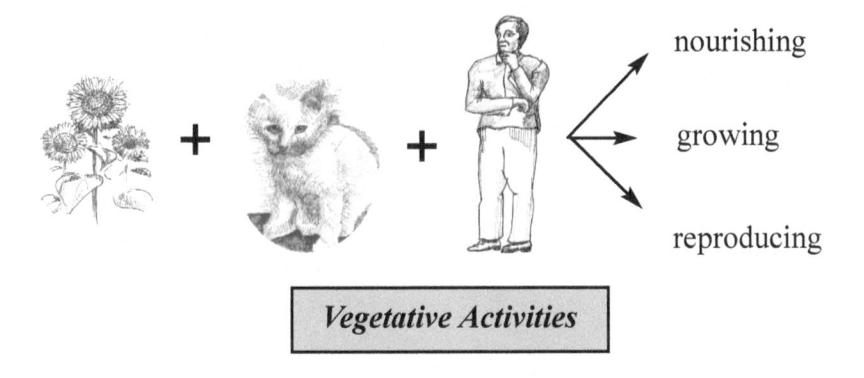

Vegetative Activities: nourishing, growing, reproducing

The vegetative powers of the human soul are not under our *direct* control. Rather, they are on "automatic pilot," so to speak. They work on their own without our having to think about them. For example, the acids in your stomach break down food without your directing them; the pituitary gland regulates your growth while you are oblivious to its operation; a baby grows and develops in his mother's womb without her controlling the process. This is all probably a very good thing, since these powers are so basic to our well-being. It would be quite an over-whelming task for one to supervise digestion and nourishment, the building up and breaking down of body tissue, the production of sperm and ovum cells, as well as the development of new little human beings!

Someone might object, "But I do have control over my procreative powers and my power to grow and be nourished." Well, it is true

NOTES

that we can *indirectly influence* these powers by our behavior, for example, by the foods we choose to eat or the sexual behavior we choose to engage in. As soon as you use the word "choose," however, you have brought into the picture a higher power of the rational soul, the free will. Plants and animals don't make such choices because they have only vegetative souls.

So, you can see that these vegetative powers are "self-directing" powers. The fact that in human beings they can be indirectly influenced by the soul's power to choose freely shows us that our higher powers influence our lower ones. It also tells us something about the dignity of the human soul itself.

Study Guide Questions:

1. How would you explain to someone <u>why</u> we think that a soul has the powers that it has? For example, why do we think the soul of a plant has the power of growth?

2. If the human soul has all the powers that the vegetative, sensitive, and rational souls have, shouldn't we say that there are <u>three</u> souls in us? Explain.

3. Why is it actually a good thing that the vegetative powers of the soul are <u>not</u> under our direct control?

CASE IN POINT

We human beings can harm ourselves by eating too much (gluttony) or by not eating the right kinds of foods (too many sweets and not enough protein).

- What harm can come to us if our vegetative powers don't work correctly?

- How can our use of our vegetative powers be offensive to God?

- Hospitals employ nutritionists to help in the care of patients. How is their work a real service to the human person, especially when someone is ill?

Chapter IV
VEGETATIVE & SENSITIVE POWERS -- Part I

Sensitive Powers

The sensitive powers of the soul enable it to relate to the world around it in more than a purely material way. This is why we consider them to be higher powers than the vegetative. The sensitive powers of the soul can be grouped into three distinct categories: sensation, appetition, and locomotion.

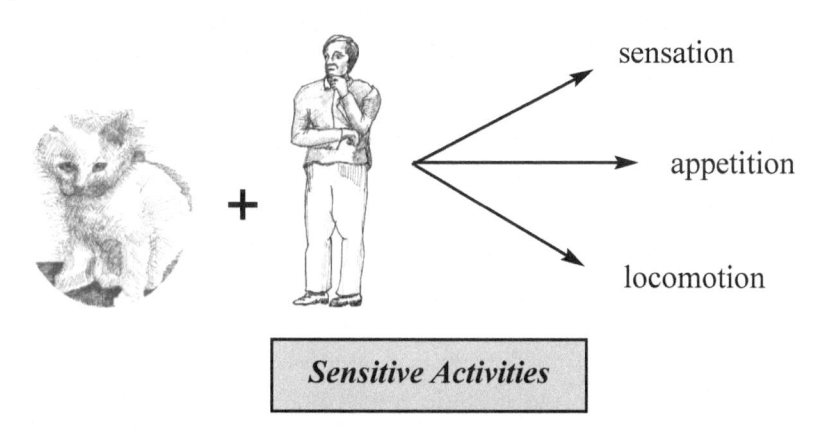

Sensitive Activities: sensation, appetition, locomotion

SENSATION

The External Senses

With the power of sensation, the soul -- by means of its body -- acquires knowledge of the world around it. This is what we mean by "sense knowledge." The five **external senses** of sight, hearing, smell, taste, and touch enable the person (soul-body unity) to "take in" the world around him. For example, through smelling we can become aware of the lily or the freshly popped popcorn. Through sight we "take in" the beauty of a sunset or the smile on a friend's face. In fact, St. Thomas says that nothing enters into the human intellect except what passes through the senses. Although the soul's sense powers are tied to bodily organs like eyes and ears, they are able to bring *into the soul* in some *immaterial* way the things of the world they experience.

Why do we say the things of the world come into the soul in some *immaterial* way? Well, think about it. When you sense the world around you -- see the sunset, smell the rose, taste the lasagna, hear the lecture -- in some way you "take into yourself" what is in the world outside of you so that you are able to *know* it. You do not take it into yourself *exactly* as it exists outside yourself; otherwise, there would not be enough room in you to hold it all! Sunsets won't fit in your head. You must be "taking it in" in such a way that space is not a problem. That is why we say that it is in some *immate-*

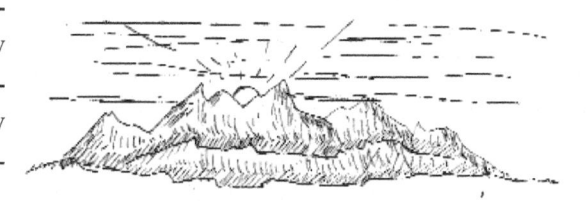

NOTES

In plants and animals, we speak of "reproductive" powers. In human beings, we refer to these same powers as "procreative." By using this term, we are acknowledging that the parents, in begetting a new human being, are cooperating with God, the Creator, who provides the human soul for the new person. This explains why we must always use our procreative powers in ways that are truly good for the person who comes into existence through them.

"Organs like the eye, the ear, the nose, the mouth present themselves in the form of receptors. They are obviously fashioned to receive the messages that come from things in the world. They are so many 'open doors,' where qualities, the shapes of sensible things, enter the soul. They are so many recesses in which the soul accumulates the numberless objects offered by the world. Thus, we 'toss' a whole, delicious 'salad' within our consciousness."

Pierre-Marie Emonet

57.

The Human Person ~ Dignity Beyond Compare

NOTES

Proper object - the end or goal of a power of a soul; that in reality which the powers of the soul were designed to know.

"For my eyes say, 'If things have a color, it was we who have brought these messages.' The ears say, 'If they gave any sound, it was from us that their revelations come.' The nostrils say, 'If they had any smell, it is through us that they have passed.' The sense of taste also says, 'Unless they had a savor, never ask me for them.' The touch says, 'Were it not a body, I handled it not; and if I never handled it, then I gave no notice to it.'"

St. Augustine, *Confessions*

"This type of burgeoning thing, these buds, translucent, these two globes charged with exquisite devices, filling the double alcove of the skull and contriving to be capable of sallying forth in all directions, this double receptive sun, by which one communes with all that is light without! It is as if the need to see had made the eye, the eye the face, the face the head, and the head this flexible neck!"

Paul Claudel

Internal senses - the common sense, imagination, memory, and cogitative (estimative) sense.

58.

rial way that we take in these things. St. Thomas said that the knower takes in the *forms* (Ex: rose-ness) of the things he knows but without their *matter*. Let us see what he meant by that.

In order to "take things in," each of the external senses has its own **proper object**, that is, its own specific aspect of the world that it is designed to "pick up" or sense. For example, the proper object of sight is color. None of the other senses can pick it up. So, if a person has been blind from birth, the word "red" will have no meaning for him because he lacks the sense of sight that picks up the color red. No one would put his hand above a cake to find out how delicious it smells. Hands can't detect odors. Only noses can do that.

The proper object of hearing is sound; for smell, it is odor; and for taste, it is savor. The proper object of touch is the tactual. This vague term "tactual" covers many things. Every human sensation that is not clearly from the other four senses is considered to be the object of the sense of touch. This would include sensations such as: pressure, pain, hot/cold, wet/dry, hard/soft, motion/rest, tired/energetic, and so on.

Now, someone might be thinking, "Isn't this power of sensation we are talking about simply the work of a bodily organ, like the ear or the eye? Why do we say the soul is involved?" That's a good question. Let us think about it for just a minute. Have you ever seen something with your eyes or heard something with your ears, but you did not *really* see or *really* hear because you were not "paying attention" to what your bodily organs were taking in? What is happening in these cases shows us that it takes *both* the body *and* soul really to see and hear. It is not enough for my eyes to be open and looking at the teacher presenting a lesson at the board. My soul needs to be attuned to what my eyes and ears are taking in; otherwise, what I am seeing and hearing doesn't really enter into my soul.

The Internal Senses

Most of us are aware of our five external senses, but few have probably heard of the **internal senses**. They are called "internal"

Chapter IV
VEGETATIVE & SENSITIVE POWERS -- Part I

because they work more from *within* us. They are not "tied to an organ" at the body's surface. Seated in the brain, the internal senses *refine* the data brought in by the external senses. This ensures that the soul receives a more complete reception of the outer world.

We can know these internal senses exist because we see activities in both animals and humans that require powers of the soul to make them happen. St. Thomas also uses the process of *introspection* to know about these senses. He *looks within himself* and "sees" the results of their activities. Using both of these methods, St. Thomas identifies the internal senses as the following:

1) <u>Common sense</u> - This internal sense is <u>not</u> what we refer to when we tell someone to use his "common sense," i.e., to use good judgment. No, this internal sense refers to the power of the soul which puts together the images which each of the external senses brings in. In doing this, it forms a unified whole of whatever is being sensed. We call this image of the sensed object we perceive the "**percept**." For example, when you sense a lemon, your common sense automatically "*puts together*" the images of its color, its taste, its odor and the rough texture of its peal. Even though we take in the various qualities of the lemon through different senses, we *perceive* them all together as aspects of the one thing, the lemon.

Percept - the image of the sensed object which is formed by the common sense.

We say, then, that the job of the common sense is to *integrate* -- to put together as a whole -- the various pieces of information our external senses give us about what we are experiencing in the world. It is called "common" because all of the external senses contribute to it and because it brings together "*in common*" all the various qualities of the one thing we perceive, such as the lemon.

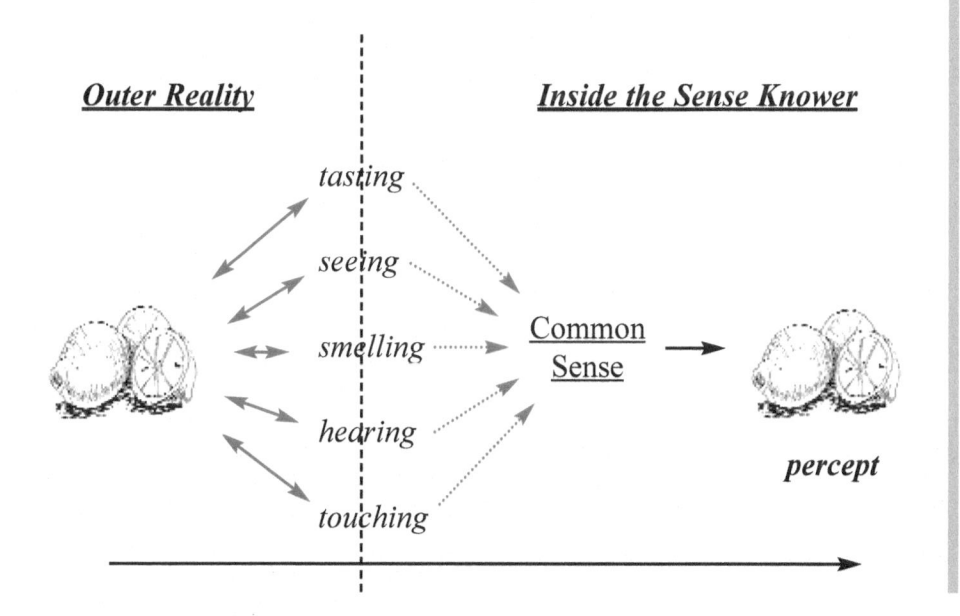

Outer Reality | *Inside the Sense Knower*

tasting
seeing
smelling → <u>Common Sense</u> →
hearing
touching

percept

59.

There is one other important function of the common sense. When the common sense puts together the different objects of sensation (color, taste, smell), it unites qualities that don't usually go together. For example, there is nothing about "yellow" and "sour" that would indicate they go together as qualities of the same thing. When the common sense puts them together as qualities of the object being sensed, it is taking the first step in acquiring knowledge that is *objective*. "Objective" simply means that the knowledge is not something we're making up. It is knowledge that is based on the *object* that exists outside of us.

Now, it is true that at times what one person perceives as sweet, another will perceive as sour. This does not deny that our sense knowledge is based on *objective* reality, however. Rather, it reminds us that sense knowledge also involves the one who is doing the knowing, the *subject*. The condition of the person (the subject) can have an affect on our ability to know. Remember how we said that a blind person cannot know the color red? Similarly, a person who has just eaten a piece of fudge will experience a lemon as being more sour than would a person who hasn't just eaten fudge.

2) <u>*Imagination*</u> - The imagination is the power of the soul which produces the very first images a knower (animal or human) has of the various sensations he is experiencing through his exterior senses. For example, the imagination forms an image of the sound or the odor or the color of the sensed object. St. Augustine writes about the imagination: "There we find countless images, brought in by every sort of perception."[1] You see, the images stored by the imagination are not just *visual* images. It stores the images received from any of the five exterior senses. St. Augustine, speaking again about the imagination:

"I distinguish the perfume of the lily from that of violets, without smelling a flower. I can prefer honey to wine sauce, the smooth to the rough, without tasting anything or touching anything."[2]

You and I can "smell" the brownies baking or "hear" the music from last weekend's concert long after the brownies have been eaten and the concert's ended. It is fascinating to realize this about ourselves!

Once the common sense "unites" the images it receives from the exterior senses, forming the percept, it is the imagination's work to use this percept to produce a completed sense image we call the

---

[1] St. Augustine, *Confessions*, 10.8.
[2] Ibid.

Chapter IV
VEGETATIVE & SENSITIVE POWERS -- Part I

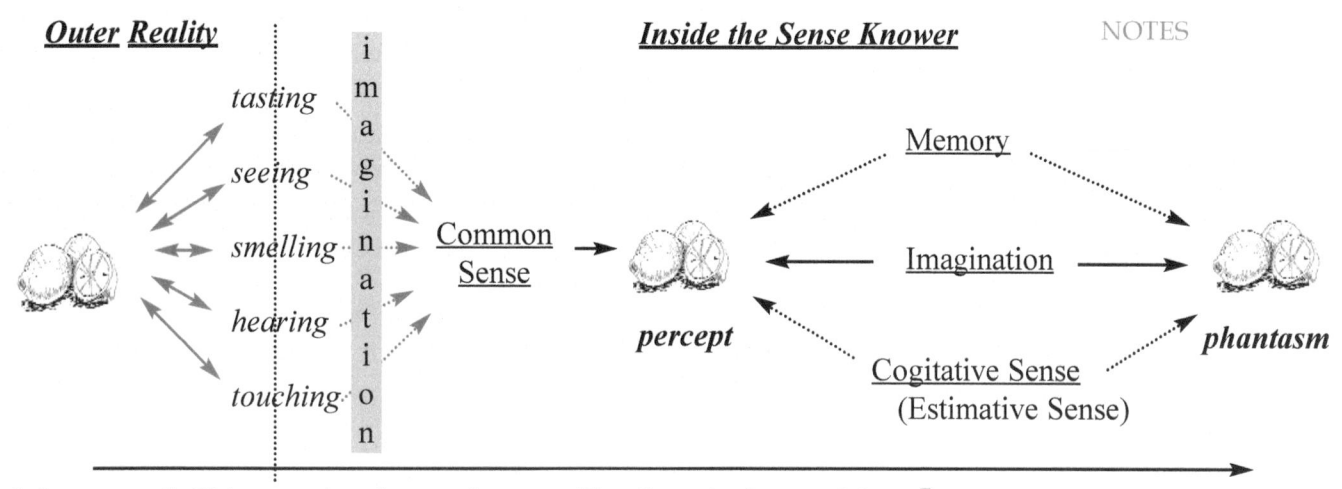

Outer Reality   *imagination*   **Inside the Sense Knower**   NOTES

tasting
seeing
smelling → Common Sense → *percept* ← Memory → *phantasm*
hearing   ← Imagination →
touching   ← Cogitative Sense
                  (Estimative Sense)

"**phantasm**." This completed sense image will reflect the input of the other two internal senses we will look at next. The *phantasm* is also the image that the knower will use if he wants to recall an image that he is not presently sensing.

You no doubt have had the experience of trying to "put things into your head" so that you can recall them as you take an exam. It is the work of the imagination actually to store the images of the things you experience through your senses. Thanks to the imagination, we are able to experience right *now* objects that are physically absent from us. And the really good news is that there seems to be an unlimited amount of storage space -- despite the fact that you might feel *full* after studying!

When the imagination recalls an image stored away, what the person actually knows is the *thing in reality* that the image represents. The image within him is the *means by which* he knows the thing in reality. For example, when I recall an image of my mother, I do not simply know the image of her. I know my mother herself. Her image within me is the means by which I know her.

Because of our rational powers, we can *direct* our imagination to recall certain images. Animals can't do this. So, the soul can have present to it, through the imagination, the world at large. Just think of it! "In a fraction of a second, I have Paris in me, I have my mother in me -- and yet she left this world more than thirty years ago!"[3] Right now, I can direct my mind to last summer's vacation or to the first Christmas I remember as a child. It's amazing, when you stop to think of it.

NOTES

Phantasm - the completed sense image which is produced by the imagination.

---
[3] Pierre-Marie Emonet, O.P., *The Greatest Marvel of Nature*, New York: The Crossroad Publishing Company, 1994, p.19.

The Human Person ~ Dignity Beyond Compare

NOTES

In human beings, the imagination can do even more than this. Thanks to the influence of our rational powers, we can use our imagination *creatively*. We can select images to recall and put them together in new ways -- in ways not found in reality. That is how we have been able to come up with such things as "mermaids," "centaurs," and countless new inventions.

There is, though, a limitation to our creative ability. The imagination cannot make up images it has not previously sensed. It can only combine previously sensed images in creative ways not found in reality.

A word of caution: The imagination is extremely spontaneous. It does not always wait for us to tell it what to recall. This explains why images -- welcome or unwelcome -- pop into our heads at all hours of the day or night. Some of them can be quite disturbing. So, if we want to control what images pop up in our minds, we need to be careful about the pictures and movies we see, the music we hear, the books we read, and the food and drink we taste. If we want to "feed" our imagination in healthy ways, then we expose it to the kinds of pictures, movies, music, etc., which will spur us on to wholesome living.

3) <u>Memory</u> - The internal sense of memory works in partnership with the imagination. The imagination makes the sense images and stores them. The memory takes these images and situates them *in time*. So, for instance, when your memory takes the image of you playing with your little brother when he was two-years-old and the one of you walking him home after his first day of school, it enables you to know that the one occurred *before* the other one. This awareness of *before* and *after* is the work of the memory. As St. Thomas says, memory enables us to "sense" time.

Animals, of course, have memory too, but in animals, memory entails only a sudden recollection of a sensed object as being "of the past." They have no control of the recollection. So when Snarles sees his master, he will remember him bringing food and respond by wagging his tail. Or when he sees someone who abused him, Snarles will remember the person as being harmful and respond by growling or barking. In human beings, however, we can **reminisce** by freely *choosing* to recall certain past images. Through memory, we can recover whole sections of our lives, making them exist in a new way *in our souls*. This is why a person can say that he delights in thinking about his childhood days.

Under the influence of the rational powers, we can use our memory as a tool to seek specific information we want to recall. Does that not usually happen to you as you try to fill in answers for a test? You

Reminisce - to recall past experiences.

might actually be able to "hear" yourself tell your memory to seek the image of the notes that you studied the night before.

With the ability to see ourselves in past images, we experience continuity in our lives and begin to understand ourselves as *enduring* in time. The memory, then, helps form what we call our *self-awareness*. It is a tool our **consciousness** uses to "gather in" our identity. So, by my memory, I can "meet myself," remembering what I did at a certain time; where I was; even how I felt as I did it!

Consciousness - from the Latin *conscire*, "to know, to be aware of;" a center or focal point of a person's awareness.

4) *Estimative / cogitative sense* - There are two names for this internal sense, depending on whether we are talking about its presence in animals or in human beings. In animals, we call it the *estimative sense*. This sense enables them to "estimate" or "size up" a situation quickly, determining whether the object sensed is helpful or harmful to them. When we speak about animal "instinct," we are referring to the work of the estimative sense. It provides a non-thinking but correct response to the situation. For example, when a rabbit senses a fox, the rabbit senses ("estimates") that the fox is dangerous and runs for its life. Similarly, a bird senses ("estimates") which material is good for building its nest.

If we were not aware of this internal sense, we might make the mistake of thinking that the animals themselves are smart, because they seem to be "thinking." Snarles does have the estimative sense, but that doesn't mean he's thinking! The One who designed him put into him well-developed instincts.

In human persons, we call this internal sense the *cogitative sense*. Although it is similar to the animal's "estimative" ability, it is significantly different in humans. This is because we humans have rational powers. Man's instinct is poorly developed, probably because he does not really need it. St. Thomas explains that what an animal knows through instinct, a human being learns by putting ideas together.[4] For example, birds know by instinct what materials to use to build their nests. A human person, however, doesn't know by instinct what

---
[4] St. Thomas Aquinas, *Summa Theologiae* I, 78, 4.

materials he should use to make his house. He can figure it out, though, by trial and error or by what he knows concerning the nature of certain materials. That is why our homes have improved over time while birds still build their nests the same way they always have.

Let us take what we have been discussing regarding these powers of sensation and try to see how it all fits together. The diagram on the next page might help to summarize and to visualize what's going on inside the one sensing an object in the outer world. For the sake of trying to picture it, though, we will be "pulling apart" the act of sensation. It's important to realize that the activity involved here happens so quickly that we hardly realize it's going on.

In the diagram, a lemon exists in reality:

1. A person senses it with at least one or more of his senses. He might see its yellow color, taste its tart flavor, feel its rough peel, or smell its odor. Once these external senses *take in* their respective objects, the internal senses go to work.

2. Thus, as you are looking at, tasting and touching the lemon, your imagination forms the images of the various sensations and stores them away. It forms images of the lemon's yellow color, its tart taste, or its oval shape.

3. The common sense then puts together these images it has received from the external senses. In doing so, it forms an image (the percept) of the lemon *inside* the knower. We refer to the percept when we ask the question, "What are you *perceiving*?" With this question we are asking: "What are you sensing right now?"

4. This sense image -- the percept -- is then refined by the memory and the cogitative sense before the imagination produces the completed sense image (the phantasm).

5. The phantasm is also the sense image that we bring to mind when we have an image of something we are not actually sensing at the time.

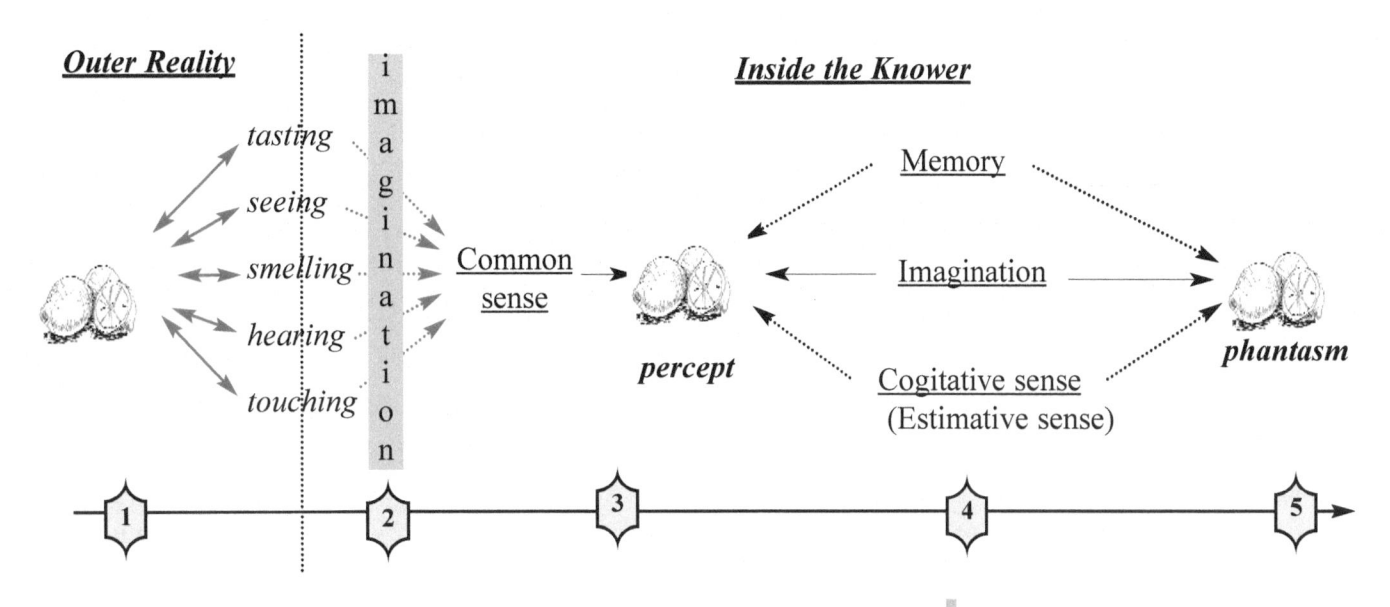

Chapter IV
VEGETATIVE & SENSITIVE POWERS -- Part I

Outer Reality   *Inside the Knower*

[Diagram showing the process from Outer Reality through imagination, Common sense → percept → Memory/Imagination/Cogitative sense (Estimative sense) → phantasm, with stages numbered 1 through 5]

For example, as you think of a hot fudge sundae which is not actually present, the image of it that you have in your mind is the *phantasm*, which is kept stored in your imagination. If I ask you to think of the last hot fudge sundae you enjoyed, your memory goes to work, locating in the stored phantasms the most recent image. The cogitative sense might also have its say about the hot fudge sundae, telling you how good it is to taste but also how much you don't need the added sugar it brings. Notice that this is not a matter of instinct for us, but of the use of our reasoning power.

NOTES

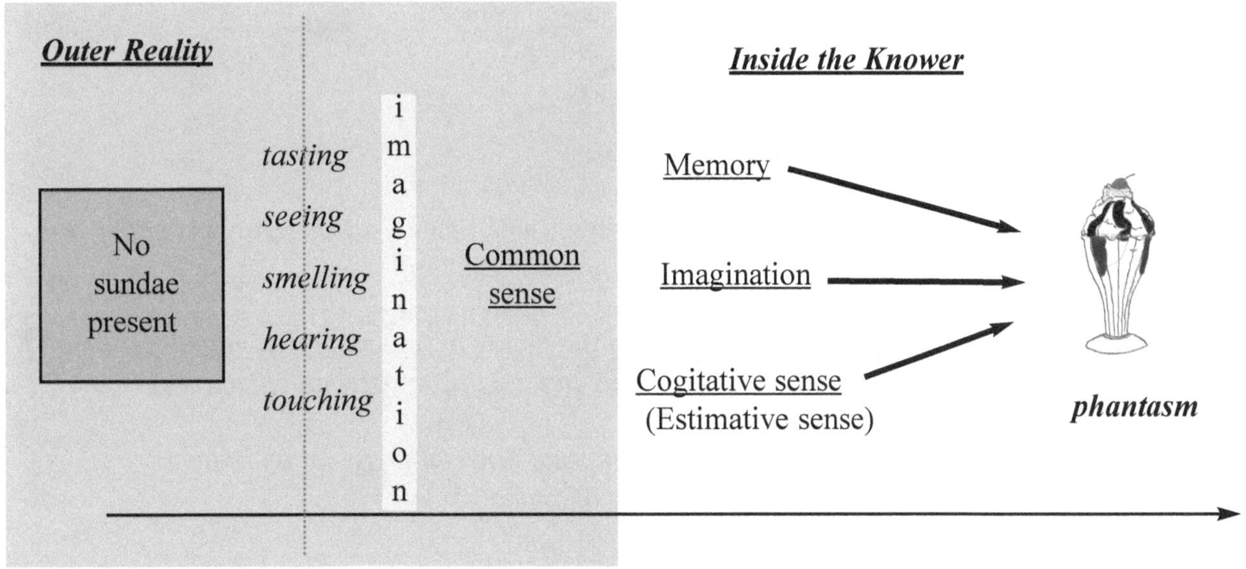

Outer Reality   *Inside the Knower*

[Diagram: "No sundae present" box, with tasting/seeing/smelling/hearing/touching, imagination, Common sense; on the right Memory, Imagination, Cogitative sense (Estimative sense) all pointing to a sundae labeled *phantasm*]

The sense image (whether as a percept or a phantasm) is **immaterial**; otherwise, it would not "fit" inside the knower. Still, it has certain material conditions. What we mean by "material conditions" is that the image of the lemon inside the knower will have a *particular*

Immaterial - from the Latin *im*, "not," and *materialis*, "matter;" without matter.

65.

size, odor, color, and texture. These material or accidental qualities are the conditions of the *matter* of this particular lemon that the knower either is presently sensing or has previously sensed.

Conclusion

We have investigated the vegetative and sensitive powers of the soul, and we have seen that:

- With his vegetative powers of nutrition, growth, and reproduction, the human person keeps himself alive;

- With his external and internal senses, the human person has the tools he needs to know the world around him.

There is still more, however. Aristotle tells us that "[w]here there is sensation, there is also pain and pleasure, and where there is pain and pleasure, there is necessarily appetite."[5] What does he mean by this? Simply that the senses enable the soul not only to know the world but also to respond to it. For example, the rabbit not only has sense knowledge of the lettuce in the garden, but it can also experience a "movement" within himself making him tend toward it. It is to these "moving powers" by which we respond to what our senses present, that we now turn our attention.

Study Guide Questions:

1. Why did St. Thomas think that knowledge always implies a certain degree of immateriality?

2. What is it about the power of sensation that might give us a clue that we are, in fact, in contact with objective reality?

3. How does the internal sense of imagination in human beings differ from that of animals?

4. How does memory contribute to our self-awareness?

5. Why does St. Thomas give the estimative sense a different name when he considers its presence in human beings?

---

[5] Aristotle, *On the Soul*, 2.423b.24.

CASES IN POINT

#1 - When Robert was a second grader preparing for the Sacrament of Penance, he learned that he could offend God by his bad thoughts as well as by his bad acts. He didn't know what that meant at the time, but now that he is in high school, he understands it better. Some of the guys in his class go regularly to R-rated movies. He went along with them once, but he found that for weeks after that, he carried around within him the images he had seen.

- What would be so bad about having images from an R-rated movie pop up in your mind every so often?

- If we don't freely bring these images to mind, then why would we be held responsible for them being there?

***

#2 - St. Augustine once wrote, "It is in the immense palace of my memory that I meet myself, that I remember myself, what I have done, the moment and place that I have done it, *[my feelings]* at that moment and in that place, as I did what I did." (*Confessions* 10.8)

- What is St. Augustine talking about regarding the memory?

***

#3 - In his book *Do Animals Think?*, Clive Wynne points out the following: "Instinct knows everything in the undeviating *[unchanging]* paths marked out for it; it knows nothing outside those paths." (p. 56)

- What instincts of animals do you find to be very impressive?

- What is Mr. Wynne saying about these impressive ways in which we see animals behaving?

Chapter V

VEGETATIVE & SENSITIVE POWERS
(Part II)

Introduction

The sensitive powers of the soul do not stop with simply knowing the world. Knowing the world around us is not enough. For the rabbit to have sense knowledge of the goodness of the lettuce growing in the garden or the harmfulness of the fox just feet away from it is not good enough. The one with sense knowledge needs to *pursue* those things in the world that are good for him and to avoid what will harm him. This is where the soul's power of **appetition**, i.e., the **sense appetites**, comes in. They are the *first step* in the soul's being able to pursue the good and avoid the harmful.

> **Vocabulary**
>
> sense appetites   end   concupiscible
> psychosomatic   privation   irascible

APPETITION

The sense appetites are the soul's ability to respond to what it knows. They enable the rabbit to *tend toward* the lettuce and *away from* the fox. Be careful here. We are not talking about *moving* toward anything yet. We are only talking about *tending* toward, which is an *inner* movement. That is, we are talking about how the soul "*feels*" about what it is sensing through its body.

Philosophers speak of feelings of the soul and feelings of the body. Hunger, thirst, cold, sleepiness, and dizziness are feelings *of the body* -- even though the soul is aware of them. They begin in the body, alerting us to our bodily conditions and needs. Love, joy, anger, and sorrow, which we commonly classify as feelings, are feelings *of the*

NOTES

Appetition - from the Latin *appetitus*, "natural desire;" an active tendency within a being towards a goal that is proper to it. The "sense appetites" refer to the active tendency within a being towards an object that the senses present to it. The various movements of the sense appetites are called *emotions* or *passions*.

"The senses are places where the soul has pleasures and pains."
    J. Joubert

The Human Person ~ Dignity Beyond Compare

NOTES

Psychosomatic - from the Latin *psyche*, "soul," and *soma*, "body;" having to do with the body-soul union.

soul -- even though the body also shares in them. These feelings begin in the soul, reflecting to us the soul's feelings about what it is sensing in the world. The soul's feelings are called *sense appetites*. They are also called *emotions* or *passions*.

Did you notice how we said that these feelings that begin in the soul are shared in by the body? For example, a person can feel such joy that the grin on his face is from ear to ear. It happens that way because we are a soul-body union. The body experiences a change *at the very same time* the soul experiences its feeling -- not a little before or after. This is why we say that the feelings of the soul are **psychosomatic** happenings. They involve both the soul (the *psyche*) as well as the body (the *soma*).

Another way of looking at this is in terms of what we learned about form and matter. Remember how we said that form permeates matter. It is everywhere present in the matter, forming it to be the kind of thing it is. So the soul gives "form" to its body, making it to be the kind of body it is. In and through its body, the soul expresses itself. We should not be surprised, then, to see the feelings of the soul displayed in its body. For example, the *anger* of the soul makes a person's face red; or the *fear* of the soul speeds a person's beating heart, enlarges the pupils of his eyes, and makes it hard for him to breathe.

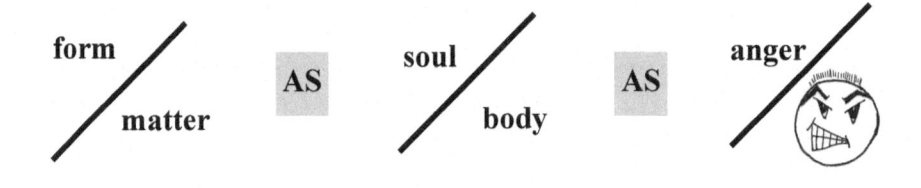

form/matter **AS** soul/body **AS** anger/😠

Emotions and Passions

The words "emotion" and "passion" are the words we commonly use to refer to the various *movements* of the sense appetites. "Movement" here refers to the soul's *tending toward* or *away from* something it senses. For example, if our sense appetites are *moved* to feel "joy" for the beautiful music we are hearing, we usually speak of experiencing the emotion or passion of joy.

Besides being synonyms for the sense appetites, the words "emotions" and "passions" also give us a little more information about them. For instance, the word "e-motion" comes from the Latin words *ex* (out), and *movere* (to move), suggesting that the emotions are moving forces, like motors, within us. Most of us are *moved from within* when we smell pizza that's just come out of the oven. That's because the soul "loves"

70.

pizza. We also know how hard it is to move ourselves to do something we "hate," like school work on a beautiful spring day. Something inside of us just seems to hold us back. That is the sense appetites at work within us. If the soul *hates* doing something, then it will *tend away* from doing it -- just as it *tends toward* what it *loves*.

The word "passion" tells us even more information about the sense appetites. Coming from the Latin *pati* (to suffer, to undergo), the word "passion" reminds us that the sense appetites are *passive* or inactive at first. They do not "turn on" until something turns them on. They are the soul's *response* to sense knowledge. This means that there needs to be "something sensed" in order for them to be activated. Do not forget, though, that memory and imagination can offer us "something sensed." So, our sense appetites can also respond to an image our imagination or memory brings to mind.

This explains why a person can experience anger long after the event occurred which first aroused his anger. He simply makes the choice with his rational powers to remember the event by calling it to mind often. This also explains what must be a part of our truly forgiving someone who has caused us harm. It means that we *choose* not to call to mind the hurtful event, if we can help it. Animals can't do this because they do not have the higher, rational powers. For example, a dog that is mistreated simply cannot forgive its abuser. As long as the memory of its abuse remains and has not been replaced by memories of kinder treatment by the same person, the dog will respond to him with anger.

Naturally Good, but Morally Neutral

Just how responsible are we for our emotions? They seem to be just automatic responses to the things we sense. A lot of people are confused about this, thinking they are responsible for how they *feel*.

It is true that the emotions are automatic responses of the soul to what we know from our senses. It is also true that we bear responsibility for something *only* to the extent that we freely choose it. So, we surely cannot be responsible for the soul responding automatically as it does

NOTES

-- <u>unless</u> we are responsible for "turning it on" in the first place. If we deliberately choose to sense something that activates our sense appetites, then we are morally responsible for the fact that they are "turned on." Let us think about this some more.

Take the example of a person who *really* likes chocolate and often craves it. He is usually not responsible for his craving because it is probably an automatic response of his sense appetites to the good taste of chocolate. However, if this same person *chooses* to take the lid off a box of assorted chocolates and put it on his desk while studying so that he can enjoy the aroma, then he begins to have some responsibility for his strong desire. He is freely choosing to do something that arouses his desire. If that strong desire leads him to eat too many chocolates or to no longer be able to concentrate on his studies, he bears full responsibility for his acts.

This is a very important point regarding the emotions. Because they are *automatic* responses, they are *naturally* good for us to have. They are simply our natural responses to whatever we are sensing. The emotions, though, are neither *morally* good nor evil. This means that the emotions do not make us good or bad people. There can only be moral good or evil if there is freedom, and our emotions are not free. This is why we say the emotions are "morally neutral." It is only when we *freely choose* to do good or evil that we either perform an act of virtue or commit a sin. So, how we *feel* about something is <u>never</u> sinful or wrong. Nor is it necessarily virtuous. What we *freely choose* <u>to do</u> about how we feel, however, might be sinful or virtuous. Our freely chosen acts will be sinful or virtuous, depending on whether or not we act in line with right reason.

For example, *feeling* hate (strong dislike) toward someone because he tells lies about you is a normal response of the soul to the evil done to you. The *feeling* is *naturally* good because it is your automatic response to the evil he is doing, but it is neither *morally* good nor evil. What you *choose to do* about that feeling will be either morally good or bad. You could go slit the tires of the person's car when he's not looking, or you could choose to go talk to him respectfully about why he says what is untrue about you. The emotion of hate *itself* is not sinful, but the action that follows from it might be sinful if you don't act reasonably. Acting "reasonably" with regard to another human person always entails acting in a way that promotes what is truly good for him.

"A truly mature existence demands a harmonious integration between emotions, thinking and willing. Only then can we experience to the fullest the joy for which we are created."
— Conrad Baars

"What you feel is one thing. What you do when you experience that feeling is an entirely different matter."
— Conrad Baars

Sin enters the picture only to the degree that our rational powers are involved and that we freely choose to do evil. That's why animals cannot sin or be virtuous. They simply, and unconsciously, act on their feelings all the time. Their feelings are automatic responses either to what they are sensing or to instinct. They *cannot* choose to take time to "think it over" because they lack both a will that can choose and an intellect that can think. They have no higher powers to guide them.

To illustrate this, imagine you are giving a party and the first guests are due in 20 minutes. You have just set some gorgeous appetizers your Mom made out on your kitchen counter. Imagine that while you are in your bedroom changing your clothes, one of the other "inhabitants" of your house enters the kitchen and discovers the appetizers.

In the first scenario, let us imagine it is your dog, Snarles, who comes into the kitchen. Remember, Snarles lives purely on the level of the senses; he lacks the rational powers we have. As he wanders into the kitchen, he smells the appetizers. His sense of smell makes him aware that they are good, and his sense appetite responds with the desire to eat them. If nothing interrupts Snarles, his next move will be to leap on the counter and have at them!

In a second scenario, imagine it is your twenty-year-old brother who walks into the kitchen and discovers your appetizers. He, too, smells the appetizers and feels the desire to eat them. But, your brother has rational powers that can step in to save your appetizers by enabling him to act reasonably. He might think, "These are Mom's famous appetizers. They must be for the party that will start any minute. I should wait until the guests come and then eat only a few." With his ability to choose, he decides to wait and not give in to his sense appetite. He acts as a rational being *should* act. (Because of his freedom, though, he could choose to act just like Snarles did!)

Study Guide Questions:

1. *How is our power of sensation related to our power of appetition?*

2. *Why do we say that the emotions are psychosomatic happenings?*

3. *What does it mean to be "morally responsible" for something? Are we morally responsible for the emotions we feel, especially emotions like despair, anger, and hate? Explain.*

4. *Why is it impossible for animals such as dogs to sin?*

NOTES

"Emotions, in and by themselves, exist for the benefit of the one who possesses them. In this sense they can be said to be selfish; they serve their owner, first and foremost. Only under the growing influence of the intellect, which provides man with much more information about the world than the primary sources of our emotions -- the senses -- can ever give us, the emotions also become oriented toward the good of others."
Conrad Baars

The Human Person ~ Dignity Beyond Compare

NOTES

CASES IN POINT

#1 - Jennie, a 17-year-old girl, is saddened when she sees homeless people every day as she rides home from school. Because her feelings have helped to make her aware of these people, Jennie decides to volunteer once a week at a soup kitchen her parish sponsors.

- How did Jennie's emotional response help her in doing the good act?

* * *

#2 - Jim, a 16-year-old boy, hates the fact that Bill, a classmate of his, makes fun of him because he's still wearing braces. Whenever Jim sees Bill at school, he feels hate because he knows Bill goes out of his way to make sarcastic remarks about him. Because he is bothered by the way he feels toward Bill, Jim decides to talk to his Dad. Jim wants his Dad's advice about how he can protect himself from Bill's cutting remarks, but still treat Bill in a way that's respectful and not hateful.

- Has Jim done anything wrong yet?

- If you were Jim's Dad, what advice would you give him, especially in view of what you have learned in this chapter?

* * *

#3 - Stephanie, a 19-year-old young woman, has been educated about the evil of abortion. She even felt strong aversion and anger regarding the killing of the innocent when she watched the pro-life film, *The Silent Scream*, with her high school class. During her first year in college, there was a major political race between two candidates with opposing views on abortion. Because she was really busy, Stephanie chose not to vote in the elections.

- Was Stephanie's emotional response to the killing of the innocent in abortion a morally good thing? How should it have affected her sense of responsibility to vote? What's wrong with Stephanie's choice <u>not</u> to vote?

Chapter V
VEGETATIVE & SENSITIVE POWERS -- Part II

The Concupiscible and Irascible Appetites

Let us zero in on those sense appetites in order to look at them in more detail. There are actually *two* sense appetites. One of them, called the **concupiscible appetite**, responds to the good or evil being sensed when there is no difficulty involved. The other one, the **irascible appetite**, kicks in as soon as some difficulty is involved in pursuing good or avoiding evil. Those words may not be easy to say, but the ideas behind them are *not* difficult. We will look at an example of how they work together once we see what movements of the soul each of them entails.

The Concupiscible Appetite

	Easy Good			Easy Evil
Response to a good whether absent or present	Love		Hate	Response to an evil whether absent or present
Response to a good which is absent	Desire		Aversion	Response to an evil which is absent but approaching
Response to a good which is present	Joy Pleasure		Pain Sorrow	Response to an evil which is present

The first movement of the concupiscible appetite and the most fundamental of all the emotions is **love**. In order for the soul to feel love for an object it senses, the soul must see it as in some way suiting his nature, that is, as being *good* for him. So we speak of a squirrel *loving* nuts, a duck *loving* water, or Tom *loving* Sally. In each case, the object loved is fitting to the nature of the lover.

As a movement of a sense appetite, love takes the soul *out of itself* to the thing it loves. For example, the one who loves chocolate is constantly on the look-out for chocolate. His love for chocolate leads him *out* to where the chocolate is. This appetitive movement of the soul which causes it to *tend toward* the object in reality is the exact opposite of sense knowledge. With knowledge, the knower takes the thing *into himself*, giving it a new kind of existence within him -- even

NOTES

Concupiscible (pronounced "con-cew-pi-si-bull") -- comes from the Latin *concupisciblis*, "desirable."

Irascible (pronounced "ear-rass-i-bull") -- comes from the Latin *irascibilis*, "able to grow angry."

75.

The Human Person ~ Dignity Beyond Compare

NOTES

though it still exists outside him. In knowing chocolate, for example, the knower takes the chocolate into himself in a non-material way. Love, on the other hand, draws the lover out of himself toward the object loved as it exists in reality.

If the lover does not actually *have* the object he loves, then the sense appetite moves the soul to **desire** it. So, we see the hungry dog scrounging around for food, or the child seeking the toy he's lost. Both demonstrate the emotion of desire. Once the lover is united with the object he loves, his soul will be moved to experience **pleasure** or **joy**.

Pleasure and Joy

Did you notice from the chart above that pleasure *and* joy are emotional responses to the good which is present? Human beings are capable of *both* pleasure and joy. Animals are capable of experiencing only pleasure in material things. Because of his rational powers, the human person is capable of more than this. Let us consider this a little more.

We respond with the emotion of *pleasure* when the *material things* we are experiencing are good, like a delicious meal, a favorite drink, a delightful fragrance, or a gentle touch. We respond with the emotion of *joy* when we are experiencing goods which are *intellectual* or *spiritual*. Such goods could be beautiful music, a gorgeous sunset, superb literature, a morally good person, or truly being in love with someone. You see, Snarles has the senses he needs to hear music and to see the colors of a sunset, but he does not have the ability to appreciate their *beauty*. You will never see a dog simply gazing at a sunset, marveling at its array of color.

"True joy is something different from pleasure; joy grows and continues to mature in suffering, in communion with the Cross of Christ. It is here alone that the true joy of faith is born."
Pope Benedict XVI,
Address to Diocesan Clergy of Aosta,
July 25, 2005

Pleasure is felt in a particular part of the body because it is a response to what the senses are bringing in. For example, delicious food delights taste buds and a gentle touch feels good on the hand. Joy, however, is not limited to the body. It is an emotional response to what the intellect knows. Think of the joy a person experiences in caring for a sick friend, or the sick person's joy in

Chapter V
VEGETATIVE & SENSITIVE POWERS -- Part II

being lovingly cared for. Joy can even be present in physical suffering. Think of the joy a woman experiences who is about to give birth, or the joy of the Martyrs in their final moments of life on this earth.

Pleasure lasts a shorter amount of time than joy. When we try to extend the experience, it sickens us. For example, too much ice cream at one time is no longer fun. Joy tends to last longer because it is not limited to sense experience. For example, a person who has been away from home can feel joy in *anticipating* seeing Mom and Dad again, in *actually being with* them again, and in *remembering* that reunion. It seems that we cannot get too much joy.

Since it depends only on material things, pleasure can be taken away. Joy, on the other hand, is not caused primarily by physical things; it cannot be stolen from us. Pleasure tends to capture the hearts of fallen human beings, and it can easily tie us down to this physical world. For example, a brownie is good, but it can quickly lead us to "pigging out" and to the sin of gluttony, if we focus only on ourselves. Finding *joy* in sharing a batch of brownies with the elderly ladies down the street, however, helps to turn our gaze beyond the good material things to a higher good, and ultimately to the Creator of all goodness.

Emotional Response to Evil

Looking back at the chart again, do you notice the various movements of the concupiscible appetite when the soul meets up with a sensed evil? It can experience hate, aversion, or pain/sorrow. In order to understand these feelings of the soul, we need to understand what "**evil**" is. Here, we do not mean moral evil. Evil in a general sense is the **privation** of good; it is the *lack of a good which ought to be present*. For example, blindness is not a moral evil, but it is an evil because it is the lack of the ability to see, which eyes should have.

It is easy, then, to see that the soul's first reaction is **hate** when the good we love is absent. We *hate* the cold because we *love* warmth. We *hate* the mess because we *love* order. This *automatic* response of hatred will occur whenever the soul senses an evil. For example, if you smell the odor of a decaying animal, taste some rotten food, or imagine the colors orange and pink side-by-side, your

NOTES

"The deepest joy lasts forever: 'Rejoice in the Lord always.' (*Phil.* 4) It begins on earth and lives through eternity."
Fr. Thomas Dubay, S.M.
Happy Are You Poor

Evil - the privation of good.

Privation - the lack of a good or a condition which should be present.

The Human Person ~ Dignity Beyond Compare

NOTES

soul will automatically respond with a feeling of hate or dislike, and your body will often express the soul's feelings with a look of disgust on your face.

If the sensible evil is absent yet approaching, our emotional response will be **aversion**. We will feel the *tendency* to want to get out of the way of the evil that is coming. We all know the feeling of wanting to move out of the way of an approaching poisonous spider. We have an *aversion* to it because we love our good health. If we cannot get away and some evil is actually *present* to us, then our souls will feel either **pain** or **sorrow**, depending on the kind of evil it is.

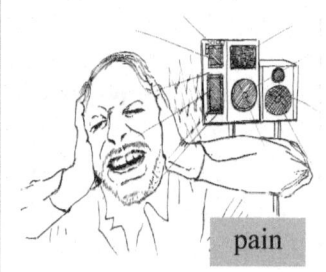

If the evil is a physical one, then we experience pain. For example, a very shrill noise will make eardrums hurt; hunger will cause stomachs to churn; and a slap will cause a face to sting. If the evil is an intellectual or spiritual one, then we experience sorrow. For example, receiving a low test grade, not making the cut for sports or cheerleading tryouts, the betrayal of a friend, or the death of a loved one would probably cause us to experience sorrow. Animals are not capable of feeling sorrow because they are not aware of intellectual or spiritual evils.

Let us look at a great example of these responses of the soul to evil. We are all probably familiar with a teacher announcing at the beginning of class that there is going to be an unexpected quiz over a reading assignment we did not take the time to do. As soon as we hear the word "quiz" come out of her mouth, our souls react with the feeling of <u>hatred</u> for the quiz. Then the feeling of <u>*aversion*</u> immediately kicks in as we consider various possible excuses for leaving the room. Once the quiz is before us and we are experiencing our ignorance, our emotional response is one of <u>*sorrow*</u>.

HATE → AVERSION → SORROW

The emotions arenot really that hard to understand, especially when we look at our own personal experience of them. There is a logic to how they work, and we can figure it out once we understand a little about each of them.

78.

Chapter V
VEGETATIVE & SENSITIVE POWERS -- Part II

The Irascible Appetite

Irascible Appetite

Difficult Sensed Good		*Difficult Sensed Evil*	
Good is absent and difficult to obtain	Hope	Courage	Evil is absent and avoidable
Good is absent and impossible to obtain	Despair	Fear	Evil is absent but unavoidable
		Anger	Evil is present and surmountable

NOTES

Let us go to the chart above now and turn our attention to the irascible appetite. This is the one that "kicks in" as soon as things get difficult, providing added "motor power" to the soul when it most needs it.

Hope or Despair

When obstacles arise that threaten to keep the soul from the good it desires, then the irascible appetite "turns on," enabling the soul to feel either **hope** or **despair**. Now do not get the impression that the sense appetite makes a *choice* between these two feelings. Remember, the sense appetites are *automatic*; they do not make choices. The irascible appetite's response of hope or despair will depend on the information provided by the senses.

Let us look at an example: A person loves the thought of having a medical degree, so he lets his *desire* (concupiscible appetite) for the degree lead him to enroll in classes at the school nearby. Midway through the first semester, he begins to feel *despair* (irascible appetite) of succeeding in his college work because of his low test grades and

despair

79.

The Human Person ~ Dignity Beyond Compare

NOTES

because he is not understanding his teachers. At this point, his rational powers should intervene and direct him to go talk with the teachers and to check with student services about getting help. After doing this, he finds out that it is not uncommon for students to have difficulty in the classes he is taking. He also is made aware of numerous helps available for him, like small study groups, tutors, and easier texts. With this knowledge, he feels *hopeful* that earning the college degree might be possible after all.

Another possibility could also have occurred. The student could have discovered the opposite, namely, that students do not normally have difficulty in the courses he is taking and that there is no help available for him. With this knowledge, his feeling of *despair* would remain or perhaps even intensify. It might lead him to drop out of school, or wait a semester and change schools.

In either scenario, the rational powers need to decide what course of action he should take. It might be a reasonable thing for him to quit trying to get a medical degree. Maybe he does not have the intellectual ability to be a doctor. If that is the case, then it would be better to stop now than to waste his time and money for another four years of failing grades. Perhaps he should consider another profession that fits his personal gifts and abilities. On the other hand, it might be reasonable for him to take steps to improve his study habits so that he can succeed in the course.

Did you notice that it is not *bad* to *feel* the emotion despair? In fact, the emotion itself is <u>always</u> a good thing because it tells the person how he is feeling about what he is experiencing. The bad thing would be simply to let the emotion of despair be "in the driver's seat" regarding making a decision about what to do. This could easily lead a person to giving up before he tries. To make a *decision*, we need the *rational* powers.

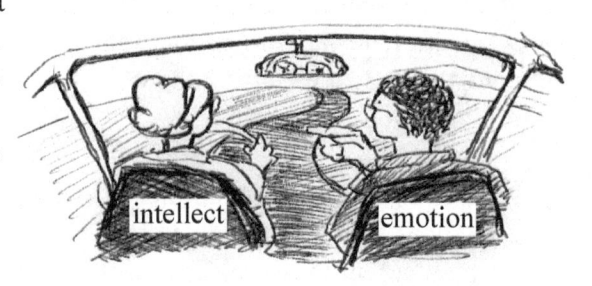

Courage or Fear

The other emotions of the irascible appetite are responses to an *evil* which is difficult to avoid. When the soul becomes aware of the difficult evil, it can respond with either of two feelings: **courage** or **fear**.

Once again, the soul's response will be *determined* by the sense knowledge it has available. It will be an automatic response in view of this information.

When we say that the *soul's* response is automatic, we are referring to how it *feels*. This does not mean that the *person's* response is automatic or determined by these feelings. For example, a soldier in battle may truly feel *fearful*, but nevertheless <u>choose</u> to continue fighting with his unit. He can do this because he has rational powers which are able to direct him to act in a way he does not *feel* like acting. He chooses to follow the guidance of his intellect rather than let fear lead him.

An animal has no choice but to act according to its feelings, but a human being is not like this. Because we have rational powers, we are able to decide whether the best way to proceed is *really* to follow our feelings. This might help you to understand better what is wrong with the saying, "If it *feels* good, do it." If we were merely talking about animals, that statement makes sense. Animals <u>cannot</u> do anything else. But when applied to human beings, the statement is telling us to act *on the animal level*. To reflect the human level, the statement needs to say, "If it *truly is good*, then choose to do it." We need our rational powers to make this judgment.

Jesus' command to us to love our enemies is another example of our need at times to act contrary to our feelings. "Our enemies" are those we do not *feel* good about. In telling us to love them, Jesus is telling us to do good to those we don't *feel* like helping. If you have ever tried to do this, then you know just how strong those emotions can be.

Anger the Sin vs Anger the Emotion

The last emotion of the irascible appetite is **anger**. The response of anger is a typical feeling of any soul that experiences an injustice done to himself or to someone he loves. A dog will *feel* angry if someone tries to take his bone away from him. A person will experience *anger* if a bully beats up his little brother. The emotion *itself* is good because it tells you how you are feeling about what you are experiencing. It also gives you the added "motor power" you will need to do something about the injustice. What you *do* about the injustice, however, should be determined not by your anger but by your rational powers.

81.

The Human Person ~ Dignity Beyond Compare

NOTES

Capital sins - Also called the Deadly Sins or Capital Vices, these "death-dealing" evils are sins in themselves as well as the causes of other sins. They are seven in number: pride, envy, sloth, lust, greed, intemperance, anger.

Locomotion - movement from place to place.

"...[W]e are moved internally by our passions so that we might then move externally, from here to there, and thus complete the work of the passions, and of the knowledge which preceded them."

— D. Q. McInerny

This is what St. Paul means when he says, "Be angry, but sin not."[1]

Now, someone might object, noting for us that anger is a **capital sin**. They are right; it is. But anger the *sin* is not the same as anger the *emotion*. Anger which is sinful is anger that leads to acts which are *both* freely chosen and unreasonable. For example, a working mother pays someone to clean her house while she is at work. Her children arrive home a couple of hours before she does and make a mess of the place. When the mother arrives home to the messy house, she *feels* angry. Because this *feeling* of anger is automatic, it is not sinful. In fact, it is actually good because it gives her the added energy she needs to discipline her children. Her anger would become sinful only if she *chooses* to punish them <u>unreasonably</u>, for instance, to deprive them of food for a week.

Are you getting the picture? All of the 11 emotions are naturally good because they are all ways the soul has of responding to the world it experiences through its body. These natural responses are morally neutral until the rational powers get involved. So, it is <u>never</u> bad to *feel* an emotion. What might be bad is how we *choose* to act on those feelings.

LOCOMOTION

As we have seen, with its sense knowledge, the soul is able to know the sensed object. With its sense appetites, the soul begins its pursuit of the good and its avoidance of the evil it senses. It does this by its inner movement of *tending toward* the good and *away from* the evil. This inner movement of the sense appetites, though, would be of no use unless a <u>third</u> sensitive power is present in the soul, the power of **locomotion**. With this power, the soul can take the *next* step of *acting* on its inner feelings. With locomotion, the soul-body union can actually move itself from one place to another.

This self-movement from place to place takes a wide variety of forms: fish swim; birds fly; snakes slither; horses trot; and human beings walk or run, etc. In every instance, even with the human, the beings move themselves because of what they have sensed and what they desire or wish to avoid. In other words, the soul moves itself locally (from place to place) because it is in

---

[1] Ephesians 4:26

pursuit of an **end** which it knows and desires. In the case of animals, the end is one they *have not* chosen; it is decided for them by sensation, appetition, and instinct. In the case of human beings, however, because we have rational powers, the end or goal of locomotion is *freely chosen*.

Conclusion

Is it not amazing what the human soul is equipped to do? Its vegetative and sensitive powers are truly impressive. What we have seen up to this point in our study of the soul's powers, though, is very little in light of what is still to come. In our next chapter, we'll investigate the rational powers - those two highest powers of the human soul which are unique to us - the intellect and will.

Study Guide Questions:

1. *What is the difference between the two sense appetites?*

2. *What is so dangerous about being a lover of pleasure?*

3. *Why do we have emotions like anger, fear, and sorrow? What good are they?*

4. *How do animals and humans differ regarding the power of locomotion?*

5. *From memory, are you able to list the eleven emotions?*

* * *

Point to Consider:

"Animals act according to their instincts and appetites. Human persons, however, are not enslaved to their passions and desires. With intellect and free will, persons can choose a course of action based on self-reflection no matter what desires may be stirring within them. For example, a very hungry man may desire to eat a ham sandwich that is offered to him, but he can choose not to follow his desire because he generously wants someone else to have the sandwich or because he has committed to fast on that particular day. A person can rise above appetites for the sake of a higher goal."

Edward Sri,
Men, Women and the Mystery of Love -- Practical Insights from Saint John Paul's Love and Responsibility, pp. 24-25.

NOTES

End - A goal for which a knowing being strives.

CASES IN POINT

#1 - Ever since Joe was a little boy, he has been told it is wrong to get angry. His parents have always punished him for any sign of anger. In spite of this, as a teenager, Joe finds that feeling angry is one of the sins he confesses regularly. He is frustrated as he realizes that he has made little progress in removing anger completely from his life.

- What advice would you offer Joe, based on what you've learned in this chapter?

* * *

#2 - "We live in a culture that tends to treat anger as taboo. A common tactic to unsettle an opponent today is to accuse him or her of being angry. It is amazing how easily humiliated and/or defensive an adversary can become in response to such an accusation. ... Rare indeed in the West is someone who will respond in a way that both admits anger and owns it as something positive and important. One way to do this would be to say, 'You're right; I *am* angry. I'm angry because I really care about this matter; I'm not just a neutral observer. I fully admit that I have an agenda, an agenda I believe in passionately. I experience grief and anger when what I value is disparaged. Yes, I'm angry; I care bout this.' ...

"Yes, love and anger are closer to each other than we moderns often realize or admit. Love says that there are certain things worth fighting for and being angry about. But the anger coming from love is not egocentric, it is 'other-centric.' It is focused on God, the truth, and the dignity of those who are meant to walk in truth."   *Msgr. Charles Pope, "The modern age hates anger, but I say we need more of it"*

- What are some of the issues today that you face which are worth getting angry about?

* * *

#3 - During Lent, Nancy decides that she wants to give up some of the pleasures she is used to enjoying. She is going to do without candy and make herself get up a half an hour earlier every morning in order to attend daily Mass with her Grandmother before going to school. Barbara, a friend of hers, doesn't understand why Nancy is doing this. She explains to Nancy that candy and sleep are good things that God would want us to enjoy.

- How would you respond to this disagreement between the two friends?

* * *

#4 - Little Tommy, a 2-year-old who lives next door, loves to run around outside. The problem is that he lives on a rather busy street, and he hasn't yet learned to stay in his own yard, away from the moving cars. When his Mom worries about the problem, she says, "Tommy has no fear!"

- What good can come from feeling fear -- for a person of any age?

Chapter VI

THE RATIONAL POWERS OF THE SOUL

Introduction

As we have seen, the human soul uses the organs of the external and internal senses in order to gather into itself the vast treasure of sensible qualities present in the things of our world. (Remember that *sensible* here means "able to be perceived by our senses.") Thus, with our five senses we are able to see, smell, and feel the rose that exists in the garden outside and to have an image of it (its form) within us.

There is more to be known about the things of our world, however, than the senses are able to gather in. For this, another power of the soul is required -- one able to go *beyond* the visible realm. We call this deeper knowing power of the human soul the **intellect**, from the Latin words *intus* (within) and *legere* (to read). In naming it "intellect," we imply that it is this power which makes it possible for us to *get at* the "more to be known" that our senses can't reach. The intellect is able "to see" the *within* of the sensible things the senses bring into the soul and to "read it" to us.

It is this knowing power of the human soul and its corresponding appetite, the **will**, which set human beings apart from all other creatures on earth, giving them a dignity "beyond compare." And it is to these two **rational powers** that we now turn our attention.

> ### Vocabulary
> intellect   essence   abstract
> will   universal   consciousness

Rational Powers

The highest powers of the human soul -- the rational -- make us unique among all living beings on earth. These two powers, the intellect and the will, enable the human person to think and to choose

---

NOTES

Intellect - from the Latin *intus*, "within" and *legere*, "to read;" the knowing power in human beings which is able to grasp the essences of physical beings.

Will - a free and active tendency within a being towards or away from an object that the intellect presents to it. It is also called the *intellectual* or *rational appetite*.

Rational - from the Latin *ratio*, "reason." Rational refers to the human way of thinking because our minds move in a step-by-step fashion from understanding one idea to understanding another one, to understanding a third. It is as if we come to knowledge in "piece-meal" fashion. Sometimes the word "rational" is used interchangeably with "intellectual," but strictly speaking they have different meanings.

freely. Unlike all other earthly creatures, the human person is able to direct himself to goals of his own choosing. Thus, he has the rare dignity of being responsible for himself and for attaining the happiness he longs to have.

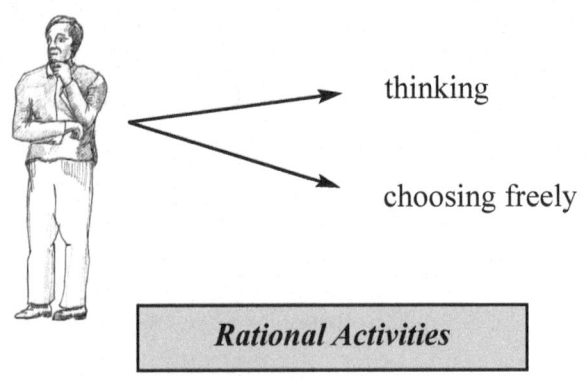

→ thinking

→ choosing freely

Rational Activities

THE INTELLECT

Getting at the Essence of Things

So, what shall we say about the intellect? First of all, we should say that it gives us more knowledge than the senses give us. It is able to do this because it "sees deeper" than the senses are able to see. The senses take in the visible qualities of physical things, but they cannot go beyond those surface qualities. They cannot reach the inner dimensions of things.

What more is there to know? Well, let us think about it. Remember what we learned in Chapter 4 about how the interior senses work within us: They take what the exterior senses bring in, refine it, and present it to the soul. The highest power of the soul, the intellect, immediately raises the question, "What is it?" In fact, the intellect raises this question about *everything* that "comes in" through the senses.

Chapter VI
THE RATIONAL POWERS OF THE SOUL

The size, sound, color, texture, or odor of a thing cannot tell us *what* the thing is. Those physical qualities just tell us what a thing looks like, tastes like, or smells like. They do not tell us *what* the thing itself is.

So, the intellect asks the deeper question, "*What* is this?" Watch small children, as they begin to notice the things around them. First they will begin to "explore" objects with their senses, by touching them, smelling them, and putting them in their mouths. As they start to get older, though, this is not enough. They will begin to ask, "*What* is this?" In fact, they will ask that question over and over about *everything* they encounter! They may not know philosophical principles or understand the process of thinking, but they are beginning to want to know more than just the outward physical aspects of the things around them. This desire *to know more deeply* will continue to grow as the child matures, even into adulthood.

"*What is this?*" Finding the answer to this question is what the intellect is designed to do. The aspects of a thing which answer that question, and which only the intellect can know, are called the **intelligible aspects** of the thing. Unlike the qualities which our senses pick up, the intelligible aspects of a thing are "*within*" it, and so they are *invisible*.

Do you remember that each of the five exterior senses has a **proper object**, such as color, aroma, sound, etc.? Well, the intellect also has its own proper object. St. Thomas tells us that the intellect seeks the **essence** of physical things as its **proper object**. Every time we sense a thing and try to figure out what it is, what it can do, or what holds it together, we are seeking its *essence*. Actually, the intellect does this *all the time*. Let us look at one example:

When you experience a rose, your five senses perceive its *exterior*, accidental qualities (its red color, thorns, pleasant fragrance and soft petals). Sense knowledge tells you that you are experiencing something that is red, smells pleasant, and has thorns and soft petals.

Looking at these exterior qualities of the thing, your intellect grasps what makes this thing to be a *rose* and not a violet or a tree. It grasps the *essence* or the "what-ness" of its accidental qualities. From its previous experience with other flowers, the intellect recognizes the particular shape of this flower, the shape of its leaves, the presence of its thorns and identifies its "rose-ness."

NOTES

Intelligible aspects - the aspects of a thing which only the intellect can know.

Proper object - the end or goal of a power of a soul; the power is directed to its proper object.

Essence - from the Latin *esse*, "to be;" what a thing is, the underlying identity or nature of a thing.

"As light to the eye, and sound to the ear, so is each and every thing to the analysis of the intellect."
Paul Claudel

The Human Person ~ Dignity Beyond Compare

NOTES

The intellect is also able to look *beneath* these exterior qualities of the rose and grasp the rose's substantial "what-ness." Aware of the rose's ability to grow, to nourish itself, and to reproduce, the intellect identifies its "plant-ness." The intellect, in other words, can know both the accidental and the substantial forms of the rose.

The *essence* or nature of a thing includes what is common to every being that is the same kind of thing. For example, every dog has the *essence* or nature of a dog. Every dog has "doggie-ness." Everything that exists has an essence because everything is a certain kind of thing. This "what-ness" of every physical being is the "intelligible object" that the intellect is designed to know. It is present in all that our senses pick up, although it is hidden from them.

"Just as the light of the sun gives colors, heretofore invisible, to be perceived, so the light of the soul gives the intelligible, hidden from the senses, to become recognizable."

Pierre-Marie Emonet

Our senses come to know only the *particular* accidental qualities of things. The senses "take in" these accidental forms of things, leaving behind the *particular* matter with which they are united in reality. But the senses cannot *completely* remove *particularity* from them. The senses cannot do this because they themselves are not completely free of matter. They are tied to bodily organs. Whatever the senses know will always be accompanied by certain *particular* material conditions. For example, the color "red" they perceive will always be a *particular* shade, and the size "large" they sense will always have *particular* dimensions. These *particular* material conditions are what enable us to form an *image* of the thing we are sensing.

Because of their connection to matter, the senses will never be able to know "rose-ness" or "doggie-ness." In other words, the senses cannot know the essence of a thing.

Truth - conformity of the mind with reality. I know the truth when what I have in my mind matches objective reality.

The wonder of the intellect is that it can do this. The intellect is able "to read" the *essence* of the rose within what the senses pick up. In being able to read the essence, the intellect can come to know the thing. It can possess the **truth** about it. In fact, the intellect has the potential to know the truth about all of reality. Let us go on to see how the intellect does this.

Chapter VI
THE RATIONAL POWERS OF THE SOUL

NOTES

Study Guide Questions:

1. What does the word "intellect" tell us about the purpose of this rational power? *it means to read within*

2. How are the intelligible aspects of a thing different from its sensible aspects? *intelligible aspects of a thing found by using*

3. What is the proper object of the intellect? *intellect the essence of things*

CASES IN POINT

#1 - Early in their senior year, Bill met Jennie at a football game with a group of friends. Right away he was attracted to her. Not only was Jennie really pretty, but she was also fun to be with. Bill decided that he wanted to ask her to join him and a small group of their classmates who regularly go bowling. The next week at school, though, before he was able to invite Jennie, Bill sat at the same lunch table with her and noticed that she often made cutting remarks about other students behind their backs, to get her friends to laugh. This made Bill feel uncomfortable, and he decided to wait awhile before inviting Jennie to join his bowling group of friends.

• What important lesson is Bill's experience teaching him?

*don't be friends with bad people**

#2 - "One danger of making emotions a measure for love is that our feelings can be very misleading. In fact, the Pope says feelings themselves are blind, for they are not concerned with knowing the truth about the other person. Thus, our feelings alone do not make a good compass for guiding our relationships."

Edward Sri,
Men, Women and the Mystery of Love: Practical Insights from Pope John Paul II's Love and Responsibility, p. 44.

• What is Saint John Paul talking about? Why does he think our emotions are blind? What should we do to overcome this blindness? *emotions can blind us from the truth overcome your emotions*

The Human Person ~ Dignity Beyond Compare

NOTES

Active and Passive Intellect

We have probably all been in a situation where we did not understand the lesson a teacher was presenting. Then, all of a sudden, we understood it! At such times, it feels very much as if a "light" within us is all of a sudden turned on, and we can see the point being made.

St. Thomas says that this experience of "not understanding and then understanding" shows us that there is something about our intellect which is *passive*. In other words, there is an aspect of the intellect that is not always "turned on." There are some times when it is "turned on" and other times when it's not. When St. Thomas writes about this aspect of the intellect that goes from "off" to "on," he calls it the "**passive intellect**."

Do not forget, though, that there is also something about the intellect that is <u>always</u> asking the question, "What is it?" concerning everything the senses bring in to the soul. St. Thomas says that this constant experience of looking for the essence of things shows us that there is something about our intellect which is *active*. In fact, we would have to say that this aspect of the intellect is always "turned on." For whenever we are aware of what is going on around us, we seem to experience a power within us seeking the essences of things. When St. Thomas talks about this "always-turned-on" aspect of the intellect, he calls it the "**active intellect**." He compares it to a "light" that is always shining, looking for the essences of things. Today, we might say it is like the emergency light that is always on in the house.

<u>*A word of caution*</u>: Do not think that the active and passive intellects are *two* intellects. St. Thomas knows that we have only *one* intellect in each of us. But this one intellect that we each have seems to have *both* an active part (always looking for

Passive intellect - that aspect of the human intellect which waits to be activated by the abstracted nature of the sensed object. It is the knowing power which forms the universal concept.

Active intellect - that aspect of the human intellect which is always activated and which has the power to abstract the essence of a thing from the completed sense image (the phantasm).

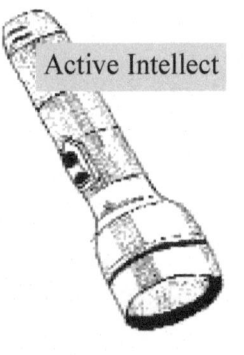

90.

Chapter VI
THE RATIONAL POWERS OF THE SOUL

essences) and a passive part (waiting to be "turned on," to understand).

From Phantasm to Concept

Let us see now if we can understand *philosophically* how the passive and active intellects work together and how they are able to "get at" the essences of physical things.

St. Thomas says that the intellect begins its work where sense knowledge leaves off. The beginning point for the intellect is the completed sense image, the *phantasm*. Once the senses present the phantasm to the intellect, the "light" of the active intellect penetrates *into the phantasm*. The active intellect finds the *essence* hidden within the phantasm and "draws it out" or **abstracts** it from the material conditions of the image in which it is embedded. This *abstracting* of the essence from the phantasm removes it *completely* from matter.

With this abstracted essence which is *completely* immaterial, the active intellect activates ("turns on") the *passive intellect*. It is then the work of the passive intellect "to read" the essence it has received from the active intellect. In "reading it," the passive intellect produces the **concept** or **idea** of it.

The concept is always "**abstract**," that is, it is free of any particular qualities that would tie it to just one concrete thing. For example, "lemon-ness" is the essence of <u>every</u> lemon, *abstracted from* the qualities which are unique to any one lemon. The concept possesses everything that any lemon must have to be a lemon. This is why we say the concept is **universal**. The one concept "lemon-ness" applies to all lemons.

Let us look at this in diagram form. *(See below.)* I have seen, smelled, touched and tasted a lemon.

1. My senses present an image (phantasm) of this lemon to my intellect.

2. My active intellect uses the phantasm of the lemon to withdraw from it its essence, lemon-ness. In this process of abstraction, the active intellect leaves behind all accidental qualities of this particular lemon (its particular size, shape, shade of yellow, etc.). It withdraws only what belongs to every lemon, the essence or nature of lemon-ness.

3. My active intellect then presents the abstracted essence to my passive intellect "to read."

4. The passive intellect "reads" the essence it receives and expresses its understanding in the concept "lemon-ness."

NOTES

"We possess within us the 'illuminating intellect,' a spiritual sun ceaselessly shining, activating everything in the intelligence, its light arousing all of our ideas in us and penetrating with its energy all of the operations of our mind. This original source of light remains invisible to us, hidden in the unconscious part of the mind."
— Jacques Maritain

Abstract - from the Latin *abstrahere*, "to bring forth or to draw away;" to separate a substance from its non-essential accidents. This separation is a mental one, not physical. The *abstract* concept which is formed by the process is the essence of the thing without any concrete particularities.

Concept - the simplest form of thought; an idea; an abstracted universal.

Universal - from the Latin *unus*, "one" and *vertere*, "to turn;" refers to the idea of the many "turned or combined into one." A mental concept is a universal because the one concept applies to the many instances of it in reality.

The Human Person ~ Dignity Beyond Compare

NOTES

Sense Image | **Intellectual Knowledge**

phantasm

Active intellect

"lemon-ness" CONCEPT

Passive intellect

→ "lemon" WORD

1　2　3　4　5

Notice what else the diagram shows:

5 The word "lemon" expresses the concept "lemon-ness."

Words have meaning only when we can connect them to an idea in our intellects. Learning a foreign language entails learning that there are words in another language that express the same concepts as words in our own language do. This explains why animals are not capable of language: they cannot form concepts. Their way of communicating is always limited to the realm of the senses.[1]

Only we human beings are able to form concepts and to share these ideas with each other. Only we human beings can think using these concepts, pondering them and wondering about the reality they represent. Only we can make judgments about the world around us by relating these concepts to each other. Only we can use these concepts to possess the *truth* about the beings we know and so enter into a wonderful union with them. Only we can know the *truth* about reality and communicate it to other people!

Study Guide Questions:

1. Why did St. Thomas speak of both an active and a passive intellect? *Sometimes we have to think to get an answer*

2. Explain the relationship between the words we use for things, the things in reality, and our thinking.

3. What does it mean to say that our concepts are "abstract" and "universal"?

"Language is as natural to man as is flight to the bird. The cry of animals in pain, the bark of dogs, the mimicry of parrots -- these sounds are not language; they follow naturally on some motor stimulus and, although they are *signs* of emotional and biological needs and reactions, they are not known by the animals themselves to be signs."

Fredrick D. Wilhelmsen

---

[1] See Dennis Bonnette, Ph.D., "Ape-Language Studies," in *Faith & Reason,* 19:2,3 (Fall, 1993), pp. 221-263.

Chapter VI
THE RATIONAL POWERS OF THE SOUL

Human Knowledge vs Animal Knowledge

Let us take a break from the technical discussion we have been having and look further at how our knowledge of the world around us differs from the knowledge that our dogs and cats have of it.

To some extent we have already discussed this when we were talking about the internal senses. Do you remember the many times we pointed out that *because of our rational powers* we are able to do more than the animals can do in using those internal senses? So, in our discussion now, let us <u>not</u> refer back to those internal senses. Let us just consider the question in terms of how the intellect *on its own* makes our knowledge different from an animal's.

My dog Snarles automatically forms sense images of all that he is sensing, just as we do. So both Snarles and I can know the *particular* things that our senses pick up from the world around us. For example, we both have sense knowledge of the oak tree in my front yard, the tulips in the vase on the table, and the people walking down the sidewalk. To say that Snarles and I have sense knowledge of them means that we "take in" the accidental forms of these things. We can both know their sizes, shapes, colors, odors, textures, sounds, etc. Because an animal's senses might actually be better than ours, the animal may even have better knowledge of these accidental forms than we do. That is why we use dogs to hunt the scent which we are unable to pick up.

Where we differ is that this knowledge of the particular aspects of things is <u>all</u> that Snarles is able to know. He is not able to know what we can know: the essences of those things. He does not know that the brown, firm, rough thing with moving green parts is a *tree*. He does not know that the purple, round-shaped, nice smelling thing is a *flower*. He does not know that the moving things with different odors and bright colors are *people*. Nor is he able to have a language that expresses these concepts.

Because Snarles does not have a clue as to *what it is* he is sensing, he is unaware that things differ in value. Thus, he will treat them all the same, unless his senses tell him otherwise. This is why we sometimes hear of a dog mistaking for a tree a person who has been standing still involved in a conversation. The dog does not know the value of the human person and so treats him as if he were a tree.

NOTES

"So in this way, the soul is the form (or blueprint) of the body. Our bodies have the design they do because of the capacities of our souls. We are able to talk because our souls have something to say. Our fingers are nimble yet strong because our souls have the capacity to work at tasks that require both strength and agility. We have highly developed brains because our souls have the capacity to think and reason. Animals have less of all this because their souls have little capacity in any of these regards. My cat, Daniel, does not speak. This is not just because he has no larynx: Daniel has no larynx because he has nothing to say. The lack of capacity in his animal soul is reflected in the design of his body."

Msgr. Charles Pope

NOTES

"We are at a place where people are angrier if a dog is killed in traffic than if a child is killed in traffic. Let me give you an example. There was a woman who was jogging in Los Angeles and she was brought down by a cougar. And they went out and shot the cougar because of human safety concerns. And a lot of money was raised for the offspring -- of the cougar! More money was raised for the cubs of the dead cougar than for the children of the dead woman."
Wesley J. Smith,
"Nihilism as Compassion"

But Snarles' ignorance does not bother him because there is nothing in him which continually raises the question, "What is it?" He has no intellect with its passive and active dimensions. Snarles rests content with his superficial knowledge of the world around him.

It is hard for us even to imagine this kind of a limitation in knowing because we do not experience it ourselves. Instead of trying to imagine it, however, many of us simply treat Snarles as if he is "one of us," though smaller. This way of treating animals shows a mistaken understanding of what they are.

Why do we think animals do not have this higher kind of knowledge? What evidence do we have for making this judgment?

Do you remember our discussion in Chapter Four about how we know that a soul has the powers that it has? We pointed out that by looking at the activities displayed through their bodies, we can know the powers of the soul which caused them. These activities tell us there must be powers, and the powers tell us something about the nature of the soul itself.

So, what kinds of activities do we see dogs and cats doing? We see them doing today the same kinds of things they have always done. They eat, drink, rest, and run after lizards or squirrels that stimulate their senses. They show excitement when the one who feeds them comes near.

What kinds of activities do we *not* see them doing? That is, what kinds of activity would we expect to see *if* they had intellectual knowledge? We would expect to see some advancement or improvement in the way they live. Why? Because concepts are universal ideas that apply in many different situations. For example, with the concept "wheel-ness," man was able to make wheelbarrows, wagons, cars, pulleys, bicycles, etc. "Shade-ness" is another good example. With that concept, we made visors on baseball caps, umbrellas, sun-glasses, and patio roofs. All are applications of the concept "shade." But did you notice the improvement? We probably first learned "shade-ness" from seeing how tree branches protect us from the sun. Then we make an advance by figuring out how we can make "shade-ness" portable or more permanent.

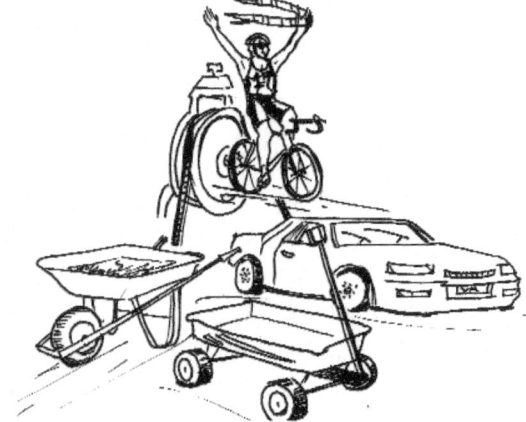

Chapter VI
THE RATIONAL POWERS OF THE SOUL

Rarely do human beings do something twice without there being some improvement. We advance from carrying a load ourselves, to devising wheel barrels, to making horse-drawn carts, to inventing engine driven trucks -- all made possible because we can form a *general idea* that is able to be applied in many different instances. There are many examples like these among human beings, but we find *not a single one* in the animal world. Dogs and cats are doing today what dogs and cats have always done. There are no new inventions or better ways of doing things in the animal world.

Now, you might respond, "Not my dog. He has a pretty little dog house with a swinging door, a fancy bowl for his food, and a beautiful collar around his neck." Yes, you are right: all of those advances are signs of an intelligent power. But in this case, the intelligent power is not in the dog itself because the advances did not come from him. His owner is responsible for them all.

It is because we humans understand "desk-ness" that we do not rest content with the first one we experience. Rather, from the first one, we understand its "what-ness," and then are able to make improved models with the same essence. So we devise desks with wider, softer chairs for comfort, and higher backs for support; areas for storing extra books, and with bigger flat surface areas for writing and using our computers.

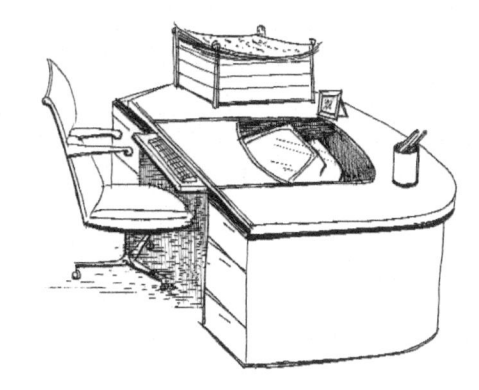

This is some of the evidence we have for realizing that humans have an intellectual power that animals lack.

Study Guide Questions:

1. In what ways are human knowledge and animal knowledge similar? In what ways are they different?

2. What evidence do we have that animals lack the power of intellect?

3. Animals do not get as troubled or bothered about things as humans do. Doesn't this seem to be a sign of their intelligence?

NOTES

"Man does not fade into the background of nature to become part of the scenery: He steps out of the world and establishes a new order of things, the order we call civilization or culture."
Frederick D. Wilhelmsen

THE WILL

Seeking Goodness Itself

In Chapter Five we discussed the *appetitive* powers of the soul, those powers that respond to what the soul knows through the senses. We called these powers the *emotions*, *passions* or *sense appetites*. Just as the senses have "appetites" which respond to what is sensed, so also the intellect has an appetitive power. This "appetite" of the intellect is called the *will*. Because the will is so closely connected with the intellect, it is often referred to as the **intellectual appetite** or the **rational appetite**. In fact, the will is so closely connected with the intellect that Aristotle once said, "The will is born in human reason."[2]

Let us see if we can make some sense out of Aristotle's statement. Remember that all of our knowledge comes through the five senses. Nothing "gets into" the intellect without coming in through the senses. In the same way, all of the movements of our will (our rational appetite) follow in some way from the movements of our emotions (our sense appetites). This means that the will acts only *after* the person has been emotionally attracted to some good he perceives.

To help in understanding this, consider an everyday example: I first smell and then see the pizza in front of me. My emotions kick in immediately. I love the good pizza and desire it for myself!

While this is going on at the level of my senses, my intellect gets involved -- but *in its own way*. The intellect forms "ideas" of the experience. Abstracting from the image the senses present to it, the intellect forms the idea "pizza-ness." From the response of the emotions to the *good* pizza, the intellect forms the idea "good-ness." These ideas are abstract and universal. "Pizza-ness" is the *essence* of any being we call a pizza.

But what is "good-ness?" The good is whatever is fitting or suitable to a being. For example, nuts are good for a squirrel, water is good for a

---

"Truth means more than knowledge: knowing the truth leads us to discover the good."
Pope Benedict XVI,
4/17/08

---

[2] Aristotle, *On the Soul*, 3.432b.5.

duck, and Sally is good for Tom. One being is "good" for another if it helps to fulfill him, i.e., if it gives him something that he *ought* to have but is lacking.

So what does the abstract idea "goodness" mean? It refers to the *essence* of the "good." This essence of the good must apply to every good thing there is, and it must leave out any particular lack or limitation of goodness. In other words, this idea "good-ness" is universal and represents the "fullness of good."

In our daily lives, we experience many particular "good things." They have *some aspects* of goodness, but they lack the total fullness of good. That is why they can't totally satisfy our will's longing for the good. Because there is no lack of good in the concept "good-ness," however, this idea "good-ness" represents what would *completely* fulfill or satisfy the human person. That is why some people have referred to this "fullness of goodness" as human "happiness."

No matter what we call it -- "fullness of goodness" or "happiness" -- the desire for it is found in every human person. Augustine says: "There's no doubt about it. We all want to be happy. Everyone will agree with me, before the words are even out of my mouth."[3]

Where does this desire that each of us has for the totality of goodness come from? It cannot come from our sense appetites, because they seek only *particular* good things. These particular good things are truly good, but they are **finite**, limited goods. Each one of them is lacking some aspect of goodness. For example, pizza is *not the best* food for a person's good health. A good nap right now is *not good* for getting work done. Listening to a good concert tonight means that I'll not be able to visit with my friend. None of these limited goods can fully satisfy us.

St. Thomas explains that the desire for **infinite** goodness -- the fullness of good -- arises from the intellect itself. Once the intellect forms the *idea* of good-ness, there springs up within the intellect itself an *appetite* for it. This *intellectual appetite* -- different from the *sense* appetites -- seeks a good which is infinite. This new appetite "in the heart of the intellect" we call the **will**.[4] Its proper object is the infinite good.

It is because we humans have this desire for infinite goodness, that is, for goodness itself, that we are never fully satisfied with limited goods. Unlike animals that rest content with the goods of this world, our wills spur us on to constantly seek for more good, for goodness itself.

---
[3] St. Augustine, *The Standards of the Catholic Church.*.
[4] Pierre-Marie Emonet, O.P., p. 69.

NOTES

"Where has happiness ever been seen, so as to be loved? Certainly it is within us. But how? I know not."

St. Augustine, *Confessions*

Finite - from the Latin *finis*, meaning end, boundary, or limit. The word refers to whatever has a limit or end point.

Infinite - from the Latin *infinire*, "not to limit;" unlimited; inexhaustible; endless.

Will - a free and active tendency within a being towards or away from an object that the intellect presents to it. It is also called the *intellectual* or *rational appetite*.

The Human Person ~ Dignity Beyond Compare

NOTES

"Is not that to which all aspire, and which no one disdains, happiness?"

St. Augustine, *Confessions*

Freedom of the Will

The intellect and will work together as partners in the human soul. In fact, their cooperation together is the starting point of all of their later activity. That starting point is the following truth: **"Happiness (the fullness of good) is what I want."** This first truth also gives the "intellect-will team" their "marching orders:" They want to find happiness!

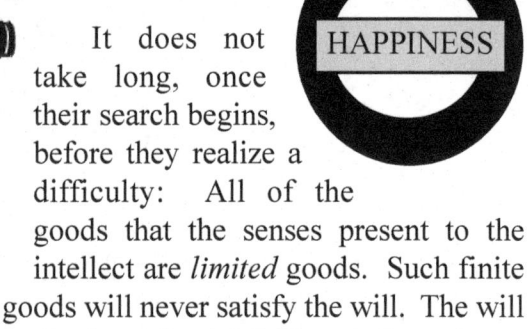

It does not take long, once their search begins, before they realize a difficulty: All of the goods that the senses present to the intellect are *limited* goods. Such finite goods will never satisfy the will. The will wants a good which is *unlimited*. It seeks the fullness of goodness. Once the will finds this being which is good in every way, it will have to "go for it" because this fullness of the good will completely satisfy its longing. The will will not be able to turn away.

Until it finds this fullness of goodness, however, the will is free to pick and choose among the limited goods that the senses present to the intellect. It is free to turn away from them or to embrace them. This ability to pick and choose from among limited goods is what we mean by the will's *freedom* or its *free choice*.

We cannot lose sight of the fact, though, that as it chooses from among limited goods, the will is looking for what will make it happy. When it chooses any good, it does so because it thinks that good will in some way lead it closer to happiness.

Perhaps an example will help us to see what we mean here. Suppose you are free to choose what to do after school today from among the following options of limited goods:

a) You can go over and spend some time at a friend's house.
b) You can hurry home and get started cutting the grass for your parents.
c) You can stop by the library and begin working on a history project.
d) You can go home and take a nap.

Each of the options presents something good to your will. But none of them presents an option which is *wholly* good. For example, if

Chapter VI
THE RATIONAL POWERS OF THE SOUL

you spend an hour at a friend's house, then you won't get started on the history project, or mow the yard for your parents, or take a much needed nap. Because it does not find an option that will completely satisfy it, the will is free to choose from among the options.

When the will chooses an option, though, it will do so because it views that option as being able to lead it to happiness. For example, you might choose to go spend time at a friend's house because you think that relaxing there will make you happy. Or, you may hurry home to work for your parents because you want to make life a little easier for them. If you choose this option, you have probably come to realize that you are usually happier when you forget about yourself and focus on helping other people.

The intellect and will work together in this decision-making process. The intellect presents the options to the will. The intellect's job is to point out to the will what is *truly* good as opposed to what is only *apparently* good. For example, it is only apparently good to eat only candy all day long. It is truly good for you to have a well-balanced diet. The will, however, has the final say. It can direct the intellect to look more closely at an option in order to determine if it is truly good, or it can direct the intellect not to consider fully an option if the will doesn't want to know the truth. Ultimately, then, the will actually decides *for itself* which limited goods it will seek. This *self-determining* power of the will is what we mean by its *freedom of choice*.

A <u>word of caution</u> about this freedom to choose: While the will has the supreme dignity of being able to determine *for itself* the limited goods it will pursue in order to achieve happiness, it can be wrong about their ability to actually bring happiness. For example, you might think that *whatever* brings you more money will make you happy. You might even make choices with money as your final goal. However, because the human person has needs that money cannot satisfy, you will not find the happiness you seek. In other words, the ultimate goal of the will's choices must <u>truly</u> be what is totally good -- objectively speaking -- or the will will not find the happiness it wants.

This is why it is so important that the intellect and will work together. The will needs

NOTES

"This freedom which is a distinctive feature of the being called man enables him to orient his life towards ... the happiness to which he is called for eternity."
Pope Benedict XVI
1/28/08

"Freedom is a delicate value; it can be abused."
Pope Benedict XVI,
4/20/08

99.

The Human Person ~ Dignity Beyond Compare

NOTES

to have the intellect present the full *truth* about the goods it sets before it. For only when the will chooses what is *truly* good will it be <u>*free*</u> to achieve the happiness it was designed to enjoy.

Human Consciousness

Because both the intellect and the will are involved in producing the free act, the "intellect-will team" knows itself as the cause of its own free act.[5] Simply put: You know that *you* are the cause of your free choice to take a nap instead of mowing the yard. This awareness of yourself as the cause of your own activity is what we mean by human **self-consciousness**.

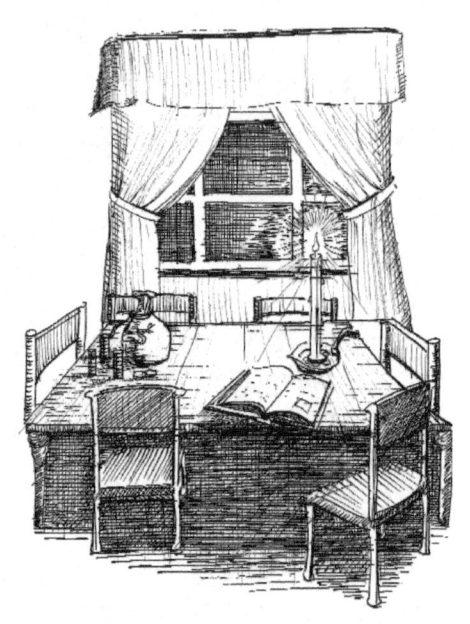

Plants and animals act *unconsciously* toward ends that are set by their natures. They are unaware of themselves. For example, plants take in water *automatically* as dictated by their nature. Animals drink *automatically* as dictated by their senses and appetites.

Self-consciousness - from the Latin *conscire*, "to know," "to be aware of;" the awareness of oneself as the cause of one's own activity.

The human person is different. He is aware of himself. He knows that he knows, and he knows that he freely chooses. With this *self-knowledge*, he can understand his freedom and his responsibility for his own actions. For example, the human person can choose either to drink or not to drink. He can dehydrate himself by refusing to drink, if he chooses. Or he can choose to drink as a means of taking care of his body and his life which have been given to him by his Creator.

You see, whether or not we move closer to the fullness of good that our wills desire is under our control. The "intellect-will team" makes this possible. With every free act, we are actually moving ourselves towards what is *truly* good for us or away from it. The choice is ours.

[5] St. Thomas Aquinas, *Summa Theologiae* I, 87, 1.

Chapter VI
THE RATIONAL POWERS OF THE SOUL

Will we use our freedom to pursue limited goods that leave us hungering for more? Or will we use it to pursue what is *truly* good and so find the happiness we seek? Our freedom is an awesome, God-like privilege which involves us in choices that will determine our eternal destiny.

Conclusion

With our study of the rational powers of the human soul, we begin to get a glimpse of the reason for our exalted dignity as human beings. Our power of intellect enables us to know reality, for we can "read" the hidden natures of things. Our rational appetite, that in-born power driving us toward the Fullness of Good, enables us to move ourselves freely in the direction which we ourselves choose. Thus, we are able to move ourselves either toward what is *truly* the Fullness of Good or away from it, toward the limited and unsatisfying goods of this world. The choice is ours!

Study Guide Questions:

1. How is the will related to the intellect?
2. What is the proper object of the will?
3. Why do we say that the will's freedom is dependent upon the intellect?
4. If a person can choose his own ends, why can we not guarantee that he will be happy with whatever he chooses?
5. How do animals and humans differ regarding self-knowledge?
6. How are plants, animals, and human beings different from each other regarding the goals in their various activities?
7. In what sense is our freedom both an awesome gift and a weighty responsibility?

* * *

Point to Consider:

"Dear young people,
... It is Jesus in fact that you seek when you dream of happiness;
he is waiting for you when nothing else you find satisfies you;
he is the beauty to which you are so attracted;
it is he who provokes you with that thirst for fullness
that will not let you settle for compromise;
it is he who urges you to shed the masks of a false life;
it is he who reads in your hearts your most genuine choices,
the choices that others try to stifle.
It is Jesus who stirs in you the desire
to do something great with your lives,

NOTES

"The great mystery of personal freedom is that even God pauses before it."
St. Edith Stein

*the will to follow an ideal,
the refusal to allow yourselves to be grounded down by mediocrity, the
courage to commit yourselves humbly and patiently
to improving yourselves and society,
making the world more human and more fraternal."*

*Saint John Paul II,
World Youth Day Address, August 19, 2000*

CASES IN POINT

#1 - St. Augustine said, "Our hearts are restless until they rest in You, O Lord." It really does seem that nothing can completely satisfy us human beings. No matter how good we have it, we always seem to want "more."

- In view of what we have studied in this chapter, can you explain this restlessness of the human heart? That is, why can't we be fully satisfied with the good things we experience?

***

#2 - "For most of us, whatever our feelings about cats and dogs, and no matter how clever a bee may turn out to be, these insects are nothing but machines. And yet what wonderful machines! A close look at the bee machine will perhaps make the notion of all animals as machines more palatable (acceptable)." Clive Wynne, *Do Animals Think?* p. 14.

- What does it mean to say that insects are nothing but machines? Why is it so hard for us to think of cats and dogs as nothing but machines?

***

#3 - "The person with a mature love is not focused primarily on what feelings and desires may be stirring inside him. Rather, he is focused on his responsibility to care for his beloved's good. He actively seeks what is good for her, not just his own pleasure, enjoyment and selfish pursuits." Edward Sri, *Men, Women and the Mystery of Love: Practical Insights from John Paul II's Love and Responsibility*, p. 80.

- Why can't mature love be based simply on the emotions? What other powers of the rational soul need to be involved if our love for others is going to be mature?

Chapter VII

THE RATIONAL SOUL

Introduction

So far we have progressed step by step to understand that: from the activities of a being we can discover its powers, and from its powers we discover the nature of the being itself.

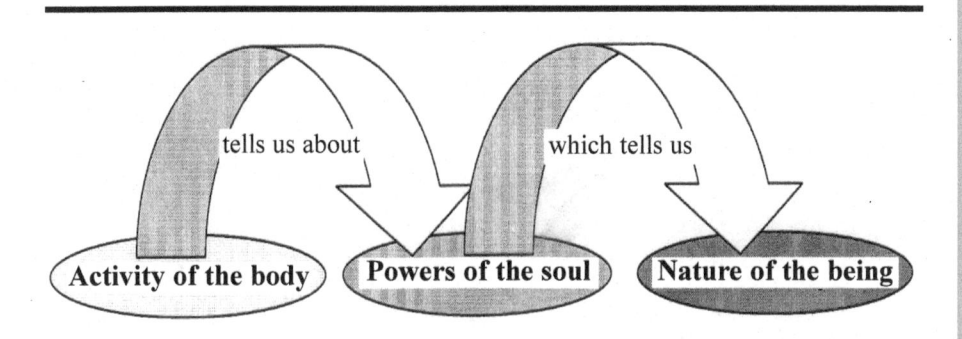

```
Activity of the body  →tells us about→  Powers of the soul  →which tells us→  Nature of the being
```

We see the activities of growth, reproduction, and nourishment in human beings. We conclude that the human soul must have the powers which cause these vegetative activities. We see the activities of sensation, sense appetition, and locomotion in human beings. We understand that the human soul must have the powers to bring about these sensory activities. Finally, we see the activities of intellectual knowing and freedom in choosing, activities which are unique to human beings. We realize that the human soul must have powers capable of producing these rational activities.

Aware then of the powers present in the human soul, we are now ready to focus our attention on the rational soul itself and to draw some conclusions about its nature.

Vocabulary

subsistent	spiritual soul	immortal
immaterial	permanent vegetative state	corporeal

The Human Person ~ Dignity Beyond Compare

The Distinction between the Soul and its Powers

The first thing we need to clarify about the rational soul itself is that it is something different from its powers. Another way of saying this is that what the soul can *do* is not the same as what the soul *is*. If this were not so, then when a person is not able to be actively thinking or freely choosing, his soul would stop existing. He would then no longer be a human being.

If the powers of the soul were identical with the soul itself, then we should expect them to be *always* activated or turned on. This means that we would be thinking and choosing *all the time*. If we were not thinking and choosing, then we would conclude that the rational soul is gone and that we are not, at that time, actual human beings.

Does this sound a little ridiculous? Just good practical thinking helps us to see that this cannot be true. When you are sleeping and not actively engaged in thinking, you are still a living human being. Your rational soul remains present, even though you are not using all of the powers of your soul.

Perhaps the terms "*first* act" and "*second* act" -- which we talked about in Chapter Two -- can help us out here. Remember that the rational soul is the *first* act of a living human body. As long as the soul is united to the body, their union will be a living, human being. Any other activities that the human being does -- nourishing himself, sensing, feeling, thinking, choosing -- are its *second* acts. These acts are caused by the powers of the soul.

Now while it is true that there would be no *second* acts without the *first* act, the opposite is not true. The absence of *second* acts does not always mean the absence of the *first* act. Simply put: A person cannot sense and think and choose unless he is a living human being, but it is possible for a human person to be living and not be sensing, thinking, or choosing. It is the powers of the soul that are responsible for the soul's second act, and these powers are not always turned on. This is why we know there is a difference between the rational soul and its powers.

Understanding this difference is extremely important, especially in today's society. Today we tend to place so much value on *what we do* rather than on *who we are* as human persons. This is why some people say that it is acceptable to kill human beings who are unborn, still in their infancy, severely mentally handicapped because of disease or old age, or in a **permanent vegetative state**. If a person cannot use his thinking powers, then some people think that he is not fully human. They think he lacks the dignity the rest of us have. Pope John Paul II refers to this problem:

> In opposition to such trends of thought, I feel the duty to reaffirm strongly that the intrinsic value and personal dignity of every human being do not change, no matter what the concrete circumstances of his or her life. A man, even if seriously ill or disabled in the exercise of his highest functions, is and always will be a man, and he will never become a "vegetable" or an "animal."[1]

A person who is disabled in the use of his highest powers will always be a human being because his rational soul remains present as long as he is alive. It is the rational soul, as the substantial form of the body, which makes the being to be the kind of being it is. Dignity is ours precisely because of the kind of beings we are, not because of any particular activity we do. Not to recognize that dignity is a grave offense against the person himself as well as against the One who bestowed this dignity upon him.

Study Guide Questions:

1. Why is the fact that a soul is something different than its powers so important?

2. Give an example of a thing's first act and its second act.

3. What causes a living being's first act? What causes its second act?

4. Why is a person who is disabled in the use of his highest powers still considered to be a human being?

---

[1] Saint John Paul, *Address to the Participants in the International Congress on "Life-Sustaining Treatments and Vegetative State,"* 20 March 2004, #3.

NOTES

Permanent Vegetative State (PVS) - the condition of a person who has shown -- for over a year's time -- no evident sign of self-awareness or of awareness of the environment, and seems unable to interact with others or to react to specific stimuli. The more prolonged in time the condition of the vegetative state is for the person, the less likelihood there is he will recover. However, there are well-documented cases of at least partial recovery even after many years.

The Human Person ~ Dignity Beyond Compare

NOTES

[handwritten: because the material organ is bound to the particular yet we grasp the universal]

CASE IN POINT

You may recall in 2005 the case of Terri Schiavo. She was a young woman from Florida whose husband petitioned the courts to allow her to be starved and dehydrated to death because she was in what was determined by some to be a "permanent vegetative state." Terri was healthy, though severely brain-damaged. She was breathing on her own. The courts made the decision, in agreement with her husband's request, to deprive Terri of food and water so that she would die.

◆ In light of our discussion in this chapter, why do we know that the courts were wrong in their decision?

The Nature of the Rational Soul

What can we conclude now about the nature of the rational soul itself? What kind of a thing is it? St. Thomas identifies two characteristics:

- The rational soul is spiritual.
- The rational soul is subsistent.

Let us look more closely at both of these characteristics. <u>First</u>, what does it mean to say that the rational soul is *spiritual*? The soul is a *form*, and <u>all</u> forms are **immaterial** -- even the forms of plants and animals. But the forms of plants and animals are sometimes called "*material* souls." We call them "material" not because the souls themselves are material, but because they need their bodies for *all* of their activities. For example, a plant soul's powers of growth, nourishment, and reproduction all depend on its body. Similarly, an animal's soul needs its body for sensing, for its sense appetites, and for locomotion. In other words, the activities of plants and animals are all *rooted in matter*.

Immaterial - from the Latin *immaterialis*, "not matter;" without matter.

Material soul - the souls of plants and animals which, although they are immaterial in themselves, are completely dependent upon the matter with which they are united.

Material souls

The rational soul, which human beings have, is different.

Chapter VII
THE RATIONAL SOUL

Whenever the rational soul forms concepts (thinks) or freely chooses (wills), it acts *as a spirit*. It does not depend on its body for these activities. That is why St. Thomas says that the rational soul is ***spiritual***.

Remember how the intellect's work begins with the abstraction of the essence of a thing from the phantasm? With this act of abstraction, the intellect begins its work *separate from matter and from any conditions of matter.* What the intellect knows is the universal essence of a thing and what the will seeks is the *universal* good. As universals, both of these objects are immaterial. Both the intellect and the will, then, are involved in activities that are completely free of the body.

Spiritual, subsistent soul

The second characteristic of the rational soul is its ability to exist *on its own* as a substance. St. Thomas uses the word "**subsistent**" to speak of this ability of the rational soul to exist independently. Thomas says the rational soul is subsistent because it has an activity that it can do without the help of its body: it can think and choose. If it can act without the body, then the rational soul must be able to exist without it. St. Thomas says, "[A] thing operates according as it is."[2]

The souls of plants and animals cannot do this. Because all of their activities are done in union with their bodies, they must exist only in union with their bodies. This means that these souls are not like substances which can exist on their own. They are non-subsistent. They are more like accidents which always require something else in order to be able to exist. The souls of plants and animals always require their bodies in order to exist. They form a substance *only* when they are united with their bodies.

Non-subsistent souls

Be careful: We are not saying that the human being is *two* substances: body and soul. The human being is *one* substance, but it is a substance because the soul shares its "act of independent existence" with its body. This means that our being able to exist independently as substances is due to our souls. With plants and animals, it is due to the union of their souls and bodies.

---
[2] St. Thomas Aquinas, *Summa Theologiae*, I, 75, 2.

NOTES

Spiritual soul - the rational soul; that soul which has both an activity and an existence which is free of matter.

Subsistent - able to exist independently or on its own.

"Each human individual is a substance thanks to the soul. This is because the soul is substance."
Pierre-Marie Emonet

107.

The Human Person ~ Dignity Beyond Compare

NOTES

Creation - the created world; the bringing of something new into existence out of nothingness.

The Creation of the Rational Soul

St. Thomas teaches that the rational soul -- unlike the souls of plants and animals -- can only come into existence **by creation**. He says this because the way a being comes into existence must be in line with the kind of thing that it is. Let us see if we can understand what St. Thomas is saying to us.

First of all, the rational soul is spiritual. Because of this, St. Thomas says that it must be created by something spiritual. We never see an effect that is greater in being than the thing which caused it. For example, anything a human being makes will be equal to or less in being than we are. So the cause of the spiritual soul, Thomas reasons, must be a spiritual being.

Secondly, for something to come into existence "by creation" is different than for it to be "made." Strictly speaking, the word "make" always entails using some already-existing materials. For example, an oil painter makes a new painting by bringing together already existing colored oils and an already existing canvas.

"Creating," on the other hand, implies that there are no pre-existing materials with which to work. Rather, to create something means to bring it into existence "from nothing." With this precise use of the terms, we quickly see that only God creates. He is the One who first brought things into existence from nothing at the beginning of time. The best we human beings can do is to make things using God's "stuff," that is, using things He has already created.

So when St. Thomas says that the human soul is created, not made, he means that each human soul comes to be directly or immediately by God causing it to exist *out of nothingness*. This is different from the way the souls of plants and animals come into existence. They come to be through the process of generation of a new plant or animal. We could say that they are *made* by the plants or animals from which they are generated. God is *ultimately* responsible for their existence, of course, but they are not created <u>*directly*</u> by Him as the human soul is.

Because it is the form of a human body, the rational soul must be created by God at the moment there is human "matter" for it to "inform." As we said in Chapter Three, science tells us that the human matter is present at the moment of fertilization. At that moment, the woman's egg and man's sperm unite to form the first 46-chromosomed cell, the human zygote. Because there is a living human body from that point until death, the philosopher knows the human soul must be present. He also knows that this soul is present only because God directly created it at that precise moment. This soul, like the body it informs, is unique and unrepeatable.

Study Guide Questions:

1. Strictly speaking, human beings cannot "create" anything. Explain.

2. If God is ultimately responsible for causing the souls of plants, animals, and human beings to exist, what is so significant about the human soul's creation?

3. Why does St. Thomas think that the rational soul has to be created directly by God?

4. What activity can the human soul do without the use of its body?

5. What does it mean for something to be subsistent? Why does St. Thomas think that the rational soul is subsistent?

6. Why are the souls of plants and animals considered to be more like accidents than like substances? Why is this not also the case for the rational soul?

The Human Person ~ Dignity Beyond Compare

NOTES

> ### CASE IN POINT
>
> The artificial reproduction of human beings is a booming business in our world today. Couples can go to fertility centers and, for a cost of about $15,000, order the kind of baby they want. They can choose its gender, its skin color, and make sure that it is disease-free and has a high I.Q. They can also select from a wide variety of already-made human embryos.
>
> ♦ In light of what we have learned in this chapter, should we not say that we are now able to "create" new human life? Where do the souls of these babies come from?
>
> ♦ Do you see anything wrong with human beings making other human beings?
>
> ♦ How does this way of bringing a human being into existence differ from the natural way?

The Immortality of the Rational Soul

Once we understand the nature of the rational soul, we do not have far to go to realize that this soul is able to live on its own once the human being dies. In order to understand this, we need to remember two things about the rational soul:

<u>First</u>, the soul is the substantial form of its body, and a form is not material. Since it is not made up of matter, the soul cannot be physically divided. A soul, then, is not able to corrupt or dissolve into parts because it is simple. It has no parts. Thus, it cannot naturally corrupt.

<u>Second</u>, because it is *spiritual* and *subsistent*, the rational soul does not depend on its body for its activity or for its existence. So, although the human body cannot live without its soul, the rational soul can continue to live without its body. This is what we mean when we say that the rational soul is "**immortal**." Once it is created and has been given its own independent existence by the Creator, the human soul will never stop existing. It cannot die.

Realizing that the rational soul cannot die is something we can know simply by using our intellects. We don't have to be people of faith

Immortal - from the Latin *immortalis*, "not subject to death;" the unending continued existence of life.

to realize it. The immortality of the rational soul is one of those truths that can be known by *both* faith and reason.

Even the ancient pagan philosopher Aristotle understood this indestructibility of the rational soul:

> "An old person who could find an eye of good quality would see just as clearly as a young person. In other words, old age is due not to any affection of the soul, but to an affection of the subject [the body] in which [the soul] resides, just as occurs in intoxication or illness. The exercise of thought and knowing, then, declines when another organ, an internal one is destroyed, but in itself the intellect is incapable of suffering decline."[3]

> **Argument for the Immortality of the Rational Soul**
>
> ◆ *That substance is immortal which cannot be corrupted of itself or by reason of something else on which it depends.*
>
> ◆ *But the rational soul cannot be corrupted of itself (it is simple), nor because of something else on which it depends (it is subsistent and spiritual).*
>
> ◆ *Therefore, the rational soul is immortal.*

So memory loss, Alzheimers, senility, etc., are not problems of the intellect. They are defects of a physical organ -- the brain. If we could get a brain transplant, the elderly could think as clearly as the young.

The "Grades" of Being

By now you are probably realizing not only that there are different *kinds* of living beings but also that these living beings are "graded." That is why we refer to *higher* or *lower* forms of life. Living beings are not all on the same level; there is an *order* (a hierarchy) among them. Some are superior to others because they possess powers which the others do not have.

Unlike the "grades" that you experience in school, the "grades of life" cannot be changed. In other words, a plant is always a plant. It cannot "graduate" and become an animal or a human person. It cannot change grades, because each grade is a unique kind of being with a soul that is unique to that grade of being.

---

[3] Aristotle, *On the Soul,* 1.4.408b.20-25.

The Human Person ~ Dignity Beyond Compare

NOTES

"Animal liberationists do not separate out the human animal, so there is no rational basis for saying that a human being has special rights. A rat is a pig is a dog is a boy. They are all mammals."
Ingrid Newkirk,
PETA (People for the Ethical Treatment of Animals)

"If you destroy human exceptionalism -- which the animal rights movement intends to do -- if you say that we are not the highest life form on the planet, if our lives do not have greater value than those of animals, then you have completely changed how we perceive ourselves. Animal rights people may think that they are raising animals to the level of people, but what they are really doing is reducing people to the level of animals."
Wesley J. Smith,
"Nihilism as Compassion"

Kind of Being	Kind of Soul	Powers of the Soul		
		Vegetative	Sensitive	Rational
Human	*Rational*	✓	✓	✓
Non-human Animal	*Sensitive*	✓	✓	
Plant	*Vegetative*	✓		

The gradation of being is easy to recognize if you look at the powers that each "grade" of living being has. The more powers a soul has, the higher its grade of being. Notice in the chart above that animals surpass plants and that humans surpass both plants and animals. This is why we say that human beings are the "highest grade" of living beings on this earth.

In order to see the human person in his rightful place, however, let us broaden our perspective. Let us look not just at living beings on this earth. Let us look at *all* beings and see where we fit in. The criterion that St. Thomas uses to understand the grades of being is the difference between potency and act. He says that being in *act* is better than being in *potency* because *act* implies actual existence and *potency* does not. So the more "in act" (actual) a thing is and the less potency it has, the higher grade of being it is. For example, an actually existing pizza is a higher grade of being than is a potential pizza.

One other thing: Remember that the form of a thing is what makes it actual. Its matter is the potency which has been actualized and which is *still* in potency to receive different accidental and substantial forms. So the less material a being is, the more "in act" (actual) it is, and the less potency it has. Thus, the more immaterial the being is, the higher is its grade of being. This is why angels (pure spirits) are higher beings than humans are.

Chapter VII
THE RATIONAL SOUL

So, let us look at where we fall in the ordering of all beings. See the chart below.

- Notice that the lowest on the scale is prime matter because it is pure potentiality.

- Non-living beings (rock, sand, metal, etc.) are higher than prime matter. This is because some of their potential has been actualized by their substantial forms.

- Plants are a grade higher than non-living beings. The vegetative powers of the plant soul enable it to be the cause of its own activities of nutrition, growth, and reproduction. Non-living beings don't have any activity of their own.

- Non-human animals are higher than plants because of their sensitive powers. Through their sense knowledge, they can "bring in" the world around them in a somewhat immaterial way. They also are able to act in response to the world they are experiencing.

- Human beings are superior to the animals. With our rational powers, we have activities which are completely free of matter: we can know and freely choose.

- Angels are above us because they are completely immaterial beings. They are below God (Pure Act), though, because they are creatures. They once did not exist, though they had potency to exist. God actualized their potential for existence when He created them.

- God is Pure Act and Pure Spirit. He has no potentiality. He has always existed and always will exist.

NOTES

"It should be enough to say that a man can have in his head stars and galaxies whirling about and the possibility of alien life and of gods; and that he can think of the remote past and of the remote future and about all species of living things he encounters. The horse, meanwhile, noble beast that it is, does not even seem to notice that there *are* stars. At least, I have never caught one gazing up at them in wonder."
Michael Augros
Who Designed the Designer?
p. 91

\	HIERARCHY OF BEING
God	*Pure Act / Pure Spirit*
Angels	*Potency and Act / Pure Spirits*
Human Persons	***Potency and Act / Spiritual and Material Beings / Rational Souls***
Non-human Animals	*Potency and Act / Material Beings / Sensitive Souls*
Plants	*Potency and Act / Material Beings / Vegetative Souls*
Non-living Beings	*Potency and Act / Material Beings*
Prime Matter	*Pure Potency*

NOTES

Corporeal - from the Latin *corpus*, "body;" means material or physical. The corporeal part of man is his body.

"Man is indeed a kind of bridge. He is the point at which the material world and the spiritual world meet and mingle and thus occupies a special place in the matrix of the created order.

Through man, the material world is lifted up into the spiritual realm, and through their combination in man we see that the two are compatible, each with the other. ...That gives him a quite special function: that is to say, sharing the responsibility for the unity of creation, incarnating spirit in himself and, conversely, lifting material being up to God -- and thereby, all in all, making a contribution to the great symphony of creation."

Joseph Cardinal Ratzinger,
God and the World

Do you notice from the chart above that we are the highest of the material beings but the lowest of the spiritual beings? St. Thomas said: "The human soul is a kind of horizon, and a boundary, as it were, between the **corporeal** world and the incorporeal world."[4] In a sense, you could say that we have a "foot" in both worlds. Our spiritual powers of intellect and will place us in the spiritual realm, while our other powers of the soul and our bodies place us in the material world.

Conclusion

In this chapter, we have seen what human reason can tell us about the nature of the rational soul, its creation, its immortality, and its high rank (dignity) among created things. Our Catholic faith affirms many of these same truths:

> The Church teaches that every spiritual soul is created immediately by God -- it is not 'produced' by the parents -- and also that it is immortal: it does not perish when it separates from the body at death, and it will be reunited with the body at the final Resurrection.[5]

Our rational soul gives us the exalted dignity of being human persons. In our concluding chapter, we will take a look at precisely what this title "person" means.

Study Guide Questions:

1. Why do philosophers like St. Thomas Aquinas think that the rational soul is immortal?

2. Why did St. Thomas think that human beings stand at the "horizon" between the spiritual and physical worlds?

---

[4] St. Thomas Aquinas, *Summa Contra Gentiles* 2.68.
[5] *The Catechism of the Catholic Church*, #366.

CASES IN POINT

#1 - Maggie is a high school senior. Her 16-year-old sister, Lucy, has Down's Syndrome. As they grew up, Maggie and Lucy spent lots of time together, and Maggie's Mom and Dad taught her and their other brothers and sisters how to look out for Lucy and include her in their fun. When Maggie had friends over, it was not unusual to find Lucy right in the middle of them, laughing and having a good time. Maggie's friends came to realize that Lucy had special gifts to share with them, even though there were many things Lucy was unable to do as they could. When Maggie told some of her friends that Lucy was going to take part in the Special Olympics at the school she attended, they decided to go and cheer her on. Lucy was thrilled to see them in the audience.

- What do you think both Lucy and Maggie have taught their friends about our dignity as human persons? How has their friendship with Lucy been good for Maggie's classmates? How has it been good for Lucy?

* * *

#2 - In an April, 2006, *National Geographic* article entitled "Where Dogs Have Their Day," author Michael Mason writes about San Francisco -- home to about 754,000 people and about 110,000 dogs. It has the lowest ratio of children to adults of any major U.S. city. Mason writes, "There is little doubt that dogs are helping fill a parental void. ... Residents are taking seriously the notion that dogs are family members, and pets are acquiring something that begins to resemble rights. The San Francisco Society for the Prevention of Cruelty to Animals established the nation's first no-kill shelter and built an adoption center with 'condos' furnished with televisions and aquariums." In the same article, he notes that San Francisco has its urban woes. "Homeless people wander the streets, housing is unaffordable, and public schools are struggling."

- A pet industry trade group says Americans spent $58 billion on their pets in 2014. $22 billion for food, $15 billion for veterinary care and $14 billion for supplies such as bowls, beds, and medicines for fleas and ticks. The fastest growing category was "other services," which includes grooming, boarding, walking, training, daycare and even trips to the spa, where pets can get facials and massages. *("Americans spent $58 billion to pamper, protect pets in 2014," The Associated Press, March 6, 2015)* What once seemed extravagant -- doggy daycares, pet cemeteries, and a wide variety of pet surgeries and treatments -- are now common place. In view of what we know about the nature of animals and humans, do you find anything worrisome about the way many Americans treat their pets?

- How does a person's responsibility for the homeless person who is a stranger to him compare with his responsibility for his pet dog or cat?

- What value do animals such as horses, dogs and cats rightfully have?

* * *

#3 - In October, 2017, five military dogs were chosen as the 2017 recipients of American Humane's Lois Pope K-9 Medal of Courage. The awards -- the nation's highest honor for military dogs recognizing their valor and service -- were presented at a Capital Hill ceremony attended by 12 members of Congress and more than 200 Congressional staffers.

"These remarkable dogs work side-by-side with the men and women of our Armed Forces, performing vitally important and life-saving work, while putting their own lives on the line for our country," Pope said. "It is high time that their valiant sacrifices and contributions to our nation and our men and women in uniform are properly recognized at the highest levels."

The following dogs received awards: Explosive detection dog Alphie; military working dog Coffee; military working dog Capa; military working dog Ranger; and military working dog Gabe (in memoriam).

(http://www.pennlive.com/nation-world/2017/10/5_us_military_dogs_ receive_med.html)

The Human Person ~ Dignity Beyond Compare

> ## CASES IN POINT *(continued)*
>
> - Does it seem reasonable for military and homeland security leaders to confer these awards on dogs? Explain your answer.
>
> * * *
>
> **#4** - The remains of a 22-year-old Virginia woman, Bethany Stephens, were found by her father in a wooded area in Goochland, Virginia. Bethany had taken her two pet dogs (pit bulls) for a walk, and it is thought that her dogs viciously mauled her to death. A man who used to work with Bethany, said that she "loved the canines and was very experienced working with animals." Others said that the dogs were "social, passive and had a 'significant bond' with the woman." The autopsy report determined that no drugs or alcohol were in Bethany's body, and there was no evidence of a gunshot, strangulation, sexual assault, or any other kind of attack. Rather, the medical examiner found defensive wounds on Bethany's hands and arms from "trying to keep the dogs away from her," and there was evidence of the animals chewing on her face, torso and arms after she died. With the family's consent, the dogs were euthanized.
>
> "Deputies watched dogs 'eating rib cage' of Virginia woman ..." *Fox News*, 12/19/2017.
"Autopsy confirms Virginia woman, 22, mauled to death by her own dogs," *Fox News*, 2/23/2018.
>
> Dan Brandon was strangled to death by his pet python, named Tiny. The 8-foot snake, which had been owned by Brandon since it was small enough to fit in the palm of his hand, wrapped itself around Brandon, crushing him and making it impossible for him to breathe. Brandon is said to have had "a special bond" with the snake.
>
> "Giant Pet Snake Named 'Tiny' Strangles Owner in his Own Home," by Callum Paton, *Newsweek*, 1/26/18.
>
> - How can we account for such vicious attacks by pets that were "loved" by their owners and who had a "special bond" with them?
>
> - What lesson should a person take from incidents such as these?

Point to Consider:

> *"When I behold your heavens, the work of your fingers,*
> > *the moon and the stars which you set in place --*
>
> *What is man that you should be mindful of him,*
> > *or the son of man that you should care for him?*
>
> *You have made him little less than the angels,*
> > *and crowned him with glory and honor.*
>
> *You have given him rule over the works of your hands,*
> > *putting all things under his feet:*
>
> *All sheep and oxen, yes, and the beasts of the field,*
> > *the birds of the air, the fishes of the sea,*
> > *and whatever swims the paths of the seas.*
>
> *O Lord, our Lord, how glorious is your name over all the earth!"*

Psalm 8:4-10

Conclusion

THE HUMAN PERSON ~ DIGNITY BEYOND COMPARE

"Beyond all the marvels of nature, the greatest is the human being."
— *Sophocles*

After all we have studied in this book, we should not be surprised to find that this quotation comes, not from St. Thomas Aquinas, but from an ancient Greek writer who lived seventeen centuries before Thomas! At the same time, we won't be surprised either to realize that St. Thomas would have readily agreed. *"The person,"* St. Thomas wrote, *"is what is most perfect in all of nature."*[1]

Why, exactly, does the person hold so high a place? Actually, in the previous chapters we have already begun to find an answer to that question. Now, as the summary and "crown" of our study, let us delve into this one last term, "person." Understanding its deepest meaning will shed light on the exalted **dignity** that is ours as *human* persons.

Origin of the Word "Person"

It is interesting to know that the concept *person*, as we understand it today, actually came into use with early Christian theologians. They used the concept as they struggled to understand the truths that God had revealed about Himself. They knew that there could be only *one* God; yet Jesus had revealed the truth that God is Father, Son and Holy Spirit. What could this mean?

There can be only one Divine Being; yet Jesus clearly spoke of Himself as the Son of God, equal to the Father. He also spoke of the Holy Spirit in a way that could only mean that He, too, must be divine. So, *"What* is God?" they asked; and *"Who* is Jesus Christ?" and "What about the Holy Spirit?" How could they understand the truth Jesus was revealing about God? How could God be both "One" and "Three" at the same time?

As they sought to understand this mystery, these early Christians turned to a concept that had originally been used in ancient

---

NOTES

Dignity - from the Latin *dignitas*, "worthiness;" of high rank or worth.

---

[1] St. Thomas Aquinas, *Summa Theologiae*, I, 29, 3.

Greek forms of drama. Instead of costumes, actors wore masks to depict the individuals they were portraying as they spoke. The story was told through the dialogue of these speakers. *"Persona"* was the word for the "mask" they wore or the "role" they assumed as they took their parts in relation to one another.

The early Christians began to see that God is One who is always "in dialogue." They knew that Scripture tells the great "drama" of the history of our salvation, in which God speaks to us and acts among us, revealing Himself. When the early Christians read Scripture, they discovered that the great drama of salvation history also involves roles and dialogue. They realized that there are places in Scripture where God speaks in the plural -- and that He speaks with Himself! For example, in the Book of Genesis, they read God's words at creation: *"Let us make man in our image and likeness."*[2] Later in Genesis, they read God's words: *"Adam has become like one of us."*[3]

They recalled this mystery of God "speaking to Himself" as they reflected on the Gospels, where Jesus speaks of God as Father, Son, and Holy Spirit. They realized that He is not just speaking of "roles" played by God. Not at all! Through Jesus Christ, God reveals the *fullest truth* about Himself. The names "Father," "Son," and "Holy Spirit" refer to actual <u>realities</u> who are in dialogue (i.e., communication) with one another.

This was the birth of the concept "person" as we understand it today. It arose from reading the Bible and realizing that God speaks: that He is in dialogue with Himself. Not only that, but He is also clearly in dialogue with the human persons whom He addresses. This is, after all, what divine revelation is: a communication in which the eternal God speaks to human persons in order to invite them into communion with Himself!

The concept of "person" continued to be developed as Christians tried to express the meaning of what had been fully revealed through the teaching of Jesus Christ: that God is one Being in three *Persons*. They knew that "person" couldn't imply "substance" (that which is able to exist on its own); otherwise, there would be three Gods. They began to realize that "**person**" could only be understood as "relation."

Let us see why it made sense for them to come to this conclusion.

---

[2] Genesis 1:26
[3] Genesis 3:22

Person - a being who is essentially relational.

Conclusion
THE HUMAN PERSON ~ DIGNITY BEYOND COMPARE

"God is Love."

One of the first theologians of Christianity was St. John the evangelist. He wrote both the fourth Gospel and three of the letters ("epistles") in the New Testament. In his first letter, as he taught about God and His love for us, John was inspired to know a most wonderful truth, one which is probably very familiar to you. John wrote: "*God is Love.*"[4] John didn't simply say, as we might expect, "God <u>loves</u>," but rather "*God is Love.*" This statement of John tells us much about the inner life of God.

The early Christians continued to gain deeper insights into God as the fullness of Being and the fullness of Love. They came to see that, while there can be only one God, this God is not "solitary." He is a **Trinity** of Persons. Mysteriously, God is *three* Persons (the Father, the Son and the Holy Spirit) in *one* Divine nature.

Another way to express this truth is to say that the one God is an *eternal communion* of three Divine Persons, related to one another in an **eternal** exchange of love. Let us take time to explore this mystery just a little:

- From all eternity, the **Father** knows Himself; and He eternally begets the Son by totally and selflessly giving Himself ("pouring Himself out") in love. The Father doesn't "lose" anything by giving Himself this way. In fact, this Self-giving of the Father to the Son is what makes Him to be "Father."

- The **Son** (the Father's "beloved") eternally knows the Father. He eternally receives the Father's love, and at the same time eternally gives Himself back to the Father in return. Here, too, the Son does not "lose" anything of Himself by giving Himself this way. Far from it. His Self-giving back to the Father is what makes Him to be "Son."

- The bond of love that's eternally shared between Father and Son is a *living* Bond, a third Person -- the **Holy Spirit**. We could say He "personifies" the Self-giving of the Father and Son One to the Other. Saint John Paul referred to the Holy Spirit, in fact, as "*Person Love-Person Gift.*"[5]

The divine Persons are so perfectly united in knowledge and love that they are actually *one* Being. Using the language of philosophy to help us, we could say that these three Divine Persons of the

---

NOTES

Trinity - The central doctrine of the Christian Faith, which states that the one God is a communion of three Divine Persons -- Father, Son, and Holy Spirit -- who share one nature. The three Divine Persons are co-equal, co-eternal, and consubstantial, and are to receive the same worship.

Eternal - without beginning or end.

"Each member of the Trinity has an especially 'characteristic' form of love:

♦ The Father -- Generosity
His free and unconditional generosity in His love of the Son.

♦ The Son -- Receptivity
His free and unconditional receptivity to the love of the Father.

♦ The Holy Spirit -- Delight
His free and unconditional delight in the giving of the Father and the receiving of the Son."

Fr. Joseph Koterski, S.J.
Inprint, Winter, 2020

---

[4] 1 John 4:8
[5] Saint John Paul, *Lord and Giver of Life*, n. 10.

The Human Person ~ Dignity Beyond Compare

NOTES

> "As a human person, man is never closed in on himself; he is always a bearer of otherness and from the very first moment of his existence interacts with other human beings...."
>
> Pope Benedict XVI
> 1/28/08

Human person - an individual substance of a rational nature.

> "It is the nature of spirit to put itself in relation, the capacity to see itself and the other."
>
> Cardinal Joseph Ratzinger

Love isn't just something God does; it's Who He is!

Trinity are three distinct *relations* existing as *one substance*. These three Divine Relations are related to one another by their mutual and total self-giving. Their mutual giving of self is so complete that they are more truly One Being than any "one being" we have ever experienced.

One modern theologian, in reflecting on the Persons of the Trinity, had this to say:

> "Amazing. Stop to think about it. Perfect love -- perfectly and eternally given, perfectly and eternally received, perfectly and eternally returned -- that's God."[6]

Do you see now how our understanding of who God is has developed our understanding of the idea "person?" The idea "person" implies a "relation toward the other." A person is one who is <u>not</u> closed in on himself; he is one who bears a relation to others.

"In Relation to Others"

What is it that enables a person to be *in relation to others?* It is the person's "spiritual existence." We know that as human beings we have a spiritual existence because we have a rational soul which is both *spiritual* and *subsistent*. So it is the rational soul with its powers of intellect and free will that accounts for the fact that we human beings are *persons*. This is why philosophically we define the **human person** as *an individual substance of a <u>rational</u> <u>nature</u>*.

You see, only a being which exists spiritually is able to *reflect back* on himself. Because he is free of physical limitations, a spiritual being can know not just the things around him. He can also know himself. In other words, *he can know that he knows*. He is *conscious of himself* at the very same time that he is *conscious of the other*. This is what enables him to be in relation with the other. He can know himself as an "<u>I</u>" in relation to the objects ("they") that he knows. And he can know that some of those "objects" that he knows are *persons* like himself.

---

[6] Christopher West, *The Love that Satisfies*, p. 11.

Conclusion
THE HUMAN PERSON ~ DIGNITY BEYOND COMPARE

Beings that have only a material existence -- like rocks, plants, and animals -- cannot do this. Their material existence ties them down. They cannot reflect back on themselves. They have no self-awareness or consciousness of themselves. Thus, they cannot know themselves *in relation to others*.

Being in relation to others is not only a matter of knowing, however. It is also a matter of loving. You see, in knowing himself, a person first of all *possesses* himself. He belongs to himself. In possessing himself, he can know the unique and unrepeatable good that he *is*. This makes it possible for him both to love himself (in the right way) and to love other persons.

Because of his self-possession and his awareness of his own goodness, a person is able to give himself away to others. This *giving of self* to others is what we mean by "love."

We can know others and know ourselves as knowing them. We can "go out of ourselves" to the good we see in them. And if I as a person can *know another*, it is also true that I can *be known* by another person! It is this mutual *knowing* of each other that is the beginning of human relations. It is also the beginning of *loving* one another.

We love others when we begin to know them and see the good in them. Love is genuine when we begin to desire for another what's truly good. As our love matures, in fact, we desire not just to *receive* the good of the other person, but also to *give* the other the good that is ourselves. (Does this remind you of the Trinity? It should!)

Are there other beings besides humans who are able to be *in relation to others* because they have a spiritual existence? Yes! We have already talked about the **Divine Persons** of the Blessed Trinity. In addition to the three Divine Persons, there are **angelic persons**. Both angels and humans are created persons, but angels are purely spiritual persons, whereas human persons have bodies. Now, it is true that when we want to picture an angel, then we usually draw it with a body. But we do that only so that we can make the concept 'angel' *visible to us*. In reality,

NOTES

"If one ever met a pig capable of knowing that it was a pig, it might be safer to baptize it, on the grounds that it must have a spiritual soul to be able to arrive at the general idea 'pig' and apply it to itself as one realization of that general idea. ... The animal's soul does nothing that leads us to feel that some higher-than-material principle must be in operation."
Frank Sheed

"Love is...a journey, an ongoing exodus out of the closed inward-looking self towards its liberation through self-giving, and thus towards authentic self-discovery."
Pope Benedict XVI, 1/28/08

"Love brings one out of oneself in order to discover and recognize the other; in opening himself to otherness, it also affirms the identity of the subject, for the other reveals me to myself."
Pope Benedict XVI, 1/28/08

The Human Person ~ Dignity Beyond Compare

NOTES

angels do not have bodies. As we have already seen, our human bodies express our persons. We relate to others in and through our bodies. Our bodies share in our dignity as human persons.

Dignity Beyond Compare

This understanding of *person* as *relation toward the other* tells us something about our dignity as human *persons*. Throughout our study here, we have mainly used human reason to see something of this marvelous dignity that we have. Let us turn to our faith once again, though, to get a fuller view. God's revelation opens up to us an even grander view of the marvel of our human dignity.

<u>First</u>, we know from *Genesis* that God brought us into being from nothing. He who is Existence Itself gifted us with existence and keeps us in existence moment by moment. (In every moment God is *desiring* me, *loving* me for who I am, and keeping me in existence! That same thing is true of *every other* person.) God gave us not the existence of a rock, a tree, or a non-human animal. Rather, He gave us the existence of one made in His very image: "*God created man in his image; in the divine image he created him; male and female he created them.*"[7]

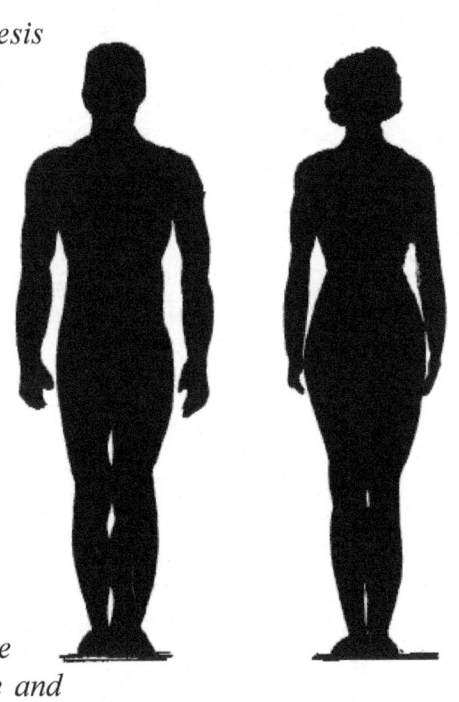

<u>Secondly</u>, we know that God loves us -- not only because He created us in the first place, but also because the Second Person of the Trinity assumed our nature. In becoming one of us, Jesus Christ, the Son of God, united Himself with each and every human person.

<u>Thirdly</u>, we know that we must surely be of immeasurable value to God, for the Father offered His Son to redeem us after we sinned. Jesus' blood offered for us on the cross reveals to us how precious we are in God's eyes and how priceless is the value of our lives.

<u>Finally</u>, we know that God sent the Holy Spirit to us so that we might share in the life of the Trinity -- in a new life that begins here on earth and is meant to last for all eternity in Heaven.

---

[7] Genesis 1:26

Conclusion
THE HUMAN PERSON ~ DIGNITY BEYOND COMPARE

Jesus Christ as our Model

Jesus Christ is both the *perfect image* of the Father and truly one of us, sharing our human nature. He shows us *perfectly* what it means to be a *person*. As a *Divine Person*, His entire being is "in relation to the Father." From all eternity He receives all that He is from His Father and gives it back in loving thanksgiving.

Jesus is also wholly "in relation" to each of us human persons. In his human life on earth, we see Jesus extending divine love to all the people He encountered each day. He gives us an example of how we ought to relate to one another. Jesus poured Himself out in selfgiving love for all of us, His human brothers and sisters. On the Cross, He made His life a gift of love back to His Father and a gift of love for each of us. Remember His words spoken at the Last Supper and lived out on Calvary: "*This is My Body, given for you. This is My Blood, poured out for you.*"[8] Jesus held nothing back for Himself. His gift was total self-emptying on our behalf and for His Father's glory.

What does this mean for us, in the way we live out our dignity as human persons? Well, unlike the rocks, the trees, and non-human animals, we are gifted with spiritual powers. With these spiritual powers of intellect and will, we can follow Jesus' example as we relate with other persons. *First and foremost,* we can be a gift returned to the Father in loving gratitude for all that we have received. We do this in union with Jesus and through the power of His Holy Spirit. *Secondarily,* we can be gifts poured out for one another in loving service, and open to receive each other as gifts into our lives.

"Become What You Are"

Unlike the rocks, the trees, and the non-human animals, which have no choice but to be what God made them to be, man can only become what he was made to be if he *chooses* to do so. This is why we were gifted with intellects and free wills, powers whereby we can know the truth and freely choose to act in accord with it. As a person, I can understand the truth of my being and choose to be the person I was created to be, that is, someone who is in knowing and loving relation to God and to other persons.

Did you ever stop to wonder what life on planet earth would be like if each of us would freely choose to live as the persons God creat-

---

NOTES

"Only in the mystery of the Word made flesh does the mystery of man truly become clear."
Gaudium et Spes, 22

-- The Son is the perfect image of the Father.
-- We are made in the image and acccording to the likeness of God.
-- Since God is a Trinity, we are made in the image and according to the likeness of the Trinity.

. . .

The Fall of Adam and Eve has damaged us and thus disordered various things within us:

♦ Instead of exhibiting the generosity especiallly characteristic of the Father, we tend to love only what strikes us as loveworthy.

♦ Instead of exhibiting the receptivity especially characteristic of the Son, we tend to fear (out of a sense that we are not loveworthy) that we will not receive the love we desire. As a result, we can either tend to be manipulative in order to try and force love, or tend to despair of ever being loved.

♦ Instead of exhibiting the delight especially characteristic of the Holy Spirit, we tend to be envious or jealous when we see others giving or receiving.

Fr. Joseph Koterski, S.J.
Imprint, Winter, 2020

---

[8] Luke 22:19-20

The Human Person ~ Dignity Beyond Compare

NOTES

"To say that I am made in the image of God is to say that love is the reason for my existence; for God is love. Love is my true identity. Selflessness is my true self. Love is my true character. Love is my name.... I who am without love cannot become love unless Love identifies me with himself. But if he sends his own love, himself, to act and love in me and in all that I do, then I shall be transformed, I shall discover who I am and shall possess my true identity by losing myself in him."

Gerald Vann, O.P.

"Jesus, in becoming human and founding His Churcvh, shows us who we are made to be, makes us members of His Body, the Church, and offers us through the Sacraments the grace that can restore what had been damaged and destroyed ... So that we can give, receive, and delight like He does, and so we can become what we are made to be from all eternity."

Fr. Joseph Koterski, S.J.
Imprint, Winter, 2020

ed and redeemed us to to be? All of us would be caught up in the life and love of the Divine Persons! There would be a "parallel" between the loving relationship among the Divine Persons and the relationships among us, as human persons living in truth and love. Just think of it: A union of love among God and ourselves that begins here on earth and is destined to last forever!

This is exactly what the *Catechism of the Catholic Church* tells us,

***"God Himself is an Eternal Exchange of Love
- Father, Son, and Holy Spirit -
and He has destined us to share in that exchange."***[9]

This is our life's work: to allow God to mold us into human *persons* who will fit right into the loving embrace of the Divine Persons. God has invited us to join him eternally -- forever sharing in His life and love -- beginning now! The *Catechism* teaches:

Endowed with a "spiritual and immortal" soul, the human person is "the only creature on earth that God has willed for its own sake." From his conception, he is destined for eternal beatitude [happiness].[10]

As we conclude our study of Part I, Saint John Paul the Great would surely look each one of us straight in the eye and say to us:

"Become what you are."[11]

---

[9] *The Catechism of the Catholic Church,* #221.
[10] Ibid., #1703.
[11] Saint John Paul, *Familiaris Consortio,* #17.

Conclusion
THE HUMAN PERSON ~ DIGNITY BEYOND COMPARE

Study Guide Questions:

1. What accounts for the fact that we are persons?

2. What does it mean to love someone?

3. Are there persons other than human beings?

4. What is the basis for our exalted dignity as human persons?

5. What does Saint John Paul mean when he tells us to "become what you are"?

CASE IN POINT

"If you ever ran into Thomas S. Vander Woude, chances are you would also see his son Joseph. Whether Vander Woude was volunteering at church, coaching basketball or working on his farm, Joseph was often right there with him, pitching in with a smile.

"When Joseph, 20, who has Down syndrome, fell into a septic tank Monday in his back yard, Vander Woude jumped in after him. He saved him. And he died where he spent so much time living: at his son's side.

"'That's how he lived,' Vanderwoude's daughter-in-law said yesterday. 'He lived sacrificing his life, everything, for his family.'

"Vander Woude, 66, had gone to Mass at Holy Trinity Catholic Church on Monday, just as he did every day, and then worked in the yard with Joseph, the youngest of his seven sons, affectionately known as Josie. Joseph apparently fell through a piece of metal that covered a 2-by-2-foot opening in the septic tank.

"Vander Woude rushed to the tank; a workman at the house saw what was happening and told Vander Woude's wife, Mary Ellen. They called 911 and tried to help the father and son in the meantime.

"At some point, Vander Woude jumped in the tank, submerging himself in sewage so he could push his son up from below

NOTES

"It is inherent in man to be a relational being. ... To form a relationship with someone else, is inbuilt in him. He is not an autarchic, self-sufficient being who develops alone, in isolation, not an island unto himself, but essentially created for relationship. Without relationship, in an unrelated state, he would destroy himself. And it is precisely this basic structure of his being that reflects God."
Joseph Cardinal Ratzinger,
God and the World

"To be human is to have the power of knowing and loving and responding to others, and, above all, to God. Only in loving relationship with God are we fully and perfectly human."
Paul Hinnebusch, OP,
The Lord's Prayer in the Light of Our Lord's Life and Preaching,
p. 33

"Man's capacity to relate is directed in the first instance to other human beings, but it is also structured in such a way as to turn toward infinity, toward truth, toward love itself."
Joseph Cardinal Ratzinger,
God and the World

NOTES

and keep his head above the muck, while Joseph's mom and the workman pulled from above.

"When rescue workers arrived, they pulled the two out. Vander Woude, who had been in the tank for 15 to 20 minutes, was unconscious. Efforts to revive him were unsuccessful, and he was taken to a hospital, where he was pronounced dead.

"For those who knew him, Vander Woude's sacrifice was in keeping with a lifetime of giving.

"'He's the kind of guy who would give you the shirt off his back,' said neighbor Lee DeBrish. 'And if he didn't have one, he'd buy one for you.'

"'They always considered Joseph a wonderful blessing to the family,' said Francis Peffley, pastor at Holy Trinity, where Vander Woude served as a sacristan and also trained altar servers. 'His whole life was spent serving people and sacrificing himself. ... He gave the ultimate sacrifice. ... Giving his life to save his son.'"*

*"Father Who Died Saving Son Known For Sacrifice," by Jonathan Mummolo, *Washington Post*, 9/10/08.

* * *

- In what ways does the above true story about Thomas Vander Woude testify to the dignity of the human person?

- After his death, a family friend wrote the following about Thomas Vander Woude:

"You lived your life quietly, humbly, faithfully, steadfastly, doing what depends on you - loving your God, your wife, and your children -- and especially that son of yours which the world has told you adds such little value in this life. But you and Mrs. Vander Woude have always known better. You showed the world how grossly pathetic it is in the way it values life, and 20 years ago you brought into this world a child, which your sons have always told me was the greatest gift God ever gave you and your wife."

-- Why would Mr. and Mrs. Vander Woude consider their son Joseph God's "greatest gift" to them?

Part II:

The Embodied Person

Chapter I

CALLED TO LOVE

Introduction

As persons, human beings are relational. We have already seen that it is the spiritual nature of the rational soul which makes it possible for human persons to be in relation with others. Our intellects are able to reflect back on themselves at the same time as they know the world around them. Thus, *we can know that we know* outer reality. We are conscious of ourselves *at the same time* as we are conscious of "the other" that we know. This is what enables us to be in relation with others. We know ourselves as **subjects** (as an "I," the center of things) and everything else in our knowing experience as **objects** (as "they," outside ourselves). To know myself as an "I" always implies there is a "you/You."

> ### Vocabulary
> personalistic norm   original solitude   original unity
> Natural Law   reciprocity   sensuality
> sentimentality   complementarity   conjugal

The Personalistic Norm

The objects in our experience vary greatly. "Object" in this general sense includes not only inanimate things such as rocks, tables, and houses, but also animate things such as plants, animals, and humans. Of the living physical objects we can come to know, only human persons are themselves also *subjects* capable of being in relation with us. This means that we can know other human persons and can be known by them. This knowing always implies a union -- the knower unites himself with the object he knows. Truly to know something (a subject in school or a person) is to "be one" with it because what I know enters into my mind and becomes one with me.

My knowledge of this person or thing gives me a type of relationship to it because I know that I know it. Because brute animals lack self-awareness or self-consciousness, they are unable to *know that they know*. Thus, they are unable to be in relation with us, though we can relate with them.

The following chart presents this understanding of the various existing things in the physical realm. Notice that it is only the human person that is *both* a subject and an object.

NOTES

Subject -- from Latin *sub* (below) + *jacere* (to throw); the one who thinks as distinguished from the object of thought; the self or ego.

Object -- from Latin *obicere* (to throw before); something perceptible, especially to the sense of touch or vision.

"No person is as such alone in the universe, but is always constituted with others and is summoned to form a community with them."
Communion and Stewardship, #41

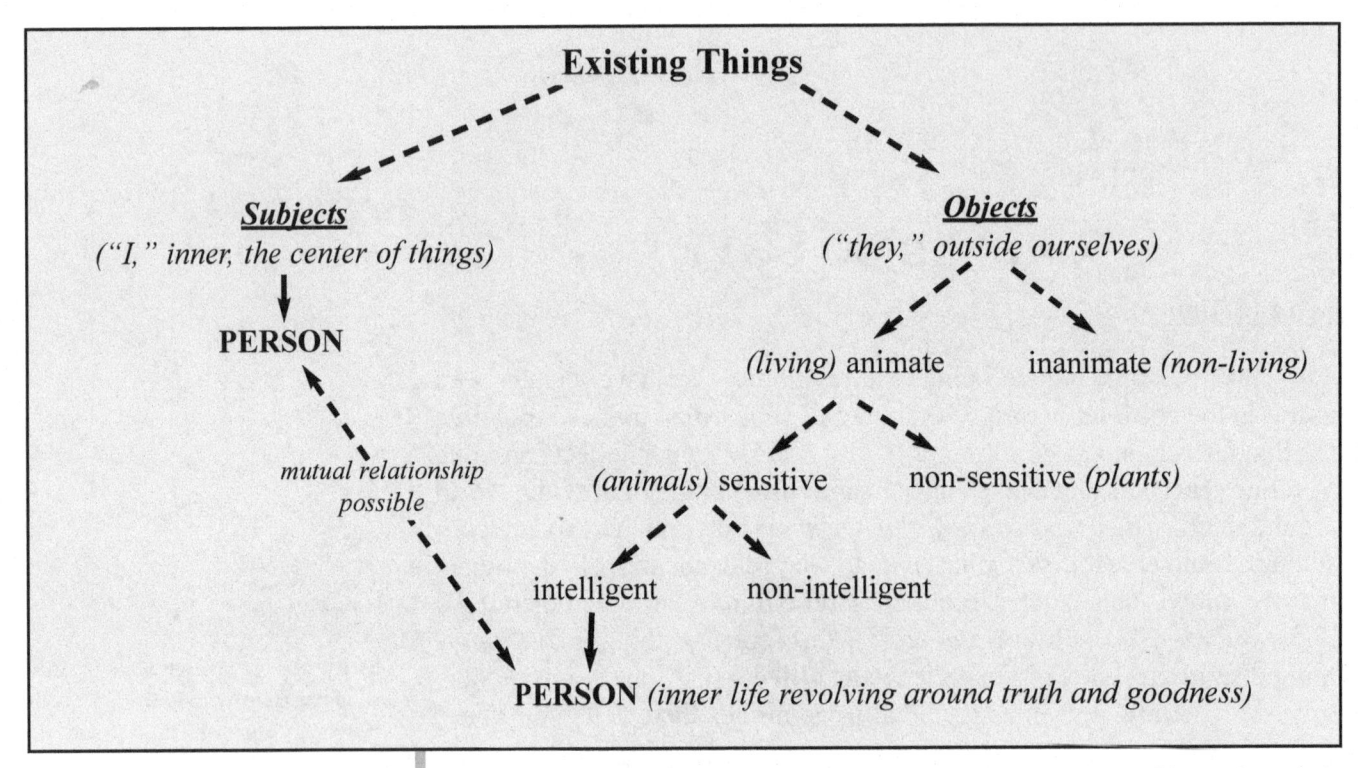

The Human Person ~ Dignity Beyond Compare

```
                        Existing Things
                       ↙              ↘
            Subjects                        Objects
   ("I," inner, the center of things)   ("they," outside ourselves)
              ↓                           ↙              ↘
           PERSON                 (living) animate    inanimate (non-living)
              ↑                      ↙          ↘
         mutual relationship  (animals) sensitive   non-sensitive (plants)
              possible           ↙        ↘
                          intelligent    non-intelligent
                               ↓
                           PERSON (inner life revolving around truth and goodness)
```

NOTES

Being in relation to others is not only a matter of knowing; it is also a matter of loving. You see, once we are conscious of ourselves, we are, in a sense, able to possess ourselves, to become aware of the unique and unrepeatable good that we are. With this knowledge of our own goodness and the goodness of other persons, we are able to go out of ourselves to them. We can actually give ourselves to them. This *giving of self* to others occurs whenever we freely will their good. In willing the good of others, we freely set ourselves to bringing about good for them -- even to the point of laying down our lives for them. This is what we mean by human love. Just as persons are able mutually to know each other, so too are we able mutually to love each other.

In fact, loving another human person is actually the *only* appropriate way of relating with him. Saint John Paul highlights this truth in what he calls the **Personalistic Norm** -- the norm or standard for dealing with any human person. The *Personalistic Norm* states that *a human person should never be used as merely a means to an end.* Rather, the only appropriate way of relating with a human person is with love.

Personalistic Norm -- Never use a human person as a mere means to an end.

The reason why it is wrong for us merely to use another human person as a means to our own ends is that it degrades the person who is being used. Every human person has his own intellect and will and thus is capable of choosing for himself the ends he wants to pursue. Not to allow him to do so is to violate his dignity as a self-determining being.

The "using scenario" looks like this: The *agent* (subject / the one acting) seeks an *end* (goal) that he wants. In order to achieve the goal

Part II -- Chapter I
CALLED TO LOVE

he uses a *means* (an object). What are most important in the scenario are the agent and the end. The means is of lesser importance because it is present only to serve the agent in achieving the end. If the agent could achieve the end without recourse to the means, he would.

Agent will use means to achieve end.

It is appropriate for humans to use inanimate objects such as vacuum cleaners, brooms, and chairs as mere means for their own ends. We humans can also use plants and brute animals merely for our own ends. Thus, there is nothing wrong with cutting down a tree because we do not like it in the middle of our front yard or killing animals to use for our food, clothing, or medical needs. We can do this because these objects are in fact inferior to us; they are lower in the gradation of being than we are.

Man uses tools to improve yard.

When the object we want to use, however, is a human person, then we may not *merely* use him, for he is a *subject* like ourselves, a person of dignity and not merely an object. Since we use people frequently to get our own ends, how do we avoid *merely* using them? Whenever we use a person in order to achieve an end, we must always seek *his* good as well as our own. In other words, we must treat him *as an end* and not <u>merely</u> as a means.

For example, I may use the paperboy to get my newspaper delivered to my door daily, but I must be as concerned for his welfare as I am for my own. In other words, I must pay him a fair wage, tip him on special occasions, and greet him when I encounter him.

Seeking the good of the other person unites the two of them in pursuit of a common good (getting me the newspaper and helping him earn a living). This common pursuit of the good establishes a special bond between them, uniting them internally. Without this bond, we tend to slip easily into merely using others for our own advantage.

NOTES

"Man as a being is an end in himself and does not exist merely to further some other end. ... [N]o one has the right to use some other person, however poor or weak he may be, simply as the means to God knows what end, however high it may be.... The basic law of human rights is just this, that no human being may become the means to any end but must retain his own inalienable dignity."
Joseph Cardinal Ratzinger,
God and the World, p. 110

"Every person is by nature capable of determining his or her aims. Anyone who treats a person as the means to an end does violence to the very essence of the other, to what constitutes its natural right."
Saint John Paul II,
Love and Responsibility

The mutual knowing and loving of other persons is the beginning of human relations. It is this ability to relate with one another that results from the fact that we are human persons, and it thus sets us apart from all other material creation.

Human persons are not just souls, however. Each of us is a body/soul unity. Our bodies, then, also have a part to play in helping us understand our ability to relate with other persons. It is to the body that we would like to turn our attention now in order to see what it has to tell us about our being persons, that is, about our being able to be in relation with others.

Study Guide Questions:

1. *In what sense can we speak of a human person as an object?*
2. *How are human persons unique as objects that we encounter daily?*
3. *Why are animals unable to be in relation with human persons?*
4. *What is meant by the phrase "human love"?*
5. *What is so bad about merely using another human person as a means to an end?*
6. *What does it mean to treat a person as an end?*
7. *Why are we ethically justified in using plants and brute animals as mere means to our ends?*

CASES IN POINT

♦ A person *(agent)* needs to travel by cab *(means)* from the airport to his hotel *(end)*. How is it possible to do this without using the taxi-cab driver as a mere means to an end?

♦ A man *(agent)* picks up a prostitute *(means)* when he is "out to have fun" *(end)* on a Saturday night. Because the man is wealthy, he pays her very well. Does the man's paying the prostitute well for her services remove the ethical problem of his using her as a mere means to his end? Explain.

♦ Bill is a rather popular guy with his classmates because he usually has plenty of money which he spends freely. He realizes, though, that a lot of the guys who hang around with him do so only because of his money. What could Bill do to find out who his real friends are?

♦ Joanne is a very pretty 16-year-old. Her radiant smile and sparkling eyes attract boys easily. This is at times a problem for her, however, for she wants them to be attracted to her person and not merely to her appearance. Is there any advice you would offer Joanne in regard to discerning those guys who are actually attracted to her person?

♦ A business executive of a large corporation makes it a point to greet the cleaning lady by name each evening when she comes in to empty his trash. He often asks her about her family and thanks her for emptying his trash. How does he avoid using her as a mere means to his end?

Part II -- Chapter I
CALLED TO LOVE

Theology of the Body

Saint John Paul has helped us greatly in rightly understanding the significance of our bodies. When he was a young priest and bishop dealing with friends and counseling hundreds of young people and married couples, Saint John Paul thought and wrote about the meaning of the human person, the body, love, and sexuality. When he later became the Vicar of Christ, Saint John Paul used his Wednesday general audiences (between 1979 and 1984) to explain to the world what has come to be called his "theology of the body." In this series of 129 talks, Saint John Paul articulated the Catholic view of the human body in an amazingly beautiful and complete way.

We will use his insights -- theological and philosophical -- as a springboard here for our investigation into the significance of the human body. Because ours is a *philosophical* rather than theological study, however, we will -- whenever possible -- use **Natural Law** and human experience to explain rather than relying solely on the Bible or on Church teaching.

The Original Experiences

Saint John Paul's reflection on the human body is an in-depth reflection on human experience. Going back to the first chapters of the Book of Genesis, Saint John Paul examines the experiences of the very first man and woman in order to retrieve God's original intention for them. He sees in these original experiences which the Bible presents something which he finds present at the basis of all human experience -- no matter the time or place. In other words, what Revelation presents here actually reflects the natural experience of every human person.

When Saint John Paul talks about the *Original Experiences* of man -- *original solitude*, *original unity*, and *original nakedness* -- he has a two-fold meaning in mind for the word **original**. <u>First</u>, he is referring to the experiences of the first man and woman (Adam and Eve) at the beginning of human history. <u>Secondly</u>, he is referring to experiences which are common to us all -- to every human being ever created -- because they lie at the basis of all of our experiences throughout our lives.

Man's first experiences with life are common to us all, although with age we have the tendency to cover them over with the many other lesser experiences of our lives. The challenge for us now is to retrieve these original experiences so that we can discern in them the meaning of our lives and the direction in which we ought to go.

NOTES

"These 129 catechetical addresses, taken together, constitute a kind of theological time bomb set to go off with dramatic consequences, sometime in the third millennium of the Church."
George Weigel

"It is an illusion to think we can build a true culture of human life if we do not . . . accept and experience sexuality and love and the whole of life according to their true meaning and their close interconnection."
Saint John Paul II,
The Gospel of Life

Natural law -- man's ability to understand how he ought to act based simply on his own understanding of his human nature.

Original -- from the Greek word *arche*, which signifies both a temporal beginning and the foundations of a building.

The Human Person ~ Dignity Beyond Compare

NOTES

"Man is 'alone': this is to say that through his own humanity, through what he is, he is at the same time set into a unique, exclusive, and unrepeatable relationship with God himself."

Saint John Paul II,
Theology of the Body

Original solitude -- man's foundational openness to God in which he realizes his sonship and his complete partnership with Him.

Original Solitude

In the second creation account in the book of Genesis[1], we see that the first man experienced that he is different from the rest of creation. No beast of the field or bird of the air was on his level. As unique and utterly distinct from everything else in the visible world, Adam realized that he was *someone* and not a mere something. He had a conscious awareness of himself as a *person*. He stood alone among created reality as a being able to relate to his Creator.

Adam knew himself as one who alone among other creatures was privileged to stand *as a son* in loving thanksgiving before the One who had given him life and who invited him to be a partner in a dialogue of love. This foundational openness of man to the Author of his life and to the One who alone can fulfill his heart's desires Saint John Paul calls **Original Solitude**.

This experience of *original solitude* that Adam and Eve had is one which every human being is capable of having. It is essentially man's awareness of his uniqueness and superiority when compared with the other kinds of beings that surround him.

The human body has a major role to play in *original solitude* since this *original solitude* is revealed in and through the body. The human body both expresses man's *original solitude* and witnesses to his superiority over other animals. A person's body is not merely a thing that he uses; rather, we say that the person *is* his body. "There is no distance between us and our bodies,"[2] writes Carl Anderson, explaining further:

> We can be dispossessed of our belongings and go on living happy lives, but we can't be dispossessed of our bodies without ceasing to be. The body, then, is not just another item in our stock of possessions, but rather the foundation of our very capacity to possess anything in the first place. Similarly, the body is not just another tool in our toolkit; it establishes the very possibility of our using instruments at all: I can wield a hammer only because I first have hands, just as I can peer through a microscope only because I first have eyes.[3]

To say that I am my body, however, is not to say that I am *only* my body. Rather, it is to say that my body is *personal*. My body is part of who I am.

---

[1] Genesis 2:4-25

[2] Carl Anderson, *Called to Love*, p. 29.

[3] Ibid.

Part II-- Chapter I
CALLED TO LOVE

Our bodies open us up to the world -- whether we want them to or not. Through our five senses we "take in" the world that surrounds us, and we are put in relationship with it. Our bodies, then, are actually very much like our homes in that we dwell intimately in them, receiving others from the outside world as our guests.

It is in this encounter with the world that we realize our *original solitude*. Before too long, we find out that we, as human beings, are unlike the rest of visible creation and that nothing in the created realm can fully satisfy us.

Yet it is also our encounter with the visible world that initiates our search for the Creator of it all. Even apart from Scripture, our bodies reveal to us that we are not our own origin. We did not cause ourselves to exist; Someone else is responsible for our being here. This Someone must be greater than our parents, whose bodies He used to fashion us into the creatures that we are. This Someone has given us life -- life as *persons* who are able to know and love, and He has given us this world in which to live.

The fact that our bodies will one day die also points us in the direction of Him who created us. Unlike any other earthly creature, we wonder about the meaning of our lives and about our impending death. This wonder helps to put us in relationship with Him who is our origin and our ultimate destination.

Original solitude, then, is man's awareness of his special dignity. Plants, animals, and inanimate objects are unable to relate to their Creator. Man alone is capable of this. Man alone has been made *a son* -- a being created in the image and likeness of his Creator. As *son*, man is invited to enter into a relationship of love with the One who brought him into being.

According to Saint John Paul, the experience of *original solitude* is not something that Adam would out-grow. Rather, it is an experience that remains in both Adam and Eve even after they have one another's companionship. Indeed, *original solitude* accompanies all of us throughout our lives because it is an essential experience of every human person -- male and female. *Original solitude* is the experience of the fact of every human being's existence: he is and always will be a *child* of God his Father. No matter his age, no one out-grows being a child in this sense.

Study Guide Questions:

1. Where did the "theology of the body" originate?
2. What two-fold meaning does Saint John Paul have in mind for the word "original" when he uses it to explain his theology of the body?

NOTES

"Man is a subject not only by his self-consciousness and by self-determination, but also based on his own body. *The structure of this body is such that it permits him to be the author of genuinely human activity.* In this activity, the body expresses the person."
Saint John Paul II,
Theology of the Body

"[M]an stands in direct relationship with God and is the direct product of God's will. One should not, therefore, regard the worship of God as an external occupation for man, as if God wanted to be praised or as if he needed to be flattered. ... Worship means accepting that our life is like an arrow in flight. Accepting that nothing finite can be my goal or determine the direction of my life, but that I myself must pass beyond all possible goals. That is, pass beyond them into being inwardly at one with him who wished me to exist as a partner in a relationship with him and who has given me freedom precisely in this."
Joseph Cardinal Ratzinger,
God and the World

3. Why should we care about the original experiences of man?
4. What is meant by the phrase "original solitude"?
5. What role do our bodies play in our experience of original solitude?

Original Unity

The unity that Adam and Eve share "in the beginning" starts before Adam and Eve actually encounter one another. In fact, it is *prior* to Eve's creation. Remember that Eve comes into existence from the side of Adam. When she came into existence, she was "taken from him."[4] This shows that Eve has already been implied in Adam (and in union with him) from his beginning.

Thus, when Adam actually encounters Eve for the first time, he comes to experience a truth about his own being:

> This one, at last, is bone of my bones and flesh of my flesh;
> This one shall be called 'woman,'
> for out of 'her man' this one has been taken.[5]

Adam recognizes at once that Eve is like him in their shared humanity. Both are equal in human dignity. However, their bodies, though alike as human, are obviously different as male and female. Their bodies complement (i.e., complete) each other. Let us examine what this means.

While every person is a whole and complete human being, no single human person is complete *as a sexual organism*. Males have only half of what it takes to function sexually; females have the other half. And the half that a male has is different from that which a female has. The two different halves need each other in order to function properly. Together they make up a sexual whole, that is, a sexual organism. This is why we say that their bodies are sexually complementary. Males and females really do *literally* complete one another sexually. The *two become one* in a very real sense when they sexually unite.

Because of the **complementarity** of their bodies, Adam better understands himself now as a *male* in reference to Eve, the *female*. In experiencing Eve's *femininity*, Adam comes to understand more clearly his own *masculinity*. The two share the very same humanity, but they do so in different ways: Adam as a man and Eve as a woman.

---

[4] Genesis 2:22
[5] Genesis 2:23

NOTES

"In the case of every other biological function only one body is required to do the job. A person can digest food by himself, using no other stomach but his own; he can see by himself, using no other eyes but his own; he can walk by himself, using no other legs but his own; and so on with each of the other powers and their corresponding organs. Each of us can perform every vital function by himself, except one. The single exception is procreation.

"If we were speaking of respiration, it would be as though the man had the diaphragm, the woman the lungs, and they had to come together to take a single breath. If we were speaking of circulation, it would be as though the man had the right atrium and ventricle, the woman the left atrium and ventricle, and they had to come together to make a single beat."

J. Budziszewski

Complementarity -- that which completes or makes perfect; that which refers to the other and can be understood only in light of the other.

Part II -- Chapter I
CALLED TO LOVE

This "difference-in-sameness" of Adam and Eve which their bodies reveal to them actually makes it possible for them to come back together *as one* to share a more profound *unity* than if they were human beings without a sexual difference:

> ... a man leaves his father and mother and clings to his wife, and the two of them become one body.[6]

How is it possible for two human persons to come back together as one? Let's take a look.

Adam is first able to "take in" the existence of Eve by using his emotions to enter into her world, to see things through her eyes, and to experience the world in union with her. Eve in turn "takes in" Adam through her emotional response to him, entering into his world, seeing things through his eyes, and experiencing the world in union with him. Both are enriched by this mutual sharing of themselves with the other. A deepening relationship forms.

Their union deepens, however, as they use their rational powers to come to know the true value of the other's goodness and to commit themselves to pursuing the good with and for the other. Thus, for example, Adam might come to appreciate Eve's gentle and respectful way of dealing with him, and Eve might come to value Adam's strength of character and his personal integrity. With this knowledge of each other's goodness, they resolve to do all they can to further each other's good.

This mutual giving of themselves to the other and receiving the other into themselves makes it possible for them to form a true *communion of persons*, as Saint John Paul calls it. It is this original communion of Adam and Eve in the garden in their being created male and female that Saint John Paul refers to as **original unity**. This *communion of persons* reaches its fullest tangible expression and realization when their two sexually incomplete bodies unite to form one sexual whole in the **marital act**.

It is in forming this *communion of persons* that Adam and Eve most fully reflect the God in Whose image and likeness they were made. Profoundly united as one with their

NOTES

"These differences (between men and women) are not irreconcilable opposites; rather, they are complementary qualities. Adam needed a helpmate, and Eve was made -- "flesh of his flesh and bone of his bone." The functional differences corresponded with certain psychic and character differences, which made the body of one in relation to another like the violin and the bow, and the spirit of one to another like the poem and meter."

Most Reverend Fulton J. Sheen, *The World's First Love*, p. 151

Original unity -- the original communion of Adam and Eve in the garden in their being created male and female.

Marital act -- the act which is proper to two persons who are united in marriage: sexual intercourse.

"The function of the image is that of mirroring the one who is the model...."

Saint John Paul II, *Theology of the Body*

[6] Genesis 2:24

The Human Person ~ Dignity Beyond Compare

NOTES

differences as male and female, Adam and Eve bear witness to the divine *Communion of Persons* who are simultaneously one God and three distinct Persons.

As a communion of *human* persons, Adam and Eve stand apart from the rest of physical creation in their openness to the Creator. It is this foundational openness to God (their *original solitude*) that enables Adam and Eve to see one another as more than merely fellow human beings. Because of their relation to the Creator, Adam and Eve are able to receive one another as the *gifts from Him* that they are. In other words, Adam understands that Eve was placed in his life by the Creator as a gift meant to enrich his life and to draw him ever deeper into a relationship with Him.

Adam and Eve's union in love, then, is meant not only to bear witness to their Creator but also to aid them in their relationship with Him. In giving themselves and receiving each other in love, Adam and Eve are invited to journey together into an ever deepening relationship with their Creator. In their unique relationship with each other, they are able to experience union in their mutual self-gift -- a reflection of the union they are each meant to have with their Creator.

Saint John Paul warns us, however, that achieving a true *communion of persons* between a man and a woman is not a quick and easy matter. Achieving the fullness and depth proper to a *communion of persons* requires time and effort. It is not simply a physical thing; nor is it only spiritual. Because the individual human person is a body/soul unity, a true communion of persons will involve both body and soul. In his book, *Love and Responsibility,* Saint John Paul explains the elements of love involved in such a relationship between a man and a woman:

> *"Man became the image of God not only through his own humanity, but also through the community of persons which man and woman form from the very beginning."*
> Saint John Paul II,
> *Theology of the Body*

1. The first element of love is *attraction*. A man and a woman are designed to see one another as a *good*. Their male and female bodies initiate the call to love because rooted in them is an *attraction* to the person of the opposite sex as a good, as one who will help to fulfill or complete them. This very basic attraction rooted in their bodies we call the **sexual urge**; it is a natural force in us all.

Sexual urge -- the basic impulse toward a person of the opposite sex for the purpose of sexual fulfillment.

Love-as-attraction always involves various powers of the soul. Some level of knowledge of the other person, even if it is only the knowledge that our senses give us, must be present. We must know to some extent what it is that we like about the other person, that is, what it is we see of *value* regarding him. The emotions, too, are highly involved in *love-as-attraction* from its very beginning because the emotions spontaneously respond to the *values* that we perceive in the other person.

Love-as-attraction can also involve the will. To be attracted to another means not only that I see the person as a *good*; it also means that I commit to thinking of him as a good. The will's commitment to think of the other as a good occurs because the intellect and will work hand-in-hand.

Love-as-attraction, then, always involves an awareness of *value*. The one who is attracted to another sees in him something which he *values as a good*. Because a human person is a complex good, the values to which a person is attracted can vary greatly. He could be attracted to certain values of her body such as her beautiful hair, her shapely figure, or her welcoming smile. Or he could be attracted by values of her soul: her gentleness, her humility, or her selflessness.

Saint John Paul warns us that it is very important that the values we find attractive about a person must be *truly* present in him and not simply the result of our wishful thinking. He also cautions us that our attraction must never be limited to *partial* values, that is, to goods of a person but not to the good of the *person as a whole*. The person himself is a value and not merely some particular good which he has. For example, it is not enough to be attracted to Bill's muscular physique. Helen needs to be attracted to Bill himself, to Bill as a person.

2. The second element of love is *desire*. *Love-as-desire* arises because a human person is a limited being who needs other beings. We are not self-sufficient. A male needs a female to complete himself, and a woman needs a man in the same way. The sexual urge is the first expression of this *objective* human need we have for one another.

Love-as-desire, then, originates in a need that a person experiences, and it seeks to find the good that it lacks. The one who experiences *love-as-desire* experiences a longing for the person whom he thinks is a good for him: *"I want you because you are a good for me."*

While *love-as-desire* is of the very essence of human love, Saint John Paul notes that *love-as-desire* can easily degenerate to a mere using of another person if it is not rooted in the **personalistic norm**. If the love between man and woman goes

"I want you as a good for me."

Part II -- Chapter I
CALLED TO LOVE

NOTES

"The sexual urge in man has a natural tendency to develop into love simply because the two objects affected, with their different sexual attributes, physical and psychological, are both people. Love is a phenomenon peculiar to the world of human beings. In the animal world only the sexual instinct is at work."
Saint John Paul II,
Love and Responsibility

"*Love as desire* originates in a need and aims at finding a good which it lacks."
Saint John Paul II,
Love and Responsibility

The Human Person ~ Dignity Beyond Compare

NOTES

"Goodwill is the same as selflessness in love...."
    Saint John Paul II,
    Love and Responsibility

"To love is to will the good of another."
    St. Thomas Aquinas,
    Summa Theologiae I-II

no further than *love-as-desire*, then it will be incomplete, or sometimes even evil, for it is not the full essence of love which should exist between persons. In order to have the full essence of love, the lover must long not merely for the person as a good for himself, but also and above all, he must long for that person's good.

3. The third element of love, then, is *goodwill*. *Love-as-goodwill* is free of self-interest; its chief concern is the well-being of the other person: *"I want what is good for you."* *Love-as-goodwill* is unconditional love; it is the purest form of love. As such, it brings both the lover and the one loved the greatest personal fulfillment.

Saint John Paul notes that *love-as-goodwill* is the form of love that should be present in all of our dealings with other human persons, but to a special degree it should be present in the love between husband and wife. While *love-as-desire* will always remain present in human love, it must never overpower *love-as-goodwill*. The lover's primary concern must be for the one he loves, rather than for himself.

"I want what is good <u>for you</u>."

Study Guide Questions:

1. *In what sense can we speak of the first humans as being equal but different?*

2. *What is original unity? In what sense is the experience of original unity dependent upon original solitude?*

3. *What is good about the sexual urge? What should we be careful about in regard to it?*

4. *What various powers of the soul does love-as-attraction involve?*

5. *What do you think causes a person to value one good rather than another in a person?*

6. *What two cautions does Saint John Paul give us with regard to love-as-attraction?*

7. *Objectively speaking, in what way do males and females need each other?*

8. *Why is love-as-desire not good enough to be the kind of love that should exist between two human beings?*

9. Why is love-as-goodwill considered to be a higher degree of love than both love-as-attraction and love-as-desire?

10. Why do you suppose that love-as-goodwill gives both the lover and the one loved the greatest personal fulfillment?

CASES IN POINT

#1 -- Joe, a college sophomore, is attracted to Jenny, a freshman who is for the first time living away from home while going to school. Joe drives a sporty car, has a very good job, dresses nicely, and is good looking. He has all of the material things that a young woman might normally find attractive, and he is showering all of his attention on Jenny. Jenny, a pretty girl, is a committed Catholic. She has not ever known a person like Joe, especially because Joe is an unbeliever who seems to take pride in the fact that he does not believe in God. When asked by a friend if she realizes that Joe has taken a liking to her, Jenny replies, "Yes, I know, but I don't want to encourage a relationship with him. I want to be attracted to the kind of man with whom I will be able to share my faith."

- *What does Jenny teach us about love-as-attraction?*
- *What values do you want to attract you in a person of the opposite sex?*

* * * * *

#2 -- Peter is the type of guy who prides himself on his physical strength and his handsome physique, and his interest in girls is always focused on their physical value. Robert is just the opposite, although he is also rather good-looking. Robert's family has helped to form him in such a way that he knows to look beyond a person's appearances to the values within the person such as virtue and integrity.

- *Compare and contrast the type of girls Peter and Robert will find attractive.*
- *What danger is there in valuing too highly the physical dimension of a person?*
- *What might Saint John Paul mean when he tells us in regard to attraction that it is "the question of the truth about the person towards whom it is felt" that is so important?*
(<u>Love and Responsibility</u>, p. 78)

* * * * *

#3 -- In each of the following scenarios, identify the element of love that is most obvious to you. Be ready to explain your choice.

Love-as-attraction　　　**Love-as-desire**　　　**Love-as-goodwill**

- *Sherry, a popular cheerleader, wants to go to the prom with Brian because he is the best looking and most popular boy in her class.*
- *Andre refuses to stop hanging around Pedro, a long-time friend of his. Even though Pedro has angered some of the guys at school because he won't take part in their practical jokes that belittle others, Andre sticks by him. He knows Pedro's goodness.*
- *Becky hasn't yet actually talked to Ben, though she is in two of his classes. She loves the way he conducts himself in class: he is respectful of others, cheerful, and always asking questions that make the class think a little deeper about things.*

NOTES

Reciprocity -- from Latin *reciprocare* (to move back and forth); a reciprocal relationship, one which involves a mutual give and take of something.

Unrequited – not repaid or not given in return.

The Problem of Reciprocity

Mature human love is something which is shared. It is not enough for Jeff to know that he loves Liz, and for Liz to know that she loves Jeff, for then there would be two separate loves. Mature love is a shared experience: Jeff and Liz need to know that their love for each other is mutual. In other words, Jeff needs to know *not only* that he loves Liz *but also* that she loves him. Instead of there being two loves -- one *in* each of the persons, there needs to be one love shared *between* them both. This is what is meant by **reciprocity** in love.

If love is not reciprocated, that is, if it is not returned, we call it **unrequited** love. Unrequited love is normally accompanied with pain and suffering for the lover. Such love usually stagnates and gradually is extinguished.

Love which is reciprocated can vary greatly, depending upon what each person brings to it. If the two persons bring only self-interest so that they merely use one another for their selfish pursuits, then their reciprocated love will last only as long as their needs are being met. Such love will be superficial and short-lived. If, however, the two bring selfless love, their shared love will be strong and lasting. It is this reciprocated *love-as-goodwill* which enables a couple to trust each other; it frees them from suspicion and jealousy. Its fruit is a profound peace and joy.

- *How might the lack of reciprocity result in suspicion and jealousy?*

- *Why is it so important that a couple verify their love before exchanging declarations and beginning to build their lives upon it?*

- *Why is the sexual act an inappropriate way to verify one's love?*

In addition to the various elements of love that we just enumerated, Saint John Paul highlights the distinction between emotional love and love which is caused by the human will. Let us examine this distinction.

Emotional Love -- Do you remember what we learned about the emotions? They are automatic responses of our sense appetites to whatever we are experiencing through either our external or internal senses. Their movements happen within us *without our direct control*. Once we receive a sense impression, our emotions respond to the *value* that sense impression has for us. For example, if I value home-made bread, then the smell of it will arouse my emotions of love and desire for it. Similarly, if I do not value getting up early for school, then the sound of my alarm in the morning will arouse my emotions of dislike and aversion.

With this understanding of how the emotions work, Saint John Paul analyzes the typical emotional response of a person to someone of the opposite sex. In his analysis, he notes that the person experiencing a sense impression of a person of the opposite sex will emotionally respond to a certain *value* in the other. Saint John Paul distinguishes between two different emotional responses according to the nature of the value to which the person responds:

1) **Sensuality** is the emotional response to a person of the opposite sex which occurs when the emotions are responding to the value of the other's body: He or she perceives the body as a *potential object of enjoyment*. The emphasis of sensuality is on fulfilling a person's desire for sexual pleasure. Thus, sensuality does not yet enable a person to connect with the other *person*; it focuses only on the sexual value of the person's body. For this reason, sensuality is **fickle**, turning toward any human body which it perceives to be an object of sexual pleasure.

In itself, sensuality is not bad; it is a natural orientation, directing a person toward the *objective* good of the body of another person. Sensuality, then, is the raw material of true **conjugal love**. If it is integrated with other nobler aspects of love, sensuality will be a vital part of authentic love.

Because sensuality is "quite blind to the person,"[7] human love needs to advance beyond this sensual level of emotional love if it is truly to be *human* love and thus to give the fulfillment human love was designed to give. If the person does not make this advance, then sensuality will degrade both persons involved. It will degrade the one who is the object of the sensual desires of another by reducing him merely to his physical qualities and to the pleasure another might experience from those qualities. It will also degrade the one who is the subject of the sensual desires in that he lowers himself to acting on the level of a brute animal rather than as the rational human being that he is.

2) **Sentimentality** is the emotional response to a person of the opposite sex which occurs when the emotions are responding to the

---

[7] Karol Wojtyla, *Love and Responsibility*, p. 108.

"An initial sensual reaction is meant to orient us toward personal communion, not just bodily union. It can serve as an ingredient of authentic love if it is integrated with the higher, nobler aspects of love such as good will, friendship, virtue or self-giving commitment."
— Edward Sri

Fickle -- characterized by erratic changeableness or instability.

Conjugal love -- from Latin *conjugalis* (spouse) and *conjungere* (to join in marriage); the love of those involved in a marital relationship.

"A man may sensuously ponder in his mind or actively seek the body of a woman as a means for sexual gratification. And he may do this without any real interest in her person."
— Edward Sri

value of the *femininity* or *masculinity* of a person. In other words, it is not merely the body that attracts; it is <u>the person as a whole</u> that is valued as a *good*. The person experiencing a sentimental response to another will long to be close to him and to be exclusive. This desire to be always alone together is not aimed at using the person. Rather, it is the source of affection and the desire to be intimate. Thus, sentimentality "keeps two people close together, binds them -- even if they are physically far apart -- to move in each other's orbit."[8]

Sentimentality engages the person's imagination and memory, thus enabling him or her *to feel* always very close to the loved one. Memories of their encounters will be crisp and clear in their minds, and images of their soon-to-be encounters will be ever playing themselves out within their imaginations. In this way, memory and imagination not only are influenced by sentimentality, but they also in turn influence it. When this happens, the lover finds that the images in his mind of the one he loves are always bigger and better than what is actually the case in reality -- although the lover is unaware of this.

Sentimentality, then, tends to enlarge the true value of the beloved. The values the lover thinks he loves in the other person are actually values which his own imagination has placed there. They are the ideal values he has always wanted to be in his beloved. This is why sentimentality is said to be *subjective*: it feeds on the values *within the subject himself.* Saint John Paul explains:

> Idealization of the object of love is a well-known phenomenon. It is particularly characteristic of young love. Here, the ideal is more powerful than the real, living human being, and the latter often becomes merely the occasion for an eruption in the subject's emotional consciousness of the values which he or she longs with all his heart to find in another person. It does not matter whether they are really values possessed by that particular person towards whom the subject feels a sentimental love.[9]

It is precisely this subjective basis of sentimentality which is the cause of **disillusionment** for the lover. The lover eventually finds out that the beloved is not the person the lover thought him to be. She might even wonder what it was that she saw in him that would have caused her to fall so head-over-heels in love with him. The values she thought he had she now realizes are not actually there, or maybe they are there, but not to the extent she had envisioned. The lover also begins to see the other's faults.

NOTES

"In the eyes of a person sentimentally committed to another person, the value of the beloved object grows enormously -- as a rule out of all proportion to his or her real value."

Saint John Paul II,
Love and Responsibility

"To exalt the objects of our love until our picture is a false one, to idealize them, to project upon them our own ideal picture of our own ideal selves is to love not a real person but a dream. The result is inevitable: sooner or later the difference between ideal and real obtrudes itself; then we feel disappointed, cheated, we feel quite unjustly that we have somehow been wronged and so what looked like love but never was turns to dislike: the unreal romance is over before it ever touched reality, and real love is still as remote as ever."

Gerald Vann, O.P.,
The Son's Course

Disillusionment -- a freeing or a being freed from a false or misleading impression.

---

[8] Ibid., p. 110.
[9] Ibid., pp. 112-113.

Part II -- Chapter I
CALLED TO LOVE

If love does not grow beyond the sentimental stage, then the lovers will not be able truly to unite *as persons* because they do not yet really know or love each other. Their love is incomplete; it lacks an objective basis: they need to know each other personally and to commit themselves freely to seek one another's good. Their wills which have been charmed and disarmed by sentimentality need to be fully engaged.

NOTES

"The question of truth about the person is crucial: Is it really so? ... Does this person really have the qualities and virtues I'm so attracted to?"

— Edward Sri

	Sensuality	**Sentimentality**
What is it?	*An emotional response to a person of the opposite sex which responds to the value of the body for sexual pleasure*	*An emotional response to a person of the opposite sex which responds to the value of the whole person of the other sex*
Characteristics	• *Drive for enjoyment* • *Directed toward the body of a person*	• *Desire for nearness, exclusivity, intimacy* • *Longing to be always alone together*
Strengths	• *A natural orientation* • *The raw material for true conjugal love*	• *The source of affection* • *No desire to use the other*
Weaknesses	• *Blind to the person* • *Fickle* • *Threatens to devalue the person* • <u>*Objective*</u> *- nurtured by the sexual value of the body of the other person*	• *Charms and disarms the will* • *Can shift into sensuality* • *Enlarges the true value of a person* • <u>*Subjective*</u> *- feeds on the values within the subject himself* • *The cause of disillusionment*
Without integration	• *No real love* • *Mere using of another*	• *Incomplete love* • *No true interpersonal union*

Men & Women Differ

It is pretty generally recognized that woman is by nature more sentimental, and man more sensual. We have indicated already one trait which is typical of sensuality: seeing the value of the other person as being in his/her body as a possible object of enjoyment. Now, this form of sensuality is more readily awakened in the man, more readily takes form in his consciousness and in his attitude. The very structure of the male psyche and personality is such that it is more readily moved to reveal and to treat as an object the hidden significance of love for a person of the other sex. This goes with the relatively more active role of the male in such love, and also imposes a responsibility on him. On the other hand, in the woman's sensuality is, as it were, hidden and concealed by sentimentality. For this reason she is by nature more inclined to go on seeing as a manifestation of affection what a man already clearly realizes to be the effect of sensuality and the desire for enjoyment.

*Paraphrase of Saint John Paul's *Love and Responsibility,* p. 111.

- *Why is it important to understand this difference between a man and woman's emotional response to one another?*

- *What responsibility do you think is imposed on a man because of his more active role in the love between persons of the opposite sex? Does a woman bear any responsibility?*

- *Why can a woman's dressing modestly be of help to a man in his emotional response to her?*

NOTES

"The subjective aspect of love is no more than a pleasurable experience happening inside of me. And these powerful sensations might actually conceal the reality of a relationship that has failed to develop fully."

Edward Sri

People who experience emotional love feel close to each other, drawn together, regardless of whether they have consciously chosen to love each other or not. This "being drawn together" happens because a person's positive emotional response to another enhances or adds to the value of the other in his eyes. In other words, a person's own emotional response to a person gives this person a "plus" (an added value) that he could easily lose if the emotion dies down.

Did you notice what the origin of that "plus" is. That is, did you notice why the lover feels so positive about the person he emotionally loves? Yes, it comes from the lover himself. The good emotional feeling says very little about the value of the person he emotionally loves. Rather, the emotion says something about what is happening *in the lover himself.* Emotional love, in other words, is *subjective.* A person who experiences only emotional love for another has not yet directly experienced the *objective* value of the person. Here, the value of the emotion is what is most important rather than the value of the person. This is true even for the sensual response, which has the objective basis of the value of the other person's body; this emotional love is still blind to the value of the person he claims to be loving.

This is why Saint John Paul says that a couple experiencing emotional love needs something more if their love is going to be a love which is fully human. It is not enough to feel close to one another, to be "in the same orbit," although these feelings are a very delightful aspect of their relationship. Emotional love is only a part of what it means to love another person. The couple needs to use their emotions as a springboard for developing a true and lasting relationship. In order to do this, the free will of both persons must be involved.

<u>Love caused by the Free Will</u> -- Because a lover needs to be in control of his love -- because love needs to be an experience he *personally* bestows on another -- his free will must take on a decisive role. Only then will his love be the kind of love of which humans are capable. St. John Paul explains: "The will is, so to say, the final authority in ourselves, without whose participation no experience has full personal value or the gravity appropriate to the experiences of the human person."[10]

This kind of love occurs when a person wills a good for the other person just as he wills it for himself. In other words, distinctly human love happens when a person experiences *love-as-goodwill* for the other person. Saint John Paul explains:

> I desire a good for you just as I desire it for myself, for my own 'I'. The content and structure of friendship can be summed up in this formula. ... Your 'I' necessarily becomes in some sense mine, lives within my 'I' as well as within itself. This is the meaning of the word 'friendship'. The doubling of the 'I' implicit in it emphasizes the unification of persons which friendship brings with it.[11]

In order for the free will to make such a commitment to a person, the lover must directly experience his value. That is, he must know the true value or the goodness *of the person himself*. It is only once a person has experienced the *objective* good of the other that he can freely choose to commit himself to him. Such a love, then, will not depend on feelings (emotions) which come and go beyond our direct control. Rather, this love will rest on the solid and

---
[10] Wojtyla, *Love and Responsibility*, p. 117.
[11] Wojtyla, *Love and Responsibility*, pp. 90-91.

Part II -- Chapter I
CALLED TO LOVE

NOTES

"True love involves virtue, friendship and the pursuit of a common good. Both people are focused on a common goal outside of themselves."
— Edward Sri

"The greater the feeling of responsibility for the person the more true love there is."
— Saint John Paul II, *Love and Responsibility*

"Love develops on the basis of the totally committed and fully responsible attitude of a person to a person...."
— Saint John Paul II, *Love and Responsibility*

"By uniting myself to another, my own life is not diminished but is profoundly enriched."
— Edward Sri

"...The love for a person which results from a valid act of choice is concentrated on the value of the person as such and makes us feel emotional love for the person as he or she really is, not for the person of our imagination, but for the real person."
— Saint John Paul II, *Love and Responsibility*

NOTES

enduring foundation of the will's commitment to an *objective* good which the person has found in another person.

Saint John Paul explains the distinction between *subjective* love and *subjectivity* in the love between persons:

> We must not, however, confuse the idea of subjective love with that of subjectivity. Love is always a subjective thing, in that it must reside in subjects, but at the same time it must be free of subjectivity. It must be something objective within the subject, have an objective as well as a subjective profile.[12]

This objectivity is so important because it is the *truth* about the other person. In order to love another, a person must know the truth about who the other is so that he can form a relationship with him. Without this *objective* dimension, the lover is unable to go out of himself to unite in love with the other person. He is locked within his own subjectivity.

The following chart compares and contrasts emotional love with the love caused by the will so that you will be able to see clearly their relationship.

"Unless a man and woman have the objective aspects of love in their relationship, they do not yet have a bond of true love."
Edward Sri

Emotional Love	Love Caused by the Will
Originates spontaneously and develops quickly	*Originates deliberately and develops over time, with effort*
Draws persons together, making them feel close to each other	*Persons move themselves toward one another, making them actually become one with each other*
Depends on emotions	*Depends on the free will*
Unites persons emotionally -- Makes them exist within the other's emotional experience	*Unites persons volitionally -- Makes them exist in one another*
<u>*Subjective*</u> *-- based on a value that comes from the lover himself*	<u>*Objective*</u> *-- based on a value that comes from the one loved*
Can create the conditions for true love to develop, but is itself not true love	*Provides the basis for a true and lasting relationship -- true love!*
Ceases spontaneously	*Ceases deliberately, if it ceases*

[12] Wojtyla, *Love and Responsibility*, p. 93.

Part II -- Chapter I
CALLED TO LOVE

NOTES

Study Guide Questions:

1. *What does it mean to say that emotional love is subjective?*

2. *Why is it so important that we be able to control our love for another person?*

3. *Why is objectivity in our loving relationships with others so very important?*

4. *What are the strengths and weakness of emotional love?*

5. *What is meant by sensuality and sentimentality?*

6. *Why must love grow beyond mere sensual and sentimental emotional responses if it is to become truly human love?*

7. *Why isn't the objectivity involved in sensuality sufficient for establishing a true communion of persons?*

8. *What can a person do to increase or develop the objective dimension of his love for another?*

The Truth of Mature Love

Certainly the love of a man and a woman for one another involves the joy of mutual support, fulfillment and deep emotional happiness. At the same time, because it is more than simply emotional love, but includes genuine self-giving, this deeper love will often entail sacrifice. Its joy will even embrace suffering for the sake of the other. As emotional love matures and deepens, it is transformed into a higher form of love. This transformation occurs as a man and woman become more aware of the value of one another *objectively*, i.e., the value of one another as persons. With this awareness, both are able to commit themselves to seeking the other's good.

Saint John Paul suggests that love's objective side can be developed by the couple's sharing in certain common activities such as: attending the same class, working in the same office, worshipping in the same Church, playing on the same team, participating in the same pro-life events, etc. These common activities give the couple the opportunity genuinely to get to know each other -- to know what the other values, how she thinks, what goals he seeks. This *objective* knowledge of the other's person will give the lover's *subjective* emotional response a firm basis in objective reality.

With this knowledge of one another, the two persons can freely choose to commit their wills to seeking one another's good. Thus, the bond of friendship develops as the two form a deep spiritual union, a true *communion of persons*.

"It's easy to love when we get a lot in return. But the objective aspect of love reminds us that true love is not merely about my experience of good feelings..., but the commitment to seek what is best for the other person even when these feelings are not there."
— Edward Sri

"A mature love ... is based not on my feelings, but on the honest truth of the other person and on my commitment to the other person in self-giving love. The emotions still play an important part, but they are grounded in the truth of the other person as he or she *really* is."
— Edward Sri

149.

The Human Person ~ Dignity Beyond Compare

NOTES

Conjugal -- from Latin *conjugalis* (spouse) and *conjungere* (to join in marriage); of or relating to marriage or the relationship of spouses.

Betrothed love -- from ME *betrouthen* (in relation to); love between persons who are engaged to be married.

"...so that they may be one just as we are."

John 17:11

"Man ... cannot fully find himself except through a sincere gift of himself."

Gaudium et Spes, 24:3

150.

Such a relationship can also go further and reach the point where they are willing to entrust themselves completely to one another. In other words, the two can choose to come together to form a **conjugal** *communion of persons* -- that is, a type of relationship where the two persons commit to giving their very *persons* -- body and soul -- to one another in a lifelong relationship. We call this **betrothed love** or marriage.

This two-in-one-flesh-union of marriage is the fullest tangible expression and realization of the *original unity* Adam and Eve experienced in their relationship with each other. In their relationship with their spouses, those called to marriage are invited to reflect on the model presented to us in Scripture of the first man and woman, who freely gave themselves to one another in conjugal union.

"And the man said,
'This at last is bone of my bones and flesh of my flesh.' ...
Therefore a man leaves his father and mother and
clings to his wife, and they become one flesh."

Genesis 2:23-24

The Nuptial Meaning of the Body

All of us are called to form a *communion of persons* with the others placed in our lives. Scripture, in the Book of Genesis, reveals that the Creator's purpose in creating man male and female at the very beginning was so that Adam would have a "helpmate suited to him."[13] In other words, the woman, a being equal to the man in her rational nature and, like the man, *having a capacity for a relationship with God*, is also created *for the man*. Likewise, the man, made for relationship with God, is created *for the woman*. *Together* -- two human persons united as one -- they represent the Creator's human masterpiece, the "one" who is made in His image and likeness.

At the very beginning, the human being comes into existence as a *person for the person*. The very design of our bodies as either male or female indicates that we are made to be in a self-giving relationship with another person. As individuals, each of us is somehow incomplete. We cannot fulfill ourselves. Our sexually incomplete bodies are a sign of this, for we need a *complementary* human body to be sexually whole. Only in communion with a person of the opposite sex can we achieve this "wholeness." Our sexual "incompleteness" is actually a blessing,

---
[13] Genesis 2:18, 20

for it enables us to realize the natural human need to be open to others rather than closed in on ourselves.

Our communion with other persons is not primarily, or even essentially, a sexual matter, of course; but our bodies, with their complementary sexual powers, act as a sort of a **paradigm** for our many other types of human relationships. The primary fact is that *we are to be involved in self-giving relationships with other persons.* This is what Saint John Paul II means when he writes that the body helps us find ourselves in a *communion of persons.*[14] In other words, our male and female bodies enable us to discover deeper truths about ourselves as human persons.

In this section we will explore the wonder of one of the most beautiful relationships of which the human person is capable in this life: the nuptial relationship, expressed in and through the body.

> ### Vocabulary
>
> | | | |
> |---|---|---|
> | nuptial meaning of the body | sexual shame | integrate |
> | original nakedness | chastity | shamelessness |
> | lust | modesty | marital act |

Our male and female bodies -- which express our persons -- speak a language. They reveal our souls, the spiritual dimension of our persons. Our bodies reveal to us that we were made to go out of ourselves to another in self-giving love. In fact, it is precisely in this giving of ourselves to another that we will discover our true identities. The search for the human identity of "the one who, at the beginning, is 'alone,' must always pass through duality, through 'communion.'"[15] Saint John Paul explains:

> The acceptance of the woman by the man and the very way of accepting her become, as it were, a first gift in such a way that the woman, in giving herself, at the same time 'discovers herself,' thanks to the fact that she has been accepted and welcomed and thanks to the way in which she has been received by the man. She therefore finds herself in her own gift of self when she has been accepted in the way in which the Creator willed her, namely, 'for her own sake,'....[16]

---

[14] Saint John Paul, *Theology of the Body*, 10:2.
[15] Ibid., 10:1.
[16] Ibid., 17:4.

Part II -- Chapter I
CALLED TO LOVE

NOTES

Paradigm – an example serving as a model; pattern.

"In this communion of persons, the whole depth of the original solitude of man is perfectly ensured and, at the same time, this solitude is permeated and enlarged in a marvelous way by the gift of the 'other.'"

Saint John Paul II,
Theology of the Body

The Human Person ~ Dignity Beyond Compare

NOTES

Nuptial -- from Latin *nuptialis* (wedding); of or relating to marriage.

Nuptial meaning of the body – that man's body is a sign of his call and capacity for making a total and irrevocable *gift of self* to another; this is how human spousal love images the spousal love between Christ and the Church.

Marital act -- the act which is proper to persons who are married: the act of sexual intercourse wherein the two sexually incomplete persons so fully give themselves to each other that they form one sexual organism.

"...so that they may all be one, as you, Father, are in me and I in you, that they also may be in us, ... that they may be one, as we are one, I in them and you in me, that they may be brought to perfection as one...."

John 17:21-23

152.

We are invited, then, to go out of ourselves in knowing and loving other persons -- to make a sincere gift of ourselves to them. And we, in turn, are invited to receive others as the gifts they are into our lives, welcoming them gratefully.

This call to self-giving love, Saint John Paul says, is the "*indispensable theme*" of our existence.[17] We were made to be one with another. Simply put, we were all made for *marriage*. This is what Saint John Paul means when he speaks of the **nuptial meaning of the body**. Let us consider what this means.

The *nuptial meaning of the body* has two dimensions: the *horizontal* and the *vertical*. The relating of man and woman to each other in marriage expresses the *horizontal* dimension of the body's nuptial meaning, that is, its meaning here and now in the created world. Their male and female bodies, wonderfully designed to fit together sexually as one, bring about their physical union as persons in the most intimate way possible. Their bodily union as husband and wife in the **marital act** makes visible the spiritual union of their persons that took place when they gave themselves to each other in marriage. Through the marital act, their bodies are expressing (literally "acting out") the language of total self-giving spoken in their marriage vows: *"I give myself wholly to you. I am totally yours!"*

There is also a *vertical* dimension of the body's nuptial meaning: the body relates us to its Creator. Our bodies invite us to receive them (i.e., our bodies themselves) as *gifts*: gifts from the Creator who longs to be in loving union with us. This was so in the beginning when Adam and Eve stood apart from the rest of physical creation in their openness to their Creator. Each of them stood in relation to Him as child to Father -- as His son or daughter.

Original solitude, man's openness to and need for union with his Creator, then, never ceases. It never truly goes away. Adam and Eve's experience of *original unity* serves only to deepen their experience of *original solitude*, for in sharing their lives with each other, Adam and Eve better understand the relationship they are invited to enter into with their Creator and Father. United in love for each other and grateful for the *gift* of one another in their lives, Adam and Eve are drawn into an ever more intimate union with the Father, the Giver of all gifts.

[17] Saint John Paul, *Theology of the Body*, 15:5.

Part II -- Chapter I
CALLED TO LOVE

Original unity deepens their experience of *original solitude* in another way as well. No human person is capable of giving all of himself to his spouse. He does not own himself; he belongs to God. While he may truly love his spouse and be bound to her, only God can truly possess him or claim his total love. Only God who is Love can own a person and take total possession of him without destroying him.

Two human persons, then, cannot ever be so united that they are only one being; their bodies cannot melt into one another. Even in their most intimate union they remain "separateness-in-union" physically as well as psychically. Aware that they remain alone even when united with the other person, they experience the inadequacy of their human love. They each are able to look at one another and say, "I love you and give myself to you; but I know you yourself are not my eternal destiny. Together we travel to our Eternal Destiny." In other words, they both realize that each of them longs for Someone more; and that, in their love for one another, they can help and support each other in their life's journey to God, who is Love.

This aloneness is an expression of their openness to God. Only the love of God will satisfy them. Through loving another human person, then, they are invited to love God more deeply and more perfectly. This is the *vertical* dimension of the body's nuptial meaning.

It is this loving union between the Creator and each human person He has created which is the ultimate goal of our lives. Our loving union with other human persons is the path to that goal. These loving relationships on the horizontal level teach us how to open ourselves up to others in love and how to give ourselves selflessly to them.

In fact, it is only to the extent that we are seeking to be united with God, the Father, that we are able to bring our love for one another on the horizontal level to its true fulfillment. This fulfillment is realized when we can lead one another to the *Greatest Good:* to Him who alone is able to fully satisfy the longing of our human hearts. In a very true sense, then, we can say that the quality of our relationships on the horizontal level are totally dependent upon the relationship each one of us has with God.

Study Guide Questions:

1. What is a conjugal communion of persons?

2. What does it mean to say that we are all called to love?

3. What does the phrase "the nuptial meaning of the body" mean?

4. What are the two dimensions of the nuptial meaning of the body?

NOTES

"Total union with one who is not God is impossible. And were it possible, it would be idolatry, giving the creature the status of the divine."
— Paul M. Quay

"Your Maker is your husband, the Lord of hosts is his name; and the Holy One of Israel is your Redeemer, the God of the whole earth he is called."
— Isaiah 54:5

"... [T]he God of Israel is also a *Bridegroom*, a divine person whose ultimate desire is to be united to his creatures in an everlasting relationship that is so intimate, so permanent, so sacrificial, and so life-giving that it can only be described as a *marriage* between Creator and creatures, between God and human beings."
— Brant Pitre

"Every marriage promises what God alone can give."
— Fulton J. Sheen, *The World's First Love*, p. 164

"We may love creatures with our whole hearts: but only if we make sure that our hearts are given to God: then we can be sure of giving those we love something greater than a purely human love: of giving a love which is indwelt by God: of loving not only with our own love but with God's."
— Gerald Vann, O.P., *The Son's Course*

The Human Person ~ Dignity Beyond Compare

NOTES

5. How did Adam and Eve's experience of original unity deepen their experience of original solitude?

6. What is the ultimate goal of each of our lives? How does loving other human persons relate to this goal?

7. Why is love of God essential for a true love of our fellow human beings?

CASES IN POINT

#1 -- "When considering the objective aspect of love, I must discern what kind of relationship exists between my beloved and me in reality, not simply what this relationship means in my feelings.

-- Am I committed to this other person for who she is or for the enjoyment I receive from the relationship?

-- Does my beloved understand what is truly best for me, and does she have the faith and virtue to help me get there?

-- Are we deeply united by a common aim, serving each other and striving together toward a common good that is higher than each of us?

-- Or are we just living side-by-side, sharing resources and occasional good times together while we selfishly pursue our own interests and enjoyments in life?

These are the kinds of questions that get at the objective aspect of love."

Edward Sri, *Men, Women and the Mystery of Love,* pp. 56-57.

◆ *Write out a list of practical things that should be present in any relationship where there is real love.*

* * * * *

#2 -- "Being in love is a good thing, but it is not the best thing. There are many things below it, but there are also things above it. You cannot make it the basis of a whole life. It is a noble feeling, but it is still a feeling…. Who could bear to live in that excitement for even five years? … But, of course, ceasing to be 'in love' need not mean ceasing to love. Love in this second sense -- love as distinct from 'being in love' -- is not merely a feeling. It is a deep unity, maintained by the will and deliberately strengthened by habit; reinforced by (in Christian marriages) the grace which both parents ask, and receive, from God. They can have this love for each other even at those moments when they do not like each other; as you love yourself even when you do not like yourself. They can retain this love even when each would easily, if they allowed themselves, be 'in love' with someone else. 'Being in love' first moved them to promise fidelity: this quieter love enables them to keep the promise. It is on this love that the engine of marriage is run; being in love was the explosion that started it."

C.S. Lewis, *Mere Christianity*, pp. 108-109

◆ *What does Lewis mean when he distinguishes between "being in love" and "love itself"?*

◆ *Why is "love itself" actually better than "being in love"?*

* * * * *

#3 -- Steve and Irene married when they were in their early twenties. In addition to his working for the Post Office and helping to raise their five children, Steve was actively involved in the St. Vincent de Paul Society, caring for the poor wherever he encountered them. After about 30 years of marriage, Steve spent the final 6 years of his life battling cancer. A few days after Steve's funeral, Irene wrote the following email to a good friend: "I woke up today about 4 a.m. feeling rested and realizing that the marrow of what Steve and I had has not left. At the end little by little we had to let go of the fluff of our marriage -- things we enjoyed like Kareoke, dancing, bike riding, meals out, even our physical intimacy. … At the very end, even the quality of our meals together and our conversations faded ... and these losses I grieved little by little as they happened. But this morning when I used Steve's prayer book, I realized that the marrow and core of our marriage -- the prayers and the connections of our souls I never had to give up, and I will NEVER have to give them up -- it brought me joy. And maybe that is why I have not (at least yet) despaired."

- *Do you think Steve and Irene had achieved a true "Communion of Persons"? Explain.*

* * * * *

#4 -- *Compare/contrast the following two married couples and their love for each other:*

a) Bruce and Lilly have 3 children and have experienced 12 years as a happily married couple before Lilly is diagnosed with bone cancer. Bruce did not expect the financial and emotional stress Lilly's illness would cause him. The self-sacrifice that Lilly's illness demands of him is not what he had envisioned marriage to be. Bruce isn't willing to make the sacrifices that are needed now to care for her and their children, so he decides to divorce Lilly and leave her and their children in order to find a new way of life that will be more fulfilling to him.

b) Michael and Sarah have been married almost 25 years when Sarah is diagnosed with multiple sclerosis. Her illness proceeds rapidly and Sarah is soon confined to a wheelchair and is unable to move her arms, hold up her head, or even talk. Throughout her suffering, Michael remains at her side, serving her as best he can -- bathing her, feeding her, talking to her, reading to her and taking her for walks. He even decides to retire from his job a few years early in order to care for her, though he knows that doing so will bring financial hardship for him later. Michael faithfully cares for Sarah until her death.

* * * * *

#5 -- "Love is:
- -- listening when you want to talk,
- -- calming fears at midnight,
- -- saying hard things in a soft manner,
- -- trusting that your teenager will come home at the agreed upon time,
- -- watching that cartoon film for the third time because it is the one thing your child really wanted,
- -- what makes you smile when you're tired,
- -- when your friend stands by you, even when you are wrong,
- -- not mentioning that you have been warming dinner for over an hour when someone comes home late, tired, and frustrated,
- -- explaining long division, slowly and patiently, for the tenth time that evening,
- -- going to your child's every game of the season, even though he never wins,
- -- listening to the practice over and over again, and still being enthusiastic at the recital,
- -- making sure not to make your mother cry as you ship out back to Iraq, knowing the cancer is going to take her before your return,
- -- helping your wife struggle into her wheelchair,
- -- holding a wounded Marine so he knows that he is not alone,
- -- writing him every day, knowing that he is serving his country, will come home soon enough, and that he loves you,
- -- joyfully bearing nine months of pregnancy,
- -- when you see your newborn child for the first time,
- -- holding the hand of someone who is sick, of someone who is dying,
- -- faith in the midst of apparent failure,
  Love is sacrifice. Love is the Crucifix!"

Fr. Michael R. Duesterhaus, Diocese of Arlington, 2010

- *What would you add to this list to identify in your own life instances where love is made manifest?*

Original Nakedness

In their original state before they sinned, Adam and Eve enjoyed a conjugal *union of persons* in which they were able to be naked and yet feel no shame in each other's company. This condition in which their unclothed bodies did not cause them sexual shame Saint John Paul calls **original nakedness**.

In order to understand this condition of *original nakedness*, then, we need first to understand **sexual shame**. The term "shame" here does not have a negative meaning associated with guilt. Rather, Saint John Paul explains that *sexual shame* involves the tendency in all of us to conceal our sexual values from the gaze of others, especially from persons of the opposite sex.[18] This tendency is related to our awareness that no human person should ever be treated as a mere object of use for another's sexual pleasure. We instinctively know that the human person has more value or worth than that.

Sexual shame, then, in its objective meaning, is a good thing; it is a "natural form of self-defense for the person"[19] against the possibility of degrading or being degraded by another. It expresses the person's need to be valued rightly, in accord with his dignity.

In their state of *original unity,* Adam and Eve did not need to worry about being degraded by each other. They enjoyed an intimate *union of persons* where each was able to give fully of himself -- body and soul -- to the other. They experienced such a mutual trust and confidence in the other's genuine love for them that they felt no need to conceal anything from each other, not even their sexual value.

When Adam experienced Eve before they sinned, he experienced the full beauty of her *person* and not just that of her body. She stood as if transparent before him, allowing him to view the totality of her being. Thus, he was not inclined to lust after her and to degrade himself and her by treating her as a mere object for his own pleasure.

Eve reciprocated in her loving response to Adam. She experienced

---
[18] Wojtyla, *Love and Responsibility,* p. 175.
[19] Ibid., p. 182.

NOTES

Sexual Shame -- the tendency to conceal sufficiently our sexual values from others so that the full worth of the person is not obscured by them.

"Adam and Eve saw each other with a supernatural perspective -- with 'the vision of the Creator'."
Edward Sri

"Free from sin, they were free to love."
Edward Sri

awe and wonder at the goodness of his *person*, given to her as a gift by the Creator. Because of this, she was able to be *personally* and not just physically naked before him. That is, she was able to let her true self be known. Within this environment of complete mutual love and responsibility, Adam and Eve experienced a true *communion of persons* which brought them intense joy and a profound interior peace.

Sexual shame, then, did not exist for them. They did not need it because they were able to see in each other's bodies an expression of their unique human dignity, and so the fear of using or being used by the other as a mere object of sexual pleasure did not yet exist. This ability of theirs to discern the dignity of the human body and to see in it an expression of the person is what Saint John Paul means by **original nakedness**.

The reason Adam and Eve were able to be naked and without shame, Saint John Paul explains, is that they had confidence in one another -- trusting that the other rightly valued them. Their confidence was not misplaced, for Adam and Eve did, in fact, have self-mastery over their lower appetites. Their emotional responses to one another were in line with right reason. Thus, they were free from **lust** and from any selfish desires which would have degraded them. They truly approached one another with the reverence that was due a person created in God's very image and likeness.

Once Adam and Eve sinned, however, everything changed for them. The severing of their union with God had an effect on their own self-mastery over their lower appetites as well as on their union with each other. Their selfish desires now rebelled against the perspective of sound reason, and **enmity** took root between them.[20] They lost their experience of *original nakedness*.

In fact, Genesis tells us that *shame* in one another's naked presence was the first consequence of their sin.[21] Now as Adam and Eve approached each other with selfish and lustful hearts, they were no longer able to trust the other's genuine love for them. *Shame* entered in, then, as a form of defense from the other.

---

[20] Genesis 3:15
[21] Genesis 3:7

NOTES

Original nakedness -- the condition of man in which his unclothed body does not cause him to feel sexual shame; man's ability to discern the dignity of the human body, viewing it as an expression of the person.

Lust -- indulging in disordered sexual desire which treats another person as a mere object.

"Adultery 'in the heart' is committed not only because man 'looks' in this way at a woman who is not his wife, but precisely because he looks at a woman in this way. Even if he looked in this way at the woman who is his wife, he would likewise commit adultery 'in his heart.'"
— Saint John Paul

Enmity -- from Latin *inimicus* (enemy); deep-rooted mutual hatred.

The Human Person ~ Dignity Beyond Compare

NOTES

"In the woman, shame expresses itself like this: 'You must not touch me, not even in your secret carnal thoughts.'"
Saint John Paul II,
Love and Responsibiity

"In the man, shame expresses itself like this: 'I must not touch her, not even with a deeply hidden wish to enjoy her, for she cannot be an object for use.'"
St. John Paul II,
Love and Responsibiity

Thus, while *shame* seems to keep two people at a distance from each other, it does so only so that they will be able to come together in a truly *personal* way.

Sexual shame, then, according to Saint John Paul, has a two-fold purpose: **(a)** It protects the person from degradation; and
 (b) It clears the way for genuine love to develop.

In order to bring about this self-protection and to enable genuine love to develop, *shame* leads a woman to cover or conceal certain parts of her body that might arouse a man's sensual response to her.

She does so because she wants the man to love her for the goodness of her *person* rather than merely because her body might bring him sexual pleasure. Once she knows that he loves her for the goodness of her *person* (because he is willing to publicly commit himself to seeking her good in marriage), then she is able to reveal to him these private parts of her body because she now has reason to trust that he will regard them appropriately.

> Stop! Love me for who I am as a person!

In order not to degrade the woman and to enable genuine love to develop within him, *shame* leads a man to try to prevent reactions to her body *within himself* which would not be in keeping with her true value as a *person*.

As genuine love between a man and a woman grows, their fear of using and being used by the other diminishes. When true love is finally present between a man and a woman and the value of the other's *person* is both understood and deeply felt by the two of them, then *sexual shame* is absorbed by love. This means that the couple will not experience *shame* because their love is complete: Each of them chooses the other based on a recognition of the goodness of his or her *person*, with a view to a lasting union in marriage and an openness to being parents together. Saint John Paul explains:

> The need for shame has been absorbed by mature love for a person: it is no longer necessary for a lover to conceal from the beloved or from himself a disposition to enjoy, since this has been absorbed by true love ruled by the will.[22]

---

[22] Wojtyla, *Love and Responsibility*, p. 184.

Saint John Paul warns, however, that love which is merely emotional might also *superficially* absorb shame and thus <u>falsely</u> lead the two to think that they have the right to physical intimacy and to sexual intercourse. This is a mistaken view, he points out, for emotional love is immature love. As such, it cannot truly provide the appropriate context for a true *union of persons* which physical intimacy and sexual intercourse require.

In fact, Saint John Paul refers to such a superficial absorption of shame as a form of **shamelessness**. *Shamelessness* is the lack of shame when and where it should be. With *original nakedness,* Adam and Eve experienced the lack of shame, but they had no need for it. *Shamelessness* is the opposite of this. When there is a need for shame and a person lacks it, we speak of *shamelessness*.

Saint John Paul distinguishes between two forms of *shamelessness*, both of which are the opposite of sexual modesty:

(a) *Physical shamelessness* -- any way of being or behaving by a person so that sexual value of a person's body is considered to be more important than the person himself. Such a person is put in a position of being an object of use.

(b) *Emotional shamelessness* -- the rejection of a healthy tendency to be ashamed of reactions and emotions which make a person merely an object of use because of the sexual value of his body.[23]

The Role of Chastity

From all that we have come to understand thus far about love, we are able to realize now that genuine love of another person -- especially a person of the opposite sex -- requires a giving of oneself and a willingness to sacrifice. Love makes demands, and sometimes entails a struggle.

We cannot allow love to remain merely at the subjective level -- that is, at the sensual or emotional levels. Nor can love remain an experience of only one of the two persons involved. Rather, mature human love requires that the various elements of love -- the sensual, the emotional, and the volitional -- be **integrated** within each of the persons and that it be shared between them so that they form *a personal and interpersonal whole.*

Without this integration, love will not rise to the level appropriate for human persons, and thus it cannot truly unite them. With this integration, however, that is, with the involvement of the intellect, will, and emotions working together, the love is based firmly on an acknowl-

---

[23] Wojtyla, *Love and Responsibility*, pp. 187-8.

NOTES

"True shame can be absorbed only by true love, a love which affirms the value of the person and seeks the greatest good for that person with all its strength."
St. John Paul II
Love and Responsibility

Shamelessness -- the lack of shame when there is a need for it; at odds with the demands of sexual modesty.

"...Sexual modesty is not a flight from love, but on the contrary the opening of a way towards it."
St. John Paul II
Love and Responsibility

"Genuine love ... is demanding; but its beauty lies precisely in the demands it makes. These demands are ... capable of making your love a true love."
St. John Paul II

Integrate -- from Latin *integrare* (to restore); to bring together into a whole.

NOTES

Chastity -- from Latin *castus* (clean, pure); the virtue by which a person affirms the true meaning and value of human sexuality.

"The essence of chastity consists in quickness to affirm the value of the person in every situation, and in raising to the personal level all reactions to the value of 'the body and sex'."

St. John Paul II
Love and Responsibility

"Chastity is love preparing to give itself ...."

Paul M. Quay

"Chastity includes an apprenticeship in self-mastery, which is a training in human freedom. ... Either man governs his passions and finds peace, or he lets himself be dominated by them and becomes unhappy."

Catechism of the Catholic Church,
#2339

---

edgement of *the value of the person*. On this firm foundation, the lover can foster within himself a whole-hearted desire for the beloved's good.

This is the reason for the importance of the virtue of chastity. The word "chaste" means "clean" or "pure." **Chastity**, then, is the virtue (good habit) that frees us from anything that would mar the pure goodness of human sexuality. Chastity disposes or inclines us to use our sexuality in a reasonable way, that is, in a way that respects the true value of the person. The chaste person is the one who *affirms the true meaning and value of human sexuality as a great good given to us by the Creator.*

Simply put, chastity is the virtue which makes it possible to use the gift of sexuality in a rightly ordered way. It requires that one engage in the act of sexual intercourse only with one's own spouse, as an expression of loving spousal commitment. Chastity necessarily also means that one avoids any actions, thoughts or situations which could in any way endanger chaste living.

- ◆ **To be chaste** is to value the person as someone to be loved, not as a body to be used.

- ◆ **To be chaste** is to love the person for who he or she is, not to use him or her for what pleasure we can receive.

- ◆ **To be chaste** is to consider the person more valuable than sexual pleasure.

- ◆ **To be chaste** is to possess the good habit (virtue) of using our sexual powers in a truthful and humanly fulfilling way.

Chastity is challenging, often difficult, and even counter-cultural -- but it is a beautifully *human* virtue, and it brings *freedom*. Chastity frees us *from*:
- sexual idolatry,
- being slaves to our passions,
- using and abusing human persons.

Chastity frees us *for*:
- self-mastery of our passions,
- becoming truly loving human persons,
- worshiping God through the right use of our bodies.

With this understanding of the virtue of chastity, we can readily see why it is a virtue that is necessary for everyone -- both the married and the unmarried. Married persons need chastity to help them use their sexuality in a reasonable manner: genuinely loving one another, persevering in fidelity, and giving totally of themselves whenever they engage in the marital act. Thus, they would never engage in the sexual act with someone to whom they are not married; they would never do anything to disorder their self-gift to one another; and they would never use one another as mere objects of lust.

Chaste unmarried persons would use their sexuality reasonably: mastering their passions so they are able to love others genuinely, refusing to use others merely for their own pleasure, and refraining from all sexual acts which would be untruthful. Thus, the unmarried would save the gift of themselves for the persons to whom they will some day commit themselves in a total and exclusive way.

The cultivation of chastity is ordinarily a life-long endeavor. This is especially true in cultures where lack of sexual self-respect is blatant, and where sex is treated as a form of entertainment. Both current forms of entertainment and styles of fashion are frequently designed so as to arouse sexual passions in disordered ways. Such an atmosphere makes it extremely difficult to value and develop the practice of personal chastity. It is therefore especially necessary for individuals to take positive steps to develop chastity in their personal lives.

Here are a few helps for living a chaste life:

- **Practice modesty** -- dress, act, and speak so as not to arouse the sexual passions of another.

- **Discipline the senses and the mind** -- guard yourself from inappropriate sexual images found in magazines, movies, and TV.

- **Guard your heart** -- be aware of situations in which you experience an emotional need for love, and recognize legitimate ways by which this need can be met..

- **Avoid occasions of sin** -- know your weaknesses and avoid companions or situations which could be a source of temptation.

- **Follow wholesome pursuits** -- get involved in activities which are enjoyable and allow you to have a good time with friends, but without focusing on the sexual.

- **Persevere in prayer** -- stay close to Jesus, Mary, and the saints.

- **Receive the sacraments of Confession and Holy Communion often** -- use these powerful sources of grace in your struggle against evil.

NOTES

"If the person is not master of self -- through the virtues and, in a concrete way, through chastity -- he or she lacks that self-possession which makes self-giving possible."
The Truth and Meaning of Human Sexuality, #16

"Chastity is a difficult, long term matter; one must wait patiently for it to bear fruit, for the happiness of loving kindness which it must bring.... Chastity is the sure way to happiness."
St. John Paul II
Love and Responsibility

The Human Person ~ Dignity Beyond Compare

NOTES

"I think many people understand chastity mainly in the negative: It's restraint; it's abstinence; it's a way of understanding what you're not doing. Of course, it has that component, because as long as there is fallen human nature, there are things we have to avoid. But the greater part of chastity is the self-forgetfulness and self-possession that leads to self-giving, and that's what the human person is made for."

Father Paul Check,
Executive Director of Courage International

"Man is not such a perfect being that the sight of the body of another person, especially a person of the other sex, can arouse in him merely a disinterested liking which develops into an innocent affection."

St. John Paul II
Love and Responsibility

Conclusion

We have come to see that knowing and loving other persons -- in particular persons of the opposite sex -- is a challenging adventure for us fallen human beings. Forming a true *communion of persons* with them, however, is precisely what we as human persons were created to do. If we persevere in the challenge and learn truly to love others, then we can expect to experience the happiness for which we as human persons were created, for we will in fact then be in the image of our Creator, Love Himself. As persons who have allowed the divine image to develop within us, we will be able to become one, for all eternity, with the divine *Communion of Persons* we call the Trinity.

Modesty Differs in Men and Women

The development of sexual modesty follows one course in women and another in men. Since sensuality is in general stronger in men, modesty and shame -- the tendency to conceal the sexual value of the body -- must be more pronounced in women. Women are less aware of sensuality and its natural orientation in men because sentimentality is stronger in them than sensuality. This is why modesty is more difficult for women. Since they are not as sensual, they do not feel so great a need to conceal their *bodies as potential objects of enjoyment*. Understanding male psychology, then, will help women become more modest.

The natural development of modesty in men differs. Men do not have to fear female sensuality; however, men are keenly aware of their own sensuality, and this is a source of shame for them. Men are ashamed above all of the way they react to the sexual value of a woman's body. Growing in modesty for a man, then, will entail his need to prevent *within himself* a reaction to the body of a woman as a mere object of use for his sexual pleasure.

*Paraphrase of Saint John Paul II's *Love and Responsibility*, pp. 176-177.

- *Why does St. John Paul think that understanding male psychology will help women with modesty?*

- *What precisely does a man need to do if he wants to become more modest?*

162.

Part II -- Chapter I
CALLED TO LOVE

NOTES

Study Guide Questions:

1. Why is sexual shame considered to be something good for us?
2. Why did Adam and Eve not experience sexual shame before they sinned?
3. What is meant by the experience of original nakedness?
4. How does sexual shame clear the way for genuine love?
5. How do males and females differ in their experience of shame?
6. What does it mean to say that shame is absorbed by love?
7. Can purely emotional love truly absorb shame? Explain.
8. Is shamelessness a good thing to have? Explain.
9. Give an example of physical and emotional shamelessness.
10. Why is chastity a very positive virtue, one that is necessary in every person's life, both married and unmarried? How would you explain to someone that chastity makes for happiness?

CASES IN POINT

#1 -- Steve realizes that he has been staring at the body of a beautiful girl in a restaurant when she suddenly turns and notices him staring. As soon as their eyes meet, Steve turns his gaze away and feels ashamed for what he was doing.

Tom, a classmate of Steve's, does the same thing to a girl he sees in his college cafeteria, except that when the girl notices Tom staring at her, Tom does not turn his gaze away. Rather, he rudely continues staring at her.

- Why do you think Steve feels ashamed? Should he?
- What is the real difference between Steve and Tom in regard to their responses to their actions?

* * * * *

#2 -- After Brenda learned that men tend to be more sensual in their responses to a woman's body, she made the following comment to her friend: "Just because men struggle with lustful thoughts, that shouldn't concern me. It's their problem. I should be free to dress in any way I choose."

- If you were Brenda's friend, what advice could you offer her regarding her comment?

(Continued ...)

"What is truly immodest in dress is that which frankly contributes to the deliberate displacement of the true value of the person by sexual values, that which is bound to elicit a reaction to the person as to a 'possible means of obtaining sexual enjoyment' and not 'a possible object of love by reason of his or her personal value.'"
Saint John Paul II,
Love and Responsibility

NOTES

*****

#3 -- Although Ruth and Joan are shopping together for some new clothes to wear to school, they have very different ideas about the kind of clothes they are looking for. Ruth wants clothes that will call the attention of boys to her body. Joan, on the other hand, is looking for clothes that simply fit well, look pretty, and are comfortable.

- *Of the two, which girl is actually dressing in a way that invites boys to get to know her personally?*

- *Though both girls would say they want to inspire and experience love, which of them has the more mature outlook and approach as a young woman? Why?*

- *Describe the kind of clothes each girl will probably buy.*

*****

#4 -- "So here is the great irony: Modesty in dress, which today is considered evidence of being 'hung up' about sex, actually permits women precisely not to be hung up about sex. It allows me to be taken seriously as a woman, without having to be desperate about it or on the other hand, having to pretend to be a man. It gives me the freedom to think about things other than *Do I look OK?!*"
   Wendy Shalit, *A Return to Modesty*, N.Y.: Simon & Schuster, 1999, p. 72.

- *Explain the irony Wendy Shalit is addressing.*
- *In what ways does modesty in dress make a person more free?*

Point to Consider:

Love is patient,
love is kind.
It is not jealous,
[love] is not pompous,
it is not inflated,
it is not rude,
it does not seek its own interests,
it is not quick-tempered,
it does not brood over injury,
it does not rejoice over wrongdoing but rejoices with the truth.
It bears all things,
believes all things,
hopes all things,
endures all things.
Love never fails.
                                        1Corinthians 13:4-8

Chapter II

LANGUAGE OF THE BODY

Introduction

We have seen that human beings, as persons, are made to be in relation with one another, and it is in and through our bodies that we relate to one another in various ways. The body expresses the person. Our bodies, then, are capable of a certain "language." They communicate a message. We have already seen that our bodies naturally tell us that we are called to form a *communion of persons*. We are *persons made for other persons*.

We have also seen that the body is capable of communicating a message to another especially when we act sexually. What is the truth the body is meant to express in the natural message conveyed by the sexual act? Is it possible to distort this message; that is, can we <u>use</u> our bodies to "tell a lie"? Is there necessarily anything wrong with doing that?

Answering such questions is the aim of this present chapter.

Vocabulary

| marriage | procreative | unitive |
| monogamy | polygamy | polyandry |

The Natural Meaning of Sexual Intercourse

From what we have already learned about the *nuptial meaning of the body*, we know that the act of sexual intercourse between a man and woman is an act that is designed to express love. In this act (called the ***sexual act*** or ***marital act***), the male and female persons go out of themselves to each other. They mutually give themselves to one another and simultaneously receive the gift of the other. The two of them, with their sexually incomplete bodies, unite as one, forming a sexual whole. In so doing, their bodies speak the language of total self-giving love, expressing physically the vows they spoke when they married: *"I am totally yours, forever!"*

NOTES

"Sexual actions symbolize marital love."

Paul Quay

"Intercourse is meant to become a type of language by which husband and wife are able to express to each other all that they wish to say in the way of love and spiritual union."

Paul Quay

The Human Person ~ Dignity Beyond Compare

NOTES

"You cannot partly give yourself, because your Self is indivisible; the only way to give yourself is to give yourself entirely. Because the gift is total, it has to exclude all others, and if it doesn't do that, then it hasn't taken place."
— J. Budziszewski

Conjugal love -- from Latin *conjugium* (yoked together); the love of a man and woman involved in a marital relationship.

"Conjugal love involves a totality, in which all the elements of the person enter -- appeal to the body and instinct, power of feeling and affectivity, aspiration of the spirit and of will. It aims at a deeply personal unity, the unity that, beyond union in one flesh, leads to forming one heart and soul; it demands indissolubility and faithfulness in definitive mutual giving; and it is open to fertility."
— Pope Paul VI, *Humanae Vitae*

From this perspective of *natural law*, that is, from the viewpoint of any human being who thinks seriously about our human nature, we can understand the natural meaning of sexual intercourse. Thus we can know our moral responsibility regarding this act.

Because husband and wife are human persons -- beings composed of physical body and spiritual (rational) soul -- their act of sexual intercourse must involve more than their bodies alone. Their giving themselves and receiving each other *physically* is meant to have a parallel giving and receiving on the *spiritual* or psychological level.

What type of spiritual union appropriately parallels the bodily sexual union? Consider the fact that the bodily union of the sexual act is naturally one in which the two persons hold nothing back from each other. Their exterior bodily nakedness symbolizes this *total* openness and transparency to one another. The interior spiritual union that is a necessary parallel to this bodily union, then, must involve a *totality* in the mutual giving of the two persons. Thus, sexual intercourse requires that the two persons freely choose to give themselves <u>only</u> *to this one person* and to no one else. They must also freely choose to give themselves *for the whole time of their lives.* In other words, they must intend their union to be both *exclusive* and *lifelong.* Otherwise, it is not a total giving of oneself. If this is <u>not</u> the case, then they are "saying" something with their bodies which they do not really mean.

Sexual intercourse between man and woman, then, is designed to express and to foster **conjugal love**. By conjugal love we mean the commitment of spouses to make a *total* gift of themselves to each other. A person can enter into many different kinds of loving relationships, but conjugal love is unique in that there are no limitations to the extent of the sharing and giving and union. The friendship of spouses is <u>total</u>. Conjugal love is the mutual commitment to share *all of oneself* with the other. And the sexual act is meant to express this *total* self-giving. In other words, the conjugal act *(marital act)* is the way the spouses say with their bodies

166.

Part II -- Chapter II
LANGUAGE OF THE BODY

what they said in their marriage vow, *"I give myself totally to you, forever."*

Another way we have of knowing about what is necessary in the spiritual dimension of a couple's union is by investigating the natural purpose of the sexual act. The sexual act has two purposes:

(a) for a man and woman to express a profound self-giving love such that the two persons become one, both bodily and spiritually;

(b) for this union to bear fruit in the conception of new life.

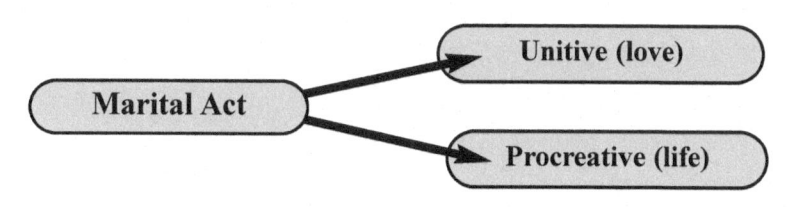

Marital Act → Unitive (love)
Marital Act → Procreative (life)

In regard to the first purpose, we know that entrusting oneself completely to another person requires that the other be a person who will truly receive and treasure the gift given. A genuine entrusting of oneself to another cannot be one-sided. There must be a mutual giving and receiving. In the language of the marital act, there is a "giving in a *receiving* way" and a "receiving in a *giving* way." There is, in other words, *reciprocity* in the entrusting of self. Such an act of mutual entrusting implies that the gift will not be taken back someday nor will it be received for a time, only to be rejected later. Love, if it is true, is forever!

With regard to the second purpose, we know that the sexual act can, if conditions are right, result in the conception of a child. The two persons engaging in the sexual act are speaking a language with their bodies which says, *"I'm willing to be a parent with you."* Since their bodies are engaged in an act which says this, their spirits need to be in accord with their act. This means that, in this act of sexual union, they must be willing to conceive and bring to birth; to love, nurture, educate and morally form the child who may be the fruit of this act. This entails a commitment requiring years of prolonged and devoted care until the child reaches maturity. In other words, they must be willing to widen the sphere of their love to form a **family**. This is a willingness to extend their self-giving beyond themselves, to embrace the life and growth of the child who is the fruit of their act of love. This is no small commitment! Raising children, nurturing their physical, spiritual and emotional growth, and sharing in their lives requires time and patience. Above all, it implies readiness to make sacrifices so that the children can grow as persons. This is the love of a lifetime.

NOTES

"In order to make the bodily union between a man and woman an expression of an even deeper personal union of love, one key ingredient is needed: a willingness to accept the possibility that through the sexual act, 'I may become a father' or 'I may become a mother.'"
Saint John Paul II,
Love and Responsibility

"Openness to the possibility of parenthood represents one of the most profound expressions of love and total acceptance of the other person in marriage."
Edward Sri

"So that life could be shared, because it is such a surpassing gift, Adam and Eve together were given by the Lord the power to co-create with Him. Sexual intimacy, according to the story of our origin, our identity, is integrally bound with fertility."
Father Paul Check,
Executive Director of Courage International

Family -- a fundamental social group in society typically consisting of a man and woman and their offspring.
American Heritage Dictionary

NOTES

"There is an unbreakable connection between the unitive meaning and the procreative meaning, and both are inherent in the conjugal act. And if both essential meanings are preserved, that of union and procreation, the conjugal act fully maintains its capacity for true mutual love and its ordination to the highest mission of parenthood, to which man is called."
Humanae Vitae

"The procreative and unitive meanings of sexuality are joined by nature; they cannot be severed without distorting or diminishing them both."

J. Budziszewski

Natural law tells us, then, that sexual intercourse is a bodily act which has an inherent meaning that requires our respect. The act has an *objective* truth to which we must conform our behavior. Part of that inherent meaning is that it is to be an act expressing *total* self-giving love, an act of the most complete union possible between two human persons. We refer to this as the **unitive** meaning of the act.

The very act which unites the couple in mutual self-giving bears within itself the possibility of bearing fruit in the conception of a child. This is so by the *very nature* of the act. In and through the act of mutual self-giving of spouses, the husband and wife become so "one-in-flesh" that through their union new human life can come into existence. God is creating new life through the unitive act of the husband and wife. We refer to this as the ***procreative*** meaning of the act.

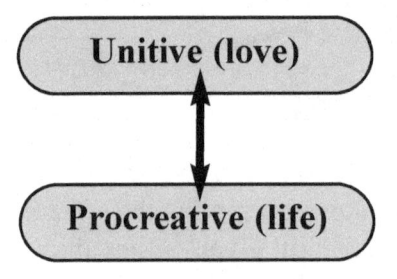

Unitive (love) ↕ **Procreative (life)**

It is important to note that the two meanings of the sexual act, the unitive and procreative, are inherently bound together: the spouses are able to unite in such a way through their mutual self-gift that their "oneness" bears fruit in a person, one who has a life of his or her own, one who can be given a person's name. The oneness of the spouses, then, is more than just a fleeting emotion or a physical sensation; it becomes a real fact, a metaphysical reality. The new human person who may be created in his parents' act of total self-giving actually *embodies* the oneness that his parents become. The child is himself a gift, the fruit of their love for each other.

Similarly, the bringing into existence of a new human being requires not only the momentary uniting of male and female bodies. It also requires their enduring partnership. As one author explains:

> A parent of each sex is necessary to make the child, to raise the child, and to teach the child. To make him, both are needed because the female provides the egg, the male fertilizes it, and the female incubates the resulting zygote. To raise him, both are needed because the male is better designed for protection, the female for nurture. To teach him, both are needed because he needs a model of his own sex, a model of the other, and a model of the relationship between them. Mom and Dad are jointly irreplaceable. Their partnership in procreation continues even after

the kids are grown, because then they are needed to help them establish their own new families.[1]

Thus, the sexual act's purpose of achieving union is not really separate from that of procreation.

In considering the natural meaning of the sexual act, we come to understand that part of the wonder of sexual intercourse is that its meaning is bound up in our maleness and femaleness. Only a man and a woman can unite in this beautiful act of self-giving, which is at the same time physical and spiritual (unitive); and only the sexual union of a man and a woman is capable of bearing fruit in new life (procreative). Only the union of a man and woman who have sealed their self-giving in the language of the marriage vows can genuinely express this truth in the language of the marital act.

Natural law thus teaches us that the marital oneness is to be *permanent*, to be *exclusive*, to be *life-giving*, and therefore, to be *faithful*. Through the marital act, the spouses commit themselves to be open to the wonder and blessing of new life that may result from their loving union. The willingness of a man and woman to have a child with one another bespeaks a willingness to share a lifetime bond. Thus we come to see more deeply why the beauty and the meaning of the sexual act is intimately bound up with the bond of marriage.

> "The couple, while giving themselves to one another, give not just themselves but also the reality of children, who are a living reflection of their love, a permanent sign of conjugal unity and a living and inseparable synthesis of their being a father and a mother."
> St. John Paul II, *Familiaris Consortio*

> "When a husband and wife are truly open to life in their marital relations, it is as if they are looking each other in the eye and saying, 'I love you so much that I am even willing to embark on the adventure of parenthood with you! I entrust myself to you so much that I am willing to become a partner with you in serving any new life that may come from this act.'"
> Edward Sri

[1] Budziszewski, J. "Designed for Sex: What We Lose When We Forget What Sex Is For," *Touchstone*, July/August, 2005.

The Human Person ~ Dignity Beyond Compare

NOTES

Marriage -- the union of a man and a woman who have publicly consented to share their whole lives in a type of relationship oriented toward the begetting, nurturing, and educating of children together.[2]

"By means of the reciprocal personal gift of self, proper and exclusive to them, husband and wife tend towards the communion of their beings in view of mutual personal perfection, to collaborate with God in the generation and education of new lives."
The Truth and Meaning of Human Sexuality

"The family is in fact a community of persons whose proper way of existing and living together is communion: *communio personarum*."
St. John Paul II,
Letter to Families

"Marriage is ... the wise institution of the Creator to realize in mankind his design of love."
The Truth and Meaning of Human Sexuality

Naturally Speaking: The Profound Good of Marriage

Even from the point of view of reason, it is easy to see why **marriage** is the natural institution which supports and protects the inherent meaning of sexual intercourse. The marital way of life involves two persons in a commitment to live in such a way that they strive to mean *in truth* what their bodies say in the sexual act: *"I give myself totally to you, forever!"* Such a mutual commitment of the two persons offers reasonable assurance that the unitive meaning of the sexual act will be protected; that is, that they will be faithful to their bond of love. It also secures for the children who might come into existence from their act, a stable and loving home in which to grow and be nurtured.

Marriage comes into existence, then, when a man and a woman pledge their word to one another that they will live every day what the sexual act symbolizes: They vow to give themselves to each other *totally*, forever! In other words, they agree to share their whole lives together in a type of relationship that expresses itself in the sexual act.

This is why a *defining feature* of marriage is the couple's ability to engage in the sexual act. What distinguishes a husband-wife relationship from any other male-female relationship (example: brother-sister, life-long friends) is precisely the sexual element. Husbands and wives have a relationship that implies *total self-giving* -- including their sexual powers.

This is not to say that a married couple *must* engage in the sexual act. It is possible for them to have a serious reason to forgo expressing their love in this way, for example, health issues, necessary absence for an extended time, or spiritual needs. They must, however, have the *ability* to engage in sexual intercourse with each other in order to get

---

[2] Patrick Lee, "The Same-Sex 'Marriage' Proposal is Unjust Discrimination, *Public Discourse*, January 20, 2012.

married. A couple who enters into marriage is beginning the type of relationship that can bring forth children.

Marriage, then, involves a commitment by a man and a woman to enter into a way of life that is oriented both toward their personal loving union and toward the begetting, nurturing, and educating of children together. The word "matrimony," in fact, actually comes from the Latin word *matrimonium* which means "to lead into motherhood." A couple who enters into marriage is beginning the type of relationship that can bring forth children.

Every human person who has the capacity to engage in sexual intercourse has the *natural* right to marry a person of the opposite sex so that he or she can be sexually complete. Notice that the right does not ultimately come from civil society or its laws. It comes from the natural law and thus from the Author of that law.

Marriage is a profound good for human beings and for society in general. It serves three important public purposes:

(a) Marriage safeguards the needs of children, particularly ensuring that they have the love and support of their father and mother.

(b) Marriage provides direction, order, and stability to adult sexual unions.

(c) Marriage especially calls males to greater maturity, deepening within them a sense of purpose that orients their lives toward virtue.[3]

Marriage is the beginning of family life, and healthy family life is the basic cell of a vibrant society. Precisely because it is so profound a good for human beings and for society in general, marriage is considered to be a *public* matter. States have universally recognized and encouraged marriage in both their laws and in their public policies. This

---

[3] Cf. The Witherspoon Institute, *Marriage and the Public Good: Ten Principles*, N..J.: Princeton, June, 2006, p. 15.

NOTES

"When marriage is strong, children and adults both tend to flourish; when marriage breaks down, every element of society suffers."
Marriage and the Public Good

"In no societies, save those decaying in the last stages of individualism, has marriage been considered a private affair."
Paul Quay

"The importance of the institution of marriage lies in the fact that it provides a justification for the sexual relationship between a couple within the whole complex of society. It does so to the extent that it creates the objective framework for a lasting union of persons."
Saint John Paul II, *Love and Responsibility*

The Human Person ~ Dignity Beyond Compare

NOTES

explains why those who enter into marriage must do so *publicly*. Having the marriage vows declared in public -- with witnesses and signed statements -- is society's way of ensuring that the man and woman involved keep their word about so important a covenant.

Study Guide Questions:

1. How does an act such as rape violate the meaning of the sexual act?
2. Why must the giving of the two persons involved in the sexual act be total?
3. What are the two purposes of the sexual act, and what does each of them mean?
4. What do the two purposes of the sexual act tell us about the spiritual dimension of the act?
5. What does it mean to say that the two meanings of the sexual act are 'inherently bound together'?
6. What is marriage?
7. Based on the principles explained in this chapter, what reasons can you offer to explain why it is wrong that persons of the same sex be issued marriage licenses by civil law?
8. What is the source of the natural right to marry?
9. Why is marriage a public affair?

Monogamy -- having only one wife at a time.

Polyandry -- having more than one husband at a time.

Polygamy -- having more than one wife at a time.

Exclusivity of Marriage

"In practice **monogamy** has been the most prevalent form of marriage even where polygamy was permitted. ...

"**Polyandry** (several husbands and one wife) and **polygamy** (several wives and one husband) are contrary to the ends of marriage because they disturb the union of love between man and wife and render their necessary cooperation in the education of the child difficult or even impossible. This contradiction is most obvious in polyandry, which is more of a hindrance than a help, not only to the education of children but even to their propagation. Polygamy is less opposed to the propagation of children than it is to their education and to the mutual love and devotion of man and wife. It also lowers the dignity of woman."
From *Christian Ethics*, pp. 446-448.

- Why do you think monogamy would be the most prevalent form of marriage?
- How do polyandry and polygamy contradict the purposes of marriage?
- How would polygamy offend the dignity of women?

Part II -- Chapter II
LANGUAGE OF THE BODY

CASES IN POINT

#1 -- Carol enjoys watching a popular TV talk show in the afternoons which often features interviews on topics related to dating, relationships, and the married life. In a recent show, an unmarried couple who were living together were interviewed. Both agreed that such a temporary arrangement is good preparation for possible marriage in a few months. Bob said, "Having sex now, before making any commitment, helps us know whether we want to marry one another, whether we'd even be happy together if we married." Jean added, "It's like a trial run, without any risks involved. We're free to work on our relationship in a deeper way." Later, when Carol is talking with some friends who also saw the show, she asks them what they think about the comments that were made.

* *If you were asked to comment about Bob and Jean's remarks, what would you say?*

* * * * *

#2 -- As seniors in college, Jack and his girl friend, Laura, are seriously considering marriage. From conversations they have had with friends on campus, they come up against what they realize are two totally different viewpoints on marriage:

(a) One view is that marriage is a really unique friendship. Sex can be part of it, if they want, but that's not the point; whether the couple wants to have children isn't the point of marriage. Marriage is about the couple developing their relationship, appreciating one another and having fun together. "There's something really neat and special about that," commented one of Laura's friends.

(b) The other view is that marriage, while certainly a special friendship, is actually a very unique "community" -- formed by a man and woman who publicly consent to share their whole lives in a very specific kind of relationship. It is a relationship that is oriented toward begetting and nurturing, raising and educating children together. This view sees children as the natural fulfillment of marriage. "It's a real commitment," remarked Jack's roommate.

* *Jack's friend Hal says the two views are just two ways of looking at the same thing, that's all. "They're not so different really. At least they're both saying marriage is good and necessary." What would you say to Hal about this?*

* *Leigh makes the point that these two views of marriage are fundamentally different and have totally different practical implications. She says, "I'd really want to be careful about which of these viewpoints the man who asks me to marry him holds!" Why do you think she would say this?*

* * * * *

#3 -- "The act of sexual intercourse is in itself bonding or unitive. It accomplishes three different kinds of bonding: that of the physical act of two bodies becoming one, that of a feeling of psychological closeness, and the spiritual or marital (and fully human) bonding of reaffirming a lifetime commitment."

Janet E. Smith, "The Morality of Condom Use by HIV-Infected Spouses"

* *What type of bonding is possible between the following people:*
    (a) Those engaging in homosexual sexual acts;
    (b) An unmarried man and woman engaging in the sexual act;
    (c) A married woman engaging in the sexual act with a man to whom she is not married;
    (d) A married couple who love each other?

Point to Consider:

*"Essential to preparing for marriage is your vocation to chastity.
I know that young people reject hypocrisy.
You want to be honest with yourselves and others.
A chaste person is honest.
When God created us he gave us more than one way
to 'speak' to each other.
Besides expressing ourselves through speech,
we express ourselves through our bodies.
Gestures are like 'words' that tell who we are.
Sexual actions are 'words' that reveal our hearts.
The Lord wants us to use our sexuality according to his plan.
He expects us to 'speak' truthfully.
Honest sexual 'language' requires a commitment to lifelong fidelity.
To give your body to another person
symbolizes the total gift of yourself to that person.
But if you are not married,
you are admitting that you might change your mind in the future.
Total self-giving would then be absent.
Without the bond of marriage, sexual relations are a lie....
Do not be deceived by the empty words of those
who ridicule chastity or your capacity for self-control."*

Saint John Paul II to the Youth in Uganda

Chapter III

Love Worthy of the Human Person: Living Within the Truth

Introduction

St. John Paul II spent much of his adult life reflecting on the meaning of human love and sharing his reflections with young people and married couples. He once wrote:

> Man cannot live without love. He remains a being that is incomprehensible for himself, his life is senseless, if love is not revealed to him, if he does not encounter love, if he does not experience it and make it his own, if he does not participate intimately in it....[1]

In our study of the Language of the Body, we have actually been using St. John Paul II's reflections on human sexuality and the human person's vocation to love. We have begun to see that human love involves a true gift of self, and an openness to the gift of the other person. In marriage this gift is express in and through the body. The body is capable of "speaking" a language of self-giving love. This self-giving is personally fulfilling to the man and woman who give themselves to one another sexually, and is capable of bearing fruit in new life. We have also seen, however, that this self-giving is much more than sexual. The sexual act which unites a man and woman physically, in fact, is meant to be the sign and expression of a much deeper reality in their relationship: a spiritual union which is both life-long and life-giving. Living within the truth of such self-giving love involves both commitment and responsibility.

When human sexuality is "removed" from this context of genuine love and responsibility, its beauty and truth are easily distorted and misdirected.

Based on the truth we have come to understand about the nuptial meaning of the body and the language that is "spoken" by the body in the sexual act, we are better able to judge acts which are not in keeping with this truth. Only sexual acts which are ordered to the truth can express a love that is worthy of the human person.

Vocabulary

adultery	*divorce*	*annulment*
contraception	*fornication*	*abortifacient*

---

[1] St. John Paul II, *Redemptor Hominis*, 10.

Adultery

In view of the natural meaning of marriage as the union of one man and one woman in total self-giving to one another, most people have no difficulty understanding that **adultery** is a disordered sexual act. Adultery occurs when a man or woman, one or both of whom are married to someone else, engage in the sexual act with one another.

Because they are inherently linked, *both* meanings of the sexual act, that is, the unitive and the procreative, are violated in adultery:

- The act which is supposed to express total self-giving becomes a *lie*. The person who is married cannot *in truth* make a total gift of self to anyone other than to his or her spouse. One who is a husband or wife has already made a gift of self in marriage. The spouses have given themselves totally to one another, and so they do not "belong to themselves" any longer. Neither of them is free to give this gift of self to someone else. Thus, in an act of adultery a person is taking what does not belong to him (or to her) and giving it to another. Such an act violates the *unitive* meaning of marriage.

- The *procreative* meaning of the sexual act is also violated. The man and woman engaging in the adulterous act are not at all prepared to welcome the "fruit" of their act and to give the baby who might be conceived the home and nurturing environment he needs and deserves. Because of this, it is very likely that they would choose to disorder the sexual act even further, so as to prevent the conception of a child. Thus the sexual act which is intended to be a beautiful expression of self-giving within marriage is doubly distorted. Ultimately, only unhappiness can be the result.

Divorce & Remarriage

Though most would probably acknowledge the disordered nature of adultery, our society has increasingly become very accepting of **divorce** and remarriage, even in cases where a couple's marriage is valid and lawful. Despite this, Christians know that Jesus Himself teaches that, "Whoever divorces his wife (unless the marriage is unlawful) and marries another commits adultery."[2] Even one who is not a Christian, however, can see the truth of Jesus' words, simply based on the natural meaning of marriage that has been discussed above.

To make a marriage vow is a sacred and binding act, a deliberate and solemn pledge of one's word, which only death can end. As we have seen, the marriage vow is a particularly solemn promise, by which a man and woman mutually pledge their very selves as an exclusive and permanent gift, one to the other. Marriage is not an arrangement they make

---

NOTES

Adultery -- sexual intercourse between two persons, one of whom is married to someone else.

"Adultery ... signifies the violation of the unity in which man and woman can unite only as spouses so closely that they are 'one flesh'."

Saint John Paul II,
Theology of the Body

Divorce -- the legal dissolution of a marriage.

"Divorce ... something like cutting up a living body, as a kind of surgical operation. ... It is more like having both your legs cut off than it is like dissolving a business partnership or even deserting a regiment."

C.S. Lewis,
Mere Christianity

---

[2] Matthew 19:9

merely for a time, "until further notice."³ Civil divorce simply cannot "undo" a vow that has been legitimately made.

The conjugal act is the physical expression of the couple's marriage vow. That is, it is an act which expresses in and through their bodies exactly what they have promised by vow: *"I give myself totally to you, forever."* To divorce and remarry when the marriage is valid and lawful is to be unfaithful to the marital vow. Engaging in the sexual act within that "second marriage" cannot be a truthful expression of exclusive and permanent self-giving. It is actually the expression of what could be called a sexual lie.

It is important to note, however, that divorce *itself* is not necessarily ethically wrong. There may be situations of physical or psychological abuse or repeated unfaithfulness that require the married couple to live apart from one another either for a time or indefinitely. Such a living apart might require that they obtain a civil divorce for reasons of safety, or in order to separate their finances and material possessions. Although civil authorities understand a divorce to mean that the marriage has come to an end, anyone who understands the nature of marriage knows that it is not possible for a valid, lawful marriage to end until one of the spouses dies.

Civil divorce, then, sometimes occurs when a married couple is undergoing very hard times, so hard, in fact, that they need legally to live apart from one another, *as if* they were not married. Although it is very unfortunate for a marriage to be in this condition, it is not necessarily sinful for a married couple to be in such a state. It is only sinful to the degree that the spouses bear any responsibility for it.

When a marriage is valid and lawful, re-marriage after a civil divorce violates not only the "one-flesh union" of the married couple. It also harms the children who have come into existence from their union. Children forever remain a *living embodiment* of their parents' marital union, and when parents are not faithful to that union, children suffer. They suffer *at least* in the fact that they do not enjoy the presence of both of their parents involved in their lives on a daily basis. They suffer also because they are not able to see their mother and father faithfully loving one another.

---

³ *Catechism of the Catholic Church*, #1646.

NOTES

"Divorce or adultery or serial polygamy stand as statements that the partner isn't irreplaceable after all. And in so saying, the inviolable dignity of the other is violated."

Mark Lowery

"The divorce rate per 1000 married women is nearly double that of 1960, but down from the all-time high of 22.6 in the early 1980s. ... Almost 50% of all marriages in the United States will end in divorce or separation. Researchers estimate that 41 percent of all first marriages end in divorce." (As of 2014, the latest year of data from the CDC)

Wilkinson & Finkbeiner
"Divorce Statistics: Over 115 Studies, Facts and Rates for 2018"

The Human Person ~ Dignity Beyond Compare

NOTES

Annulment -- a judgment by the Catholic Church that an apparent marriage was in fact never a true marital covenant.

What is an Annulment?

An **annulment** is <u>not</u> the same thing as a divorce. A divorce is a claim by some human beings that a valid marriage has come to an end. An annulment is a judgment by the Catholic Church that what *appeared* to be a marriage was in fact never a true marital covenant. In other words, there was something *essential* missing *from the beginning* of what appeared to be a marriage, and thus the marriage never truly took place. In such a case, the Catholic Church issues a "declaration of nullity," a statement of the fact that there was not a marriage in the first place.

Because the matter is such an important one, issuing a declaration of nullity requires a judicial investigation before a Church tribunal. This court of the Church determines, based of the evidence gathered, whether or not it has been sufficiently proven that the bond of marriage never existed. A judgment of nullity by one Church court must be confirmed by a higher Church court before the persons involved are free from the former (invalid) bond and able to marry someone else. If the two courts do not agree in their judgment, or if one of the persons wants to appeal the decisions, the case can go to the Roman Rota, the highest appeal court of the Church.

When a petition for a declaration of nullity is presented to a tribunal, the one petitioning is assigned an advocate to plead his or her case. An official of the tribunal whose mission it is to ensure that the arguments in favor of the validity of the marriage are not neglected is appointed as the "Defender of the Bond." A party who opposes nullity can also request an advocate.

The Church is careful to protect the "right of defense" of both parties. They are properly informed of the grounds of nullity proposed and are allowed to give evidence and present witnesses.

Some of the factors that can lead to the judgment that an apparent marital bond was nonexistent or null would be any of the following:

- Impediments such as insufficient legal age or an existing marital bond.

- One of the persons refused to be open to having children or to being faithful until death.

- One purposefully deceived the other about some quality important to marriage, such as the fact that he or she is sterile.

- One lacked the psychological ability to give free consent to marriage vows.

If a marriage is annulled, then both persons are free to marry because the apparent marriage was found to be nonexistent. Because there had been a valid civil marriage contract, however, and the spouses were legally considered to be married, the children of an annulled marriage are legitimate.

Part II -- Chapter III
LOVE WORTHY OF THE HUMAN PERSON

Study Guide Questions:

1. What is adultery?
2. How does adultery violate the two meanings of the sexual act?
3. Divorce itself is not necessarily sinful. Explain.
4. How is divorce and remarriage similar to adultery?
5. In what ways do children always suffer when their parents divorce?
6. How does an annulment differ from a divorce?

CASES IN POINT

#1 -- Christie is a young woman in her early 20's. She remembers when she was growing up how her parents would often argue. Many of her friends' parents had already divorced or were in the process. Christie tells how she and her three sisters thought that surely their parents would also divorce. She remembers one day asking her mother about it. Christie said, "Mom, why don't you just divorce Dad since you two can't get along?" Christie will never forget her Mom's response: "Honey, underneath the appearances that you see of your father, there is a man I dearly love and I intend to love him all the days of my life." Ten years later, reflecting back on this incident, Christie recalls the impact her Mother's words had on her. To this day, her parents remain living together as husband and wife, and they are currently getting along rather well, she says.

♦ *Author Diane Medved speaks to the experience of 75% of divorced people who would not now recommend divorce to others. They wish they had not jumped so quickly out of marriage. What do you think enabled Christie's parents to persevere in their marital commitment?*

* * * * *

#2 -- Mark remembers how unhappy his parents were with each other when he was growing up. There was often great tension in the house, and words between them were scarce. Mark and his brothers tried to spend as much time out of the house as they could. One morning when his Dad didn't return home after being out all night, Mark got so concerned that he rode his bike by his Dad's office on his way to school. When he peeked in the window to see if his Dad was there, his father saw him and motioned for him to come in. Mark will never forget the conversation they had that day: "Dad said that he didn't know why Mom gets so suspicious and angry with him, but at times like that it makes him so angry that he needs to get away. When that happens, Dad said that he comes here to his office and sleeps on the couch. When I asked him if he and Mom would divorce, his eyes watered and he said, 'Listen to me, son. Marriage has its highs and lows. Your

NOTES

"A permanent and exclusive union states boldly that the other is not an object that can be replaced or substituted, but a person of inviolable worth."

Mark Lowery

NOTES

"It is through devotion, effort and sacrifice, especially when made for the sake of others, that people grow and mature most; that way each one comes out of himself or herself and rises above self. Loyalty to the commitment of married life -- to be mutually faithful, to persevere in this fidelity until death, and to have and rear children -- contributes more than anything else to the true good of the spouses."

Cormac Burke

Mom and I are at a low point right now, but we'll come out of it. I love your Mother, and we both love you kids. So we will work our way out of the slump we're in. Our marriage has been a challenge, but it's been good, and I'm in for the long haul. You can count on me.'"

Cf. "What If They Tough It Out?", *Time*, September 25, 2000, p. 88.

- *What did Mark's Dad teach him about marriage?*

* * * * *

#3 -- "The promise made when I am in love and because I am in love, to be true to the beloved as long as I live, commits one to being true even if I cease to be in love. A promise must be about things that I can do, about actions: no one can promise to go on feeling in a certain way. He might as well promise never to have a headache or always to feel hungry. But what, it may be asked, is the use of keeping two people together if they are no longer in love? There are several sound, social reasons: to provide a home for their children, to protect the woman from being dropped whenever the man is tired of her."

C.S. Lewis, *Mere Christianity*, pp. 83-4

- *What exactly is it that married couples promise to one another? Is it something they are truly able to do?*

- *Can you think of other reasons why two people joined in marriage ought to stay together if they are no longer emotionally in love?*

* * * * *

#4 -- Phil and Marge had been married for 20 years when Phil decided he wanted "a change." He was tired of his lifestyle and didn't want the responsibility of raising their three children. He decided to divorce Marge and marry a younger woman (Betty) whom he had met through his work. Phil and Betty enjoyed four fun-loving years together traveling around the world before Phil was diagnosed with pancreatic cancer. The doctor gave him only 6 months to live. Because Betty did not want to care for a dying man, she quickly divorced Phil and moved on with her life. Phil appealed to Marge to forgive him and take him back. Marge did forgive him, and she nursed Phil until the day of his death.

- *Should Marge have taken Phil back? Explain.*

* * * * *

#5 -- Chuck divorced Ellen after 12 years of marriage because he had found another woman. He left Ellen with their four children. Ellen found a job and struggled to make ends meet as she continued to raise their children, ultimately putting all of them through college. She remained faithful to Chuck throughout it all: she never dated another man and never remarried.

- *What lessons about marriage do you think Ellen's children learned from their parents?*

Fornication

Just as adultery violates the *truth* of the sexual act, a sexual lie is also told when a man and woman who are not married engage in the sexual act. We refer to this distorted act as an act of **fornication**. We could also refer to it as *pre-marital* or *non-marital* sex. Such an act is disordered because it violates both the divine and the natural law. For our purposes here, we will examine how it violates the natural law. It does so in four ways:

First, *fornication* is a sexual lie. The two people engaging in the act are saying with their bodies something which is not true. Their bodies are saying, "I give myself totally to you," but their minds are saying, "not really." Through pre-marital sex the couple engages in an act which, in itself, is supposed to express total self-giving, but they refuse to give all of themselves, spiritual as well as physical. In so doing, they deny the *unitive* meaning of the conjugal act.

Second, in *fornicating*, a person belittles himself because he is giving himself to another without adequate assurance that the other is worthy of such a trust.

Third, in *fornicating*, a person belittles the other person by receiving him/her without making the necessary commitment to safeguard his/her good.

You say that you and David love each other, but what does it really mean to love someone? Love means wanting what's best for the other person. How do you know when somebody really loves you? When that somebody wants what is best for your welfare, your happiness. Not just your happiness at this moment, but in the future as well.

Is sex between unmarried persons really an act of love? Is it truly what's best for you and the other person, now and in the future? What are the dangers? Pregnancy is one. Sexually transmitted diseases is another. A third is emotional hurt, which can last for years after a break-up and is usually more severe if sex was involved. Then there are spiritual consequences -- your relationship with God. So ask yourself: Can two people really claim to love each other if they're willing to gamble with each other's health, life, happiness, and spiritual welfare?

True love will never put the other in danger of having to face consequences like these, consequences that could change your lives forever. If it's love, you'll wait.[4]

Fourth, in *fornicating*, a person disregards the rights of the child

---

[4] Tom and Judy Lickona, "How to Tell Your Children the Truth About Sex," *New Oxford Review*, November, 1996, p. 24.

NOTES

Fornication -- the sexual act between two persons who are not married.

"Only a permanent as well as exclusive union befits or is commensurate with the dignity of each spouse."
  Mark Lowery

"The difference between prostitution and love is that in the former there is the offering of the body without the soul. True love demands that the will to love should precede the act of possession."
  Fulton J. Sheen
  The World's First Love, p. 161

"Living together in a sexual relationship before marriage is a three-fold lie of unity, life and love. It says the couples' lives are one when they are not; it says they are ready for children when they are not; and it says they love one another, even while the couple is destroying (one another's) relationship with God."
  Father Jerome W. Fasano

The Human Person ~ Dignity Beyond Compare

NOTES

"The child ... is given a tremendous security by the permanent commitment of his parents."
    Mark Lowery

"Marriage used to be the principal pathway into parenthood, but that is changing. About a third of all children and more than two-thirds of African-American children are born out of wedlock. In addition, there has also been an 850% increase in the number of cohabitating couples who live with children."
    R. Albert Mohler, Jr.

"Children raised ... without the benefit of a married mother and father are two to three times more likely to experience serious negative life outcomes such as imprisonment, depression, teenage pregnancy, and high school failure...."
    The Witherspoon Institute

"The new report shows that from 2017-2018, there were increases in the three most commonly reported STDs:
- There were more than 15,000 syphilis cases. The number of primary and secondary syphilis cases, the most infectious stages of syphilis, increased 14 percent to more than 35,000 cases, the highest number reported since 1991. ...
- Gonorrhea increased 5 percent to more than 580,000 casesm the highest number reported since 1991.
- Chlamydia increased 3 percent to more than 1. million cases, the most ever reported to CDC."

"New CDC Report: STDs Continue to Rise in the U.S."
CDC Newsroom, Oct. 8, 2019

182.

---

that can be conceived in the act. Every child has a natural right to be born and raised in the secure and loving atmosphere of his parents' committed love. The fornicating couple is thinking only of themselves and not of the other person who will suffer from their disordered act. Fornication violates the *procreative* meaning of the sexual act.

Disordered acts have bad effects!

Disordered acts have bad effects. Let's look at some of the bad effects that come from fornication.

1. **Out-of-wedlock births** hit an appalling high in 2012 when 41% of the babies born in the United States were delivered to unwed mothers. In 2018, that percentage had dropped to 39.6%, but so too had the overall birth rate dropped.[5] Most of these children will spend the majority of their childhood in a single parent home. This denies the children the opportunity to have their two parents present daily to secure their material and emotional well being. "Children whose parents fail to get and stay married are at increased risk of poverty, dependency, substance abuse, educational failure, juvenile delinquency, early unwed pregnancy, and a host of other destructive behaviors."[6]

These out-of-wedlock births also have negative consequences for the mothers and fathers. Unmarried women who bear children are significantly more likely to experience poverty, to drop out of high school, and to have difficulty finding a good marital partner. Unmarried men who father children are significantly more likely to fail educationally, to earn less, and to have difficulty finding a good marital partner.[7]

2. Over **61 million abortions** in the United States since 1973. Currently, about 24% of U.S. women will have an abortion by age 45. More than half of all U.S. women having abortions in 2014 were in their 20s; adolescets made up 12% of all abortions. Women who have never married and are not cohabiting account for 45% of all abortions.[8]

3. An **explosion of sexually transmitted infections (STI).** There are about 25 sexually transmitted infections today. Prior to 1960 there were only two. The rates of STIs reached an all-time high in 2018 among both sexes. People aged 15-24 account for nearly half of the new cases of STI's each year.[9]

---

[5] The National Center for Health Statistics

[6] The Witherspoon Institute, pp. 13, 25.

[7] Ibid., p. 25.

[8] Guttmacher Institute, 2017, www.guttmacher.org

[9] U.S. Department of Health and Human Services, "Sexually Transmitted Diseases," 2020.

Part II -- Chapter III
LOVE WORTHY OF THE HUMAN PERSON

4. **Destructive psychological consequences** of temporary sexual relationships. Many people deeply regret their sexual involvements and feel profound guilt concerning them. These are some of the problems they have encountered because of them: lowered self-esteem; a despairing sense of having been used; the self-contempt for having been a user; the embarrassment of being known as one who lacks true integrity; the unease of having to lie and sneak around in order to hide one's sexual activities; the difficulty of breaking the cycle of compulsive sexual behavior; the self-hatred of repeatedly seeking people to seduce in order to bolster up one's fading self-image.[10]

Often times people feel that they are not as free to end a relationship they want to end because of the sexual intimacy they have experienced with the person. By its very nature the sexual act bonds the two people involved. That bond can become a "shackle" when one wants to move on. A priest alludes to this lack of freedom in the following statement:

> At the sacred moment when a couple pronounces their wedding vows, they need to be able to do so in perfect freedom; so much so that they should still feel free until they speak their vows to call it off. But if they have engaged in premarital sex, they are not really free. From my experience of officiating at weddings, there is something special present at the marriage of those couples who have not slept or lived together. That quality stems precisely from the sense of freedom the couple still possesses.[11]

5. **Flashbacks / comparisons / lack of trust in future marriages.** If a person has engaged in pre-marital sexual relations with someone other than his spouse, he should not be surprised when he suddenly experiences a flashback of that previous experience. The flashback could likely come at a time when he least wants it. A person might also find himself easily, and beyond his control, comparing his spouse with someone with whom he had had a previous experience.

Another experience a person could easily have if he has engaged in premarital sex is a lack of trust in his future marriage. A person could easily think the following: "I know how Bill was willing to sneak around and lie in order to be with me sexually, I wonder if he is doing the same thing now?" Compare that line of thinking with what might go through the mind of spouses who did not engage in premarital sex: "I know how much Bill wanted to be with me sexually before we were married, but he simply would not do it because he knew that it was wrong and that it could harm me in some way. He refused to sneak around and lie. I know that I can trust him now!"

NOTES

"I realize now that this is a very big step in a girl's life. After you've done it, things are never the same. Sex is not for entertainment. It should be a commitment. My advice to other girls is to be smart and save yourself for someone you wouldn't mind spending the rest of your life with."
Tom and Judy Lickona

"Those who stay chaste and bond themselves with one person only bring a simplicity to the relationship. There is no excess baggage, no memories of past affairs, no past histories to deal with."
Julia Duin

"Premarital sex can lead to boredom with married sex, because before marriage you conditioned your body to respond to the forbidden aspect of sex, no longer present after marriage."
Tom and Judy Lickona

"There is no greater gift that a man and a woman can give each other on their wedding night than the gift of their virginity. And it's a gift you can give only once."
Molly Kelly

---
[10] Tom and Judy Lickona, p. 25.
[11] Ibid., p. 28.

NOTES

6. **Greater chance of divorce in marriage.** Some people have the false idea that living together before marriage can serve as a kind of "trial marriage" that will help them determine whether or not they are compatible. This, they claim, will help them to know each other better and to be sure that they want to spend the rest of their lives together. Contrary to this way of thinking, however, the evidence proves otherwise: premarital sexual relations make it harder, not easier, to discern a marital partner. Study after study confirms the fact that those who live together before marriage are more likely to divorce than those who do not.[12]

One reason some people want a "trial marriage" is because they compare making the commitment to marry with making other major life decisions, like buying a car. "If we test-drive a car, why can't we test-drive the marriage?" they ask. The problem with this way of thinking is that they are trying to deal with a *person* as they would deal with an *object* like a car. If the object is not suitable, they discard it. Or if the car does not run smoothly, then they do not invest further in it. This conditional approach, however, is the opposite of what marriage requires. The marital commitment is absolute and unconditional: *"No matter what, I will love you forever!"*

"The person who does not decide to love forever will find it very difficult to really love for even one day."

St. John Paul II,
The Love Within Families

"Most studies find that cohabiting couples who go on to marry face a higher risk of divorce, compared to couples who marry without cohabiting."

The Witherspoon Institute

A Link between Premarital Sex and the Divorce Rate?[13]

• Taking part in a sexual relationship which is dissoluble, temporary and closed to life will not prepare a person for a sexual relationship which demands indissolubility, life-long fidelity, and an openness to life.

• Engaging in gravely disordered acts and inviting one's partner to do so as well does not prepare these people to love one another *authentically*, that is, with a readiness to sacrifice everything for the other's good.

• Accepting sex outside of marriage inclines a person to adultery once he marries, and adultery is one of the main causes of divorce.

• Establishing a pattern of *self-indulgence* through premarital sex ill prepares a person for the *self-giving* and *self-sacrifice* required in a healthy marital relationship.

• Being sexually intimate with another clouds a person's judgment about his or her *objective* value.

• Doing without the fullness of God's grace in life because of gravely sinful acts makes it impossible for a person to love another person as marriage requires -- in imitation of Christ Jesus.

---

12 Tom and Judy Lickona, p. 27.
13 Christopher West, *Good News about Sex & Marriage*, p. 72.

Part II -- Chapter III
LOVE WORTHY OF THE HUMAN PERSON

Study Guide Questions:

1. *In what ways is fornication a disordered act?*

2. *How does fornication violate the procreative meaning of the sexual act, especially if the couple intends to love the child they conceive?*

3. *Why are out-of-wedlock births considered to be problematic?*

4. *What is meant by the destructive psychological consequences of fornication?*

5. *What is harmful about having sexual flashbacks or making comparisons between sexual partners?*

6. *Why is it reasonable to think that those who engage in premarital sex stand a greater chance of divorcing once they marry?*

NOTES

CASES IN POINT

#1 -- Compare and contrast the following two scenarios:

a) Tara and Nick are engaged to be married in another two months. They have bought a new house and at present are living in it together. In a letter to one of her friends, Tara writes, "Oh, how I am looking forward to the BIG DAY!

b) Danielle and Paul have been dating seriously for about a year, and they, too, have set the date for their wedding, three months away. Although they are anxious to begin living life together as husband and wife, they are firmly committed to avoiding any sexual involvement with each other until the day of their wedding. Danielle tells her friends, "I want my wedding day to be the day when *in truth*, Paul and I become *one*, *totally* and *forever*."

♦ *Both Tara and Danielle are looking forward to their weddings. How do you think they differ in regard to what they are anticipating?*

♦ *Which of the two couples, in your opinion, will be better prepared for marriage? Explain your answer.*

NOTES

"It only stands to reason that those engaging in the conjugal act must provide a context within which the potential child can be nurtured, and this context above all else entails a permanent commitment between those using their generative faculties in the conjugal act. Without this permanence, the dignity of the child is violated."

Mark Lowery

"Contraception contradicts the *truth* of conjugal love."

St. John Paul II,
9/17/83

#2 -- Jenny became pregnant when she was dating Mike during their college years. Mike said that he intended to marry Jenny once the baby was born and that all would be well for the three of them then. Once baby Sarah was born, however, Mike found out that Jenny had changed her mind about marrying him. Mike tried to be positive after hearing the news. He insisted to his friends that he would still look after his daughter. As the months passed on, however, Jenny revealed to Mike that she intended to marry another man and that Sarah would not need two dads. She suggested that Mike move on with his life. For the good of his daughter, Mike decided to get out of Sarah's life. He moved to another state and has not seen her since.

- *How has Sarah been harmed by her parents' premarital act of sexual intercourse?*

- *Do you think it would have been a good idea for Jenny and Mike to marry <u>because</u> they had conceived a child together, that is, for the good of the baby? Explain.*

- *Looking as we are from the "outside" at Jenny and Mike's situation, can you offer a good solution to their problem?*

Contraception

Contraception is yet another way that people use their bodies sexually to lie to each other. The lie is not difficult to see once we rightly understand the meaning of the sexual act.

As we have already noted, sexual intercourse is an act of total mutual self-giving wherein the man and woman are engaging in an act that naturally means *"I give myself totally to you."* In this act, the married couple use their bodies to say to one another, *"I am wholly yours; I give myself totally to you, and I receive you totally."* Cormac Burke explains why this act is the most significant expression of affection between the spouses:

> ... what happens in that marital encounter, ... is not just a touch, not a mere sensation, however intense, but a *communication*, an offer and acceptance, an exchange of something that uniquely represents the gift of oneself and the union of two selves. ... Giving one's seed is much more significant, and in particular is much more real, than giving one's heart. 'I am yours, I give you my heart; here, take it,' remains mere poetry, to which no physical gesture can give true body. But, 'I am yours; I give you my seed; here, take it,' is not poetry, it is love. It is conjugal love embodied in a unique and privileged physical action whereby intimacy is expressed -- 'I give you what I give no one' -- and union is

achieved: 'Take what I have to give. This will be a new me. United to you, to what you have to give -- to your seed -- this will be a new 'you-and-me,' fruit of our mutual knowledge and love.'[14]

When the couple chooses to contracept their act of sexual intercourse, however, they are doing something that makes this natural message untrue. Their bodies engage in the act that means total self-giving, yet they have done something precisely so that they <u>cannot</u> give themselves totally. Instead of accepting each other totally, the contracepting spouses reject a part of each other. They reject each other's fertility.

Now it is true that the couple might *feel as if* they are giving themselves totally while using contraceptives, but objectively speaking they are not. In fact, the point of using contraceptives is precisely to *withhold* something of their sexual capacity from one another: the woman, her egg and the man, his seed. They are doing something deliberately to prevent the union of egg and sperm.

This, then, is the disorder that contraception brings about: It takes the act that naturally means total self-giving and uses it to reject each other's fertility. The two persons do not become one flesh, one sexual organism, although they go through the motions of doing so. Neither the unitive nor the procreative aspect of the sexual act is achieved.

The couple engaging in a contracepted sexual act are actually contradicting themselves. With their bodies they are engaging in an act which says, "We are uniting as one (sexual organism)." But they have done something precisely so that they do not unite as one. They do not really want to unite sexually as one because if they do, they know that a child might come from their union.

A Clarifying Example

Perhaps an example might help to clarify the point about contraceptive intercourse. Imagine a young man and woman who love each other and are very gifted with beautiful singing voices. They decide to sing a duet together to express their love for each other. When they open their mouths to begin the song, however, no sound of music passes their lips. Their mouths and tongues move *as if* they were singing to each other, but they do **not** let their vocal chords produce any intelligible sound.

Contraceptive intercourse is very much like this silent duet. The couple acts as if they are giving themselves to each other sexually, but they refuse to let their bodies communicate sexually with one another. "They go through the motions of a love-song, but there is no *song*."[15]

Because contraception is now so widely accepted in our culture,

---

NOTES

"True conjugal intercourse unites. Contraception separates...."
— Cormac Burke

"Contraceptive intercourse ... is disfigured body-language; it expresses a rejection of the other."
— Cormac Burke

"Contraception is in fact not just an action without meaning; it is an action that contradicts the essential meaning which true conjugal intercourse should have as signifying total and unconditional self-donation."
— Cormac Burke

"The conjugal act has been turned into a different kind of act, an act that is rendered incapable of new life, and even an act incapable of fully uniting the two people involved because they are now withholding a substantial part of who they are."
— Mark Lowery

"Contraception in fact turns the marital act *into self-deception or into a lie*."
— Cormac Burke

---

[14] Cormac Burke, "Marriage and Contraception."
[15] Ibid.

The Human Person ~ Dignity Beyond Compare

NOTES

a couple may not be aware of the fact that their use of contraception violates the truth of the sexual act. Nor may they be aware of its bad effects. They may have legitimate reasons for wishing to limit, at least for a time, the size of their family. Perhaps these are related to financial circumstances, poor health of one of the spouses, or other serious conditions. If such situations arise in a marriage, a couple should know that there is an effective and morally good method for regulating the conception of children, without using the disordered means of contraception.

This legitimate method, known as Natural Family Planning, simply requires periodic abstinence from sexual intercourse during that time within the wife's cycle when she is able to conceive a child. The couple does nothing to prevent conception whenever they engage in the sexual act. They simply do not engage in the sexual act at all during the time of the month when it is possible for the wife to conceive.

This natural method of regulating conception enables the couple to grow together in a spirit of mutual respect and self-sacrifice, while drawing them to express their love for one another in other ways during the time when they are abstaining from sexual intercourse. Their willingness to make this sacrifice also becomes a means of self-giving.

Natural Family Planning (NFP)

NFP uses a woman's knowledge of her own body to *scientifically* determine whether or not she is fertile. By "reading" the signs of her body, a woman can know when she has a good chance of conceiving a child through the sexual act. Some married couples who have difficulty conceiving a child use this knowledge in order to improve their chances of conceiving. Other use the knowledge to abstain from the sexual act in order not to conceive a child.

A couple using NFP might have the same *intention* as does a couple using contraception. The intention not to conceive a child -- because of some serious circumstances -- is not a problem. A couple is not required to conceive as many children as they physically can. Rather, in recognizing that children are a great good, couples are encouraged to be as generous as they can be in bringing forth new life.

What then is the difference between using NFP and using contraceptives? The difference lies in the *acts*. A couple using NFP never disorders the sexual act. Whenever they have sexual intercourse, they allow their bodies to "speak" honestly, for they truly are giving themselves totally to each other. They hold nothing back from one another when engaging in an act that means *total* self-giving. They give all that they have to give at that time. In so doing, they form one sexual whole. If they are unwilling to conceive a child for some serious reason, then they do not engage in the sexual act. While it is true that NFP can be used selfishly by couples who do not have serious reason to avoid conceiving a child, the problem here is not with NFP itself but with their selfish use of it.

The act of a couple contracepting their sexual intercourse is very different. Their act always involves disordering the sexual act because they do something to make the act not work. They do not give themselves totally to one another although they are engaging in an act that means total self-giving. Thus, they use their bodies to speak a lie. Their sexual lie mars the beauty of the marital act.

Disordered acts have bad effects. The disordered act of contracepting has bad physical, marital, and societal effects.

Physical Bad Effects

> **Disordered acts have bad effects!**

It is not surprising that when we try to make a well-functioning bodily system not work, we might cause some other problems. This is exactly what happens with contraceptive use. As one doctor explains:

> "In modern medicine, contraception is the only 'treatment' that is given because the patient is in fact healthy. A well-functioning system is rendered malfunctional by chemical or mechanical means.... There is no other example in medicine where a physician is permitted intentionally to damage healthy tissue to prevent its function."[16]

A quick look at some of the more popular forms of contraceptives will illustrate the doctor's point.

A **vasectomy** and **tubal ligation** permanently damage normally functioning tissues in the male and female. Other forms like **intra-uterine devices** (IUDs) and barrier methods involve the use of non-sterile foreign bodies within the sterile environment of the human body, thus increasing the possibility of infection and disease.

The IUD also functions as an **abortifacient**. It is put in a woman's uterus not to stop conception, but to stop the already conceived human being from implanting in his mother's womb.

There are also contraceptive jellies that act as **spermicides** (chemicals that "kill the sperm"). Sometimes these jellies only maim the sperm and so can harm the child who is conceived from the deformed sperm.

Finally, there is "**The Pill**," the most well-known of the contraceptives. The Pill is a chemical contraceptive which uses hormones to stop a woman's ovaries from releasing eggs. These hormones also make the lining of her uterus incapable of receiving and properly nourishing an embryo, if one is conceived. When the pill has this effect, it is acting as an abortifacient.

Some significant physical side effects of using the Pill are the following: blood clotting, strokes, increased infertility, and cancer. The day-to-day minor side effects women experience in using the Pill are increased irritability, propensity for depression, and weight gain.

---

[16] Sister Mary Diana Dreger, M.D. "Talking about contraception: The Catholic physician in the exam room." *Linacre Quarterly.*

Part II -- Chapter III
LOVE WORTHY OF THE HUMAN PERSON

NOTES

"The link between hormonal contraceptives and breast cancer has been known for over thirty years.... The largest metaanalysis (54 studies with over 150,000 women) found that women who use oral contraceptives before age 20 have almost double the risk of developing breast cancer before age 30, compared to women who do not use them as teens."
　　　　Susan E. Wills,
　　　　November, 2011

A study which followed 1.8 million Danish women for more than a decade found that newer hormonal contraceptives have a similar link to breast cancer as did those their mothers used. The same elevated risk is present no matter the formulation.
The New York Times, 12/6/2017

Vasectomy -- a surgical procedure which severs and seals a man's vas deferens tubes to prevent sperm from entering the seminal stream.

Tubal ligation -- the severing or blocking of a woman's fallopian tubes to disrupt the movement of the egg to the uterus for fertilization.

Intra-uterine devices -- foreign bodies introduced into a woman's uterus to prevent implantation of the human embryo.

Abortifacient -- a substance or device used to induce abortions.

Spermicides -- substances inserted vaginally prior to intercourse to prevent pregnancy by killing the sperm.

The Pill -- a chemical contraceptive which uses the hormones estrogen and progesterone to suppress a woman's normal cycle.

Marital Bad Effects

Use of contraceptives has negatively affected marriage. Between 1960 and 1980, the time immediately following the social acceptance of widespread contraceptive use, the divorce rate more than doubled in the United States, from about 20 to 45% of all first marriages.[17] There are reasons to think that contraceptive use played a significant part in this increase in divorce.

First, whether a couple is aware of the fact or not, contraception actually degrades the sexual act. The sexual act should be the most significant expression of marital love because it is a communication, an offer, an acceptance and an exchange of something that uniquely represents the mutual gift of the spouses, that is, the union of the two persons through surrendering to one another their capacity to transmit human life. For the woman, this entails the gift of her egg; for the man, that of his seed. If egg and seed unite and develop in a healthy way, a new human life, the fruit of their union, comes into existence. Through contraception, however, something is deliberately done to prevent this union from taking place. When the procreative end of sexual intercourse is thwarted in this way, its authentic unitive end is also negated. The act that was designed to symbolize their total self-gift risks becoming merely an exchange of pleasure.

Second, contraception could make it easier for a spouse to give in to the temptation to infidelity. Using contraceptives, they need not consider to worry about whether an adulterous act will bear fruit in the conception of a child. Sadly, few married couples remain together after adultery occurs.

Third, use of contraceptives makes it possible for the married couple to have fewer children or to delay having children until later in marriage, whether or not they have serious reasons for doing so. The attitude can easily arise that babies are an obstacle to growth in the married couple's relationship, a hindrance to their marriage, especially in the early years -- and even simply an "inconvenience." Actually, however, children are a help to their parents' relationship and to their fidelity in marriage. This is so especially in the early years, when the original emotional high begins to lessen and husband and wife more readily notice one another's faults. If they are focused together on caring for their chil-

---

NOTES

"When the idea that 'I may become a father'/'I may become a mother' is totally rejected in the mind and will of husband and wife, nothing is left of the marital relationship, objectively speaking, except mere sexual enjoyment. One person becomes an object of use for another person, which is incompatible with the personalistic norm."

Saint John Paul II, *Love and Responsibility*

"Contraceptives convey the message that while sexual intercourse is desired, there is no real desire for a permanent bond with the other person. The possibility of an everlasting bond has been willfully removed from the very act designed to best express the desire for such a relationship."

Janet Smith

"Contraceptives have made sexual indulgence far less costly within marriage and far safer outside it than ever before, and public opinion is less hostile to illicit unions and even to perversion than it has been since Pagan times."

C.S. Lewis

---

[17] The Witherspoon Institute, p. 24.
[18] Cf, Janet Smith, "Contraceptives are Abusive to Women."

dren, the tendency to pay undue attention to each other's weaknesses is more likely to diminish, for they are centered in the common purpose of loving and raising their children.[18]

Fourth, there is something about caring for their children that helps parents to become better people. This is probably the case because children tend to be self-centered and are completely dependent upon their parents. Parents, then, are naturally challenged to be other-centered, to mature, and to deny themselves for the good of their children.

Fifth, with fewer children at home, women are able to be more independent. They can have jobs outside the home and earn their own income. When difficulties arise within the marriage, they find it easier now to walk away rather then trying to work things out. Men, too, find it easier to walk away because their wives are not as dependent upon them financially.

Sixth, in cases when there is serious need to limit the conception of children, use of contraceptives makes it easier for a couple to communicate less than if they were using Natural Family Planning. Lack of communication is always harmful in a marriage. When using NFP, the couple must necessarily talk together about whether to engage in the sexual act during the wife's fertile period each month. As they do so, they will tend to discuss the deepest and most serious aspects of their married lives: whether they can legitimately manage to have another child right now; the pressures each of them is experiencing; about where their marriage is headed; about things that are really important to them, etc. This necessary communication helps them to become more and more sensitive and attentive to one another. Couples using contraceptives, on the other hand, need not have these kinds of conversations, having already made the decision not to have babies for a determined amount of time. Lack of such deep and personal communication is actually harmful to the marriage and to the growth of mature love between husband and wife.[19]

The evidence is abundant: The presence of children in a marriage becomes a natural help for husband and wife to remain faithful to their marital commitment.

Societal Effects

Widespread use of contraceptives has had a profoundly negative effect on American society. Contraceptives are, to a great extent, responsible for the onslaught of what has come to be known as the "sexual revolution." A revolution entails a complete change, a "turning around." Contraceptives have changed the way people view the sexual act. Before their use became so prevalent, people simply understood that a couple engaging in the sexual act might conceive a child. There was, in other words, a link in our thinking between the sexual act and the con-

---

[19] Ibid.

NOTES

"Children change us in a way we desperately need to be changed. They wake us up, they wet their diapers, they depend on us utterly. Willy-nilly, they knock us out of our selfish habits and force us to live sacrificially for others; they are the necessary and natural continuation of the shock to our selfishness that is initiated by matrimony itself. ...

In the natural course of things, if we willfully refuse the procreative meaning of union, then union is stunted. We are changed merely from a pair of selfish me's to a single selfish us."

J. Budziszewski

"When contraceptives became widely available, we had the igniting of the sexual revolution which separated having babies from having sex."

Janet Smith

ception of new life. With the use of contraceptives, however, people need not take this connection into account. Because of this, for many people, engaging in sexual intercourse has become "recreational," -- no longer linked to marriage and family, to the possibility of conception of babies or to life-long commitment.

This recreational view of the sexual act has led to a sharp increase in unwanted pregnancies, to millions of abortions, to epidemic venereal disease, to the prevalence of AIDS, and to a doubling in the divorce rate. Society is thus affected in deeply regrettable ways!

Use of contraceptives can "free" both the man and woman from considering the natural consequences of the sexual act, thus making it easier for men to use women as mere objects of their sexual enjoyment. This fact also helps to explain why extra-marital affairs and fornication are often the norm today rather than the exception.

Premature and **promiscuous** sexual activity prevents many people from establishing faithful marriages and strong families. Stable and secure family life nurtures the growth of persons who are more likely to be emotionally and psychologically healthy. A healthy society needs healthy families!

Children: the Supreme Gift!

Children are a living manifestation of their parents' two-in-one union. They are the supreme gift of marriage and a living embodiment of their mother and father's love for one another.

Sadly, there is an attitude today that considers children a burden, even a liability. True, children require their parents' time and attention. They can be very demanding, and their needs, especially when they are younger, challenge their parents to mature self-giving. Children not only need their parents' physical care, but they also depend on their parents to fill their emotional needs. Most importantly, children invite their parents to love them, to desire and provide what is good for them -- and, in so doing, at times even to deny themselves. For these very reasons, as well as others we have discussed in these pages, children are a tremendous good, a gift!

NOTES

"The public consequences of 'private' sexual behavior now threaten to destroy American society. In the past thirty-five years the federal government has spent four trillion dollars -- that is $4,000,000,000,000 -- on a variety of social programs designed to remedy ills which can be attributed directly or indirectly, to the misuse of human sexuality."
Philip F. Lawler

Promiscuous -- from the Latin *promiscuus* (mixed up); characterized by indiscriminate mingling or association, especially having sexual relations with a number of partners on a casual basis.

"Children are the supreme gift of marriage and contribute to the greatest extent to the good of the parents themselves."
Gaudium et Spes, #50

"... [P]arents themselves must be careful, when they limit conception, not to harm their families or society at large, which has an interest of its own in the optimum size of the family.
Saint John Paul II,
Love and Responsibility

Part II -- Chapter III
LOVE WORTHY OF THE HUMAN PERSON

NOTES

Children are living works of art. Often we hear of someone who wants to leave for posterity a gift that will embody something of themselves, and that will be of value to the next generation: perhaps an artistic creation, a piece of music, a beautiful painting, etc. There is no more beautiful gift for a married couple to leave for posterity than a human person they have brought into the world, one whom they have nurtured and raised to know, love and serve God. Such a person will be a tremendous blessing for the world.

Children are a joy for parents in their old age. When children are young, their parents are called upon to give and give and give of themselves in caring for them. When parents are old, however, then it is the children's turn to give and give and give of themselves -- emotionally, psychologically, financially and physically -- to their parents. What joy grandparents find not only in the love and care they receive from their own children but also in the playful visits they have with their grandchildren.

Lastly, children are an eternal gift. When parents die, they will not be able to take their material possessions into eternal life. The lives of the children they have borne and raised, however, are precious goods, gifts that are destined to endure beyond time and into eternity.

It is precisely because children are so great a good that a married couple should not, without serious reason, deliberately seek to avoid

"Children are a gift from God to their parents, a gift that helps them become adults and gives great meaning to their lives."
Janet Smith

"When a man and woman have a child together, it's an act that changes the cosmos: something has come into existence that will never pass out of existence; each soul is immortal and is destined for immortal life."
Janet Smith

"In 1950 there were 335 million Toddlers (0-4 age group) and only 131 million Elders (65-and-over age group). Due to very low birthrates in developed countries and declining birthrates in most developing countries, today Elders are rapidly closing the gap. After Toddlers peak at about 650 million, sometime between 2015 and 2020, 'for the first time in history, the [number of Toddlers] will deline' while Elders keep growing in number, reaching 714 million in 2020. By 2050, there will be 2.5 times more Elders than Toddlers -- a complete reversal of the 1950 demographics."
Susan E. Wills,
The Witherspoon Institute
November 9, 2011

NOTES

"Worldwide, birthrates have been halved in the past 50 years. There are now 59 nations, with 44% of the world's population, with below-replacement fertility."
LifeZone
2018

"Today's population growth is due to two factors: 1. higher fertility rates in the 1950s and 60s and 2. people are living longer than ever before. The thing to remember is that declining birthrates will equal a declining population worldwide that will be very rapid and almost impossible to reverse.

... Worldwide there are 6 million fewer children, 6 and under, today, than there were in 1990. If present trends continue, the United Nations estimates that by 2050 there will be 248 million fewer children in the world than there are now."
LifeZone
2018

"The US birth rate has hit a new record low, with women in nearly every age group giving birth to fewer babies than a year ago. New figures show just 60.2 babies were born in 2017 for every 1,000 women of 'childbearing' age -- a low not seen in the US since officials began charting national birth rates decades ago."
Peter Dockrill,
"US Fertility Rates Have Plummeted..."
Science Alert, May 21, 2018

---

conceiving them. It would be unreasonable for a married couple to give up so great a good as a child because they prefer some lesser goods.

Study Guide Questions:

1. What is the disorder in the contracepted sexual act?

2. Must a married couple always intend to conceive a child when they engage in the sexual act? Explain.

3. How does Natural Family Planning differ from the use of contraceptives?

4. What are some of the physical bad effects of contraceptives?

5. When a couple is using Natural Family Planning, how can their abstinence from sexual intercourse during the wife's fertile period actually be another form of self-giving?

6. What effects has contraception had on marriage?

7. What do we mean when we say that contraception is responsible for the start of the sexual revolution?

8. Why does a married couple need to have a serious reason if they intend to avoid conceiving a child?

9. Why are children a "supreme good"? Why is it considered a good thing that the care of children often demands self-denial and sacrifice on the part of the parents?

But Don't We Have a Population Problem?

"According to the U.N. Population Database, the world's population in 2010 will be 6,908,688,000. The land mass of Texas is 268,820 square miles (7,494,271,488,000 sq. ft.).

"So, divide 7,494,271,488,000 sq ft by 6,908,688,000 people, and you get 1084.76 sq ft/person. That's approximately a 33' x 33' plot of land for every person on the planet, enough space for a town house.

"Given an average four person family, every family would have a 66' x 66' plot of land, which would comfortably provide a single family home and yard -- and all of them fit on a landmass the size of Texas. Admittedly, it'd basically be one massive subdivision, but Texas is a tiny portion of the inhabitable Earth.

"Such an arrangement would leave the entire rest of the world vacant. There's plenty of space for humanity."

Population Research Institute

tad:

NFP Video
Jackie and Bobby Angel
▶ Why We Love Natural Family Planning

1. What is NFP? How effective is it when trying to avoid pregnancy?

   Using the womans body to know when you are fertile or infertile 99.8 percent

2. What do you think Jackie means by "charting," and how does it help?

   by calculating or putting data in a chart

3. How does NFP respect a woman's body?

   it teaches the couple about her body

4. How is NFP different from contraception?

   its like to study for a test, insted of cheating

5. What are the benefits of NFP?

   • less change for divorce
   • more intimacy

6. What's the challenge of NFP?

   women need to use self control when they want sex the most

Part II -- Chapter III
LOVE WORTHY OF THE HUMAN PERSON

CASES IN POINT

#1 -- A medical doctor speaks from her experience in treating patients:

"One young man, at the end of a visit with me, asked me if I could make a referral for him to get a vasectomy. I explained to him that this procedure was one that destroyed parts of his body that were working normally, that were actually healthy. I told him that if he asked me to cut off his finger because he didn't want it, even if there was nothing wrong with it, I could not support him in that request. ...

"Again when patients are taking oral contraceptives prescribed by others, or ask if I will prescribe them, I simply say that I can't support that kind of medication. My role as a healthcare provider is to support the proper functioning of their body. I would not give them a pill to stop the functioning of the heart or of the lungs, and so I cannot support them in using a pill that stops the function of their ovaries."

Sister Mary Diana Dreger, M.D. "Talking about contraception: The Catholic physician in the exam room," *Linacre Quarterly*.

- *Would you say that the doctor's comments are based only on her Catholic faith? Could a physician who had no faith at all, but whose reasons were based solely on his medical knowledge give the same response?*

- *What role do reason and faith play in knowing about the evil of contraception?*

* * * * *

#2 -- Carl Djerassi, the 85-year-old Austrian chemist whose research led to the development of the birth control pill, says he regrets the demographic catastrophe that has resulted from people using the contraceptive device to separate reproduction from sexuality. Today, Austria's population includes more people over age 65 than under 15. Djerassi said that his country will soon face an impossible situation as the working class becomes too small to support the needs of the elderly. (Erin Roach, "Pill Creator Regrets Population Decline," Baptist Press, 2/5/09)

In an address to his fellow Italian bishops, Cardinal Angelo Bagnasco lamented his nation's slow demographic suicide. He noted that over 50% of families today are without children, another quarter have only one child, while just 5.1% have three or more. (*Catholic World News*, 5/28/10)

- *Can you envision any other problems that might occur, or that are occurring, as a result of the declining population?*

NOTES

"The 2010 World Population Data Sheet ... says that a shrinking pool of working-age populations is jeopardizing social support and long-term health care programs for the elderly, and points to a decrease in the populations of developed countries. The report states that worldwide in 1950, there were 12 persons of working age for every person age 65 or older. By 2010, that number had shrunk to 9. By 2050, this elderly support ratio ... is projected to drop to 4."

Thaddeus M. Baklinski

"Social Security will spend more than it collects this year ... as it slides toward insolvency by 2034. Medicare's main trust fund is in even worse shape, scheduled to hit insolvency in 2026....

Republicans pointed to longer-term forces: the aging population and a relatively smaller share of people in the workforce to support those seniors."

The Washington Times,
June 5, 2018

Human Sexuality and Same-Sex Attraction

The occurrence of same-sex attraction is certainly not a new phenomenon. What is new in recent years, however, are the increasingly insistent claims that homosexual relationships are legitimate and normative. Such claims have called into question the very truth about the human person. From these claims have come the demand that marriage between persons of the same sex be legalized. The Supreme Court's legalization of "same-sex marriage" is a consequence of this. To accept homosexual relationships as a natural expression of human love, and to redefine marriage based on this acceptance, is to change radically the understanding of both marriage and family which have been at the core of human civilization for thousands of years. The ramifications of this decision by the Supreme Court are far-reaching.

In order to live rightly in the midst of this cultural upheaval, we have all the more need to think correctly about the human person and human sexuality. Human sexuality, as we have seen, has a meaning and a purpose, a design that is in keeping with the nature of the human person and the beauty and truth of human love. This truth can be recognized by human reason.

In discussing our identity as human persons who by nature are specifically either male or female, we have seen that our sexual incompleteness is actually a blessing. Through it, we experience the natural human need to go out of ourselves, to seek communion with an-other of the opposite sex. Our sexual identity, our "maleness" or "femaleness," is integral to who we are as persons, and is therefore a tremendous good.

As we have seen, the body expresses the person. The fact that this incompleteness is expressed in the sexual design of our bodies is the physical expression of a fundamental truth about our human nature, and therefore about each human person. This is the fact that we are relational beings, made to be involved in self-giving relationships with other persons. In order for this self-giving to be expressed sexually, the two persons involved must be of the opposite sex.

NOTES

"This universal definition of marriage as the union of a man and a woman is no historical coincidence. Marriage did not come about as a result of a political movement, discovery, disease, war, religious doctrine, or any other moving force of world history -- and certainly not as a result of a prehistoric decision to exclude gays and lesbians. It arose in the nature of things to meet a vital need: ensuring that children are conceived by a mother and father committed to raising them in the stable conditions of a lifelong relationship."
                Chief Justice John Roberts

"The majority's decision [in *Obergefell v. Hodges*] is an act of will, not legal judgment. The right it announces has no basis in the Constitution or this court's precedent."
                Chief Justice John Roberts

"Homosexuality was diagnosed and treated as a psychiatric illness -- abnormal behavior -- until 1973, when it was removed from the Diagnostic and Statistical Manual in psychiatry because of political pressure."
                Dr. Richard P. Fitzgibbons,
                Psychiatrist

It can sometimes happen that a man or woman may feel a strong physical and emotional attraction toward a person of the same sex. This same-sex attraction, or homosexual inclination, may be very real and deeply felt. The situation of one who feels this inclination can be the source of a difficult personal struggle, and he or she may feel isolated and alone. At the same time, however, freely choosing to act on these feelings and to engage in sexual activity has serious moral ramifications. Such acts distort the beautiful message of self-giving love which the human body is naturally designed to offer in and through the sexual act. It is important to understand this correctly and with sensitivity, in light of the truth about the human person. As we seek to do this, three aspects of same-sex attraction must be considered:

a) the homosexual *inclination*;

b) the homosexual *act*; and

c) the *person* who has a homosexual inclination.

The Homosexual Inclination

The homosexual inclination refers to one's conscious physical attraction toward persons of his or her own sex. Such an attraction, because it inclines a person to engage in acts which are not in harmony with human nature, is misdirected. For this reason, we say that it is an *objectively* disordered inclination. In other words, it is outside the right order of our nature as human persons.

Another way of looking at this is in terms of objectivity and subjectivity. *Objectively speaking*, a man and a woman's bodies are sexually ordered to each other. *Subjectively speaking*, however, a man or a woman might not *feel like* he or she is ordered to a person of the opposite sex. It is this *subjective* tendency of a person to act in a way which is contrary to the *objective* orientation of his or her body that is the disorder to which we refer when we speak of the same-sex orientation or inclination.

From the moment of conception, a person is *physically* male or female, and he or she develops physically until they reach maturity at puberty. Another development, however, must also take place. Every person must develop *psychologically* as a male or female From approximately the age of two and throughout childhood, a person grows in his understanding of his own sexual identity and becomes secure in it. As the child becomes **psychosexually** secure, he or she is able to grow, mature, and develop confidence in relating appropriately to persons of the opposite sex. If, for some reason, the young child does not develop this healthy understanding of his or her sexual identity as male or female, then the same-sex attraction could arise.[20]

The causes of same-sex attraction are not fully known. Despite

---

[20] John F. Harvey, *The Homosexual Person*, pp 38-43.

> NOTES
>
> "Every human person is ontologically (in his or her very being) oriented toward the opposite sex."
> — Christopher West
>
> "In our clinical work over the past 34 years, we have found that the most common cause of same-sex attractions in males is an intense weakness in masculine confidence that is associated with strong feelings of loneliness and sadness."
> — Dr. Richard Fitzgibbons
>
> **Psychosexual** -- of or relating to the mental, emotional, and behavioral aspects of sexual development.

NOTES

"Numerous, rigorous studies of identical twins have now made it impossible to argue that there is a 'gay gene.' If homosexuality were inborn and predetermined, then when one identical twin is homosexual, the other should be, as well. Yet one study from Yale and Columbia Universities found homosexuality common to only 6.7 percent of male identical twins and 5.3 percent of female identical twins."

Mark Hodges,
"Are gays 'born that way'? Most Americans now say yes, but science says no"

"Every person has emotional and developmental needs. If these are properly met by both family and peers, it would be highly unlikely that the homosexual orientation would develop."

Catholic Medical Association, "Homosexuality and Hope"

---

media reports in the early 1990s claiming that scientists had found a genetic cause for same-sex attraction, the truth of the matter is that studies have shown that a person's genes have little to no effect on his sexual orientation.[21] In other words, no one is 'born gay.'

Science tells us that human sexuality and sexual inclination are among the most complex aspects of the human person. Most respected scientists agree that same-sex attraction is due to a combination of social, psychological, and biological factors.[22] The many possible contributing factors to the development of such attractions can vary from person to person; but, as one author points out, it is possible to identify repeated "patterns" that show themselves among persons with same-sex attraction, such as: "sexual trauma, emotional wounds, poor father or mother relationships, poor body image, etc."[23]

Because same-sex attraction is a disorder which a person does not ordinarily freely choose, it is not sinful in itself. In other words, although the same-sex attraction is disordered because it inclines a person toward a disordered act, it is not in itself morally wrong. Rather, it is an inclination, a condition from which the person suffers due to situations beyond his or her control. Same-sex attraction is an *inclination*, not an *act*. Sin is involved only when one freely chooses to act in accord with this inclination and engage in sexual activity not in accord with human nature.

Certainly the homosexual orientation never means that the person himself or herself is "disordered," or that he or she has less value. Precisely because every human person has a dignity beyond compare, it is essential that men or women who experience same sex attraction also experience the love, understanding and compassion that each of us needs in our human lives. In particular, it is important that they receive professional and spiritual help in understanding this inclination within themselves, and come to realize that acting on it (and thus reinforcing it) can**not** lead to genuine human fulfillment and happiness.

It is also important that research continue which will lead to a deeper understanding of the origins of same-sex attraction within a person. Such knowledge will not only lead to understanding, but it will also make it possible to develop ways to help persons experiencing this attraction to understand and overcome its disordered effects.

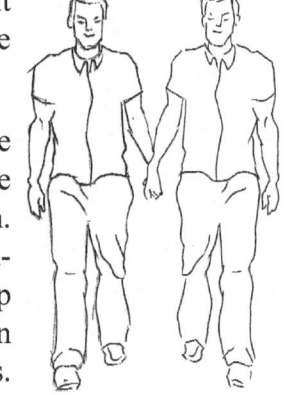

---

[21] N.E. Whitehead, Ph.D., "Latest Twin Study Confirms Genetic Contribution to SSA is Minor," www.narth.com.

[22] Cf. Peter Sprigg and Timothy Dailey, *Getting it Straight: What the Research Shows about Homosexuality,* Family Research Council, 2004, pp. 1-34.

[23] Father Paul Scalia, "Same-sex attractions: Part II - The Church's pastoral response," *Arlington Catholic Herald,* October 13, 2010.

The Homosexual Act

With regard to the homosexual act, one can easily know from natural reason that the act is disordered, i.e., not in accord with human nature. As we have already seen, the natural meaning of the sexual act is to express physically the mutual, total self-giving love of husband and wife. It is an act in which they literally "become one flesh" -- coming together to form "one sexual whole."

In the homosexual act, however, there can be no true sexual union. The two persons do not have complementary male and female bodies enabling them to unite sexually with each other. Certainly there may be some sort of physical union between the homosexual couple, and this may bring about a shared fleeting emotion or physical sensation; but it cannot bear fruit in new life. It is sterile.

We have already made the point that homosexual acts, because they are outside the right order of our nature as human persons, are disordered. The dis-order is clear: two persons of the same sex are simply not able to engage in a sexual act which will truly unite them sexually and bring forth new life. Neither the unitive nor the procreative purposes of the sexual act can be realized by persons of the same sex. Anyone who with full knowledge and freedom chooses to engage in a disordered sexual act sins gravely by doing so.

Living a lifestyle in which one engages in homosexual acts actually defeats the innate human desire for happiness. "Any action that is contrary to the design of the gift of our humanity," writes one author, "is going to put us at cross-purposes with ourselves."[24]

The Person with Homosexual Inclination

In seeking to understand the truth about same-sex attraction, the most important consideration is always the person. Having a sexual attraction to someone of the same sex never means that the person has less value. All human persons have the same inherent dignity. Each individual, without exception, has an unrepeatable worth and is deserving of love and respect. Each individual, without exception -- and with all his or her strengths and weaknesses -- is to be loved and welcomed. Although we cannot condone same-sex activity, it is seriously wrong to say or do anything that conveys unkindness or disrespect toward the persons themselves.

In this regard, it is important that we not refer to persons as "gays" or "homosexuals," as if such words specify who a person *is*. Using these terms as nouns makes them into a sort of identity, as if the

---

NOTES

"It's simply impossible for two people of the same sex to have sex."

Christopher West

"We are born male and female, but we grow into a masculine or feminine character based on a number of different things. I think, in some ways, the most important and really the first one is the way our fathers love our mothers and our mothers love our fathers. ...

"A boy very naturally wants the joy of his father and to be able to see in his father's eyes that his existence, the son's existence, is able to produce that joy."

Father Paul Check,
Executive Director of Courage International

"To love people with same-sex attractions is to love them for their God-given and Christ-redeemed dignity. They are not less than any of the Father's children. Like everyone, they deserve more than sentimentality. They deserve compassion ... compassion founded on the truth of their humanity."

Father Paul Check

---

[24] Father Paul Check, "Homosexuality, Identity and the Grace of Chastity," *Catholic World Report,* Sept. 3, 2013.

NOTES

"Love is important, but not all love is intended to be sexual. Even for the heterosexual only the marital relationship is intended to be sexual."

Dr. Elizabeth Moberly
*Homosexuality:
A New Christian Ethic*

inclination or attraction defines the person. As we have come to see, the human person is a rich and complex being. No person should ever be reduced to an inclination.

To love a person is always to desire his or her true good. Genuine compassion seeks to understand and truly to help others. To love persons with same-sex attraction, one must seek to understand the persons themselves, as well as their suffering. At the same time, if there is the opportunity and openness, one should try compassionately to help them see the truth about their disordered attraction and support them in their efforts to live chaste lives.

Genuine truth and genuine love are never at odds with one another. It is always important that we sincerely seek to maintain love for both the *person* and the *truth*. Happiness lies where truth and love meet.

"...[T]ruth finds its most accurate expression in love -- and the best way to love is in the truth."[25]

Only One Sexual Orientation?

"Although our culture speaks about various "orientations," there is really only one: heterosexual. This is simply another way of expressing the truth that human sexuality is ordered and designed for a purpose. It is oriented toward heterosexual union for procreation and marital bonding. Anything apart from that is a dis-orientation -- meaning it is not oriented to the proper purposes of sexuality.

"Further, once we lose sight of the one orientation of human sexuality, we simply create confusion. We do not end up with two orientations but with sexual chaos. And so now we have a seemingly endless proliferation of 'orientations': gay, straight, bisexual, pansexual, polysexual, transgendered, transsexual, queer, questioning, etc. Again, the rejection of the truth about sexuality has not created freedom but dissolution and disorder."

Fr. Paul Scalia
"Same-Sex Attractions: Part II -- The Church's pastoral response,"
Arlington Catholic Herald, October 13, 2010.

Study Guide Questions:

1. Why is it necessary to understand same-sex attraction within the context of the truths we have been considering about the human person and human sexuality? Why do you think this is especially important in our day?

2. What three essential aspects of this issue must be considered if we want to have a full understanding of the truth?

---

[25] Father Paul Scalia, "Same-Sex Attractions: Part IV -- Fidelity to Both Love and Truth," *Arlington Catholic Herald* (October 27, 2010.)

Part II -- Chapter III
LOVE WORTHY OF THE HUMAN PERSON

3. *How does the ethical evaluation of the same-sex act differ from that of the same-sex attraction?*

4. *In what way is the same-sex act disordered?*

5. *What do we know regarding the cause of the same-sex attraction?*

6. *What is the only appropriate response toward persons with same-sex attraction? Why?*

7. *Explain what it means to say that "...truth finds its most accurate expression in love -- and the best way to love is in the truth."*

CASES IN POINT

#1 -- Shortly after Jim and Renee's youngest child started college, he told them that he had strong sexual desires for other men. As devout Christians, Jim and Renee were shocked and saddened as they listened to their son. They prayed about how they could best help him.

- *What advice would you offer Jim and Renee?*

* * * * *

#2 -- Lexi and Samantha are cousins whose families got together occasionally when they were growing up. Lexi remembers Samantha as being a somewhat quiet girl with a good sense of humor. As young adults, the two cousins have seldom seen each other. Lexi was taken by surprise the other day, however, when she received an invitation from Samantha asking her to attend her "wedding" to another young woman.

- *If you were Lexi, would you attend the "wedding"? Why or why not?*

* * * * *

#3 -- Taken from a letter by a student to her school community: "We are taught to love the sinner but hate the sinful acts he might commit. It seems to me that, when it comes to the issue of homosexuality, this means that we don't call our fellow human beings degrading names - names I've heard in the very hallways of my school, and in our classrooms. I am a girl who has a boyish haircut, just because I like it that way; and I'd rather wear jeans or slacks than skirts. I resent being called disgusting names, even if people think they're just trying to be funny. It's not funny. It's demeaning. My hairstyle and my clothes have nothing to do with my sexual orientation, or with my dignity as a person. I happen to be attracted to guys. Being made fun of like this, though, lets me know from personal experience what it feels like to be put down by others. It's wrong to do that to people. We need to realize the impact that every single thing we say can have on other people."

- *What do you think this student means when she says that what we say has an impact on others? Is her concern valid?*

NOTES

"Truth without love can be hostility, and love without the truth is sentimentality. We must in all things -- and especially in this most controversial issue -- maintain fidelity to the truth and love for the person."

Fr. Paul Scalia

"Compassion should never lead us to compromise what's true, but it should lead us to affirm those with same-sex attraction as human beings."

Christopher West

"Do not accept anything as love which lacks truth."

Edith Stein

NOTES

"On a purely biological level, the human generative faculties are not built to handle homosexual types of acts, acts which cause serious disease, physical damage, or both. It is against the purely physical nature of the human person to engage in homosexual activities."
Mark Lowery

Human Experience and the Deeper Questions

Perhaps it could seem an unfair judgment to claim that living a homosexual lifestyle cannot lead to genuine happiness. This is one reason it is important to be aware that there is objective research which supports, through looking at actual human experience, the principles we are considering.

• Significant professional studies have found that persons involved in homosexual acts are far more likely than married men and women to suffer from:

-- Psychological disorders
-- Ideas of or attempts at suicide
-- Substance abuse and addictions such as those to drugs, alcohol or cigarettes
-- Unstable, unfaithful relationships
-- Health problems, especially cancer and STD's, including HIV
-- Sexual abuse, rape or domestic violence[26]

• Fr. John F. Harvey, the founder of *Courage* and one who has counseled persons with a homosexual orientation for 32 years, said the following: "I have yet to meet a practicing homosexual person who could be called 'gay' in the sense of joyful."

• Other important research[27] indicates a high rate of promiscuity among those who engage in a homosexual lifestyle.

Serious consideration of such findings, rather than leading us to condone homosexual acts and relationships, should rather cause us to ask ourselves deeper questions:

1. *How do such real life experiences offer evidence that these relationships do not lead to fulfillment of the human need for love?*
2. *What is it that these persons are searching for, but not finding?*
3. *What could be the reasons beneath such promiscuity?*

As we become aware of the findings from studies such as these, it is important to keep in mind that authentic compassion never pretends that disordered acts can make us happy. Nothing contrary to our human nature can be truly good for us; nor can it lead to the happiness we seek.

---

[26] Cf. Dale O'Leary, *One Man, One Woman,* N.H.: Sophia Press, 2007.

[27] See, for example, Timothy J. Dailey, Ph.D. "Comparing the Lifestyles of Homosexual Couples to Married Couples," Family Research Council, March 24, 2004; "Development and Validation of the Sexual Agreement Investment Scale," *Journal of Sex Research*, 47:1,24-37, April 2009. [Cf. Joseph Nicolosi, Ph.D., "An Open Secret: The Truth About Gay Male Couples."]; David Morison, *Beyond Gay*, pp. 18-19.

Masturbation and Chastity

By now, we have come to understand more clearly what a tremendous gift we have in our sexual faculties, and how they are an amazing power for self-giving. We have seen, too, that as we discover this capacity that is ours as male and female, we are called to respect our sexual faculties and use them chastely -- that is, in a way that is in keeping with our dignity and their purpose. Valuing our own sexual powers entails using them in the way for which they were designed, never using them in a way that is disordered. To rightly use our sexual powers is to safeguard our ability to give ourselves in true self-giving love.

Masturbation is the deliberate stimulation of the external sex organs without intercourse, with the purpose of producing the highest point of sexual pleasure. Totally directed toward oneself rather than being an act of self-giving, masturbation is a sexual practice that might begin at a time of stress or isolation, or at times of weakness or suffering. Masturbation, nevertheless, is a disorder, for it negates the message of self-giving love that the body is designed to express in the sexual act. Such behavior is potentially addictive, thus contributing to further isolation. Very often motivated by loneliness and fear, this behavior actually points to underlying interior personal problems which need healing before one can truly give oneself in love.

It is important to understand how masturbation is a misuse of one's sexual powers. We have seen that our sexual faculties "invite" us to go out of ourselves in self-giving love. In an act of masturbation, however, one uses these very powers, not to "go out of self" in love, but rather to turn back in on self. It is therefore a *misdirected* practice, ordered to satisfying oneself with pleasure rather than to giving oneself in love. If this behavior grows to be habitual, the gift of self becomes more and more difficult.[28]

Because of confused attitudes toward human sexuality in our society, many see masturbation as harmless, or at least as "better" than such practices as fornication. In reality, however, masturbation causes deep-seated harm to a person, leading to loneliness and isolation. One can eventually become so obsessed with the pleasure of the act

NOTES

"Masturbation is a symbol of fear and anxiety -- of fear to love, of anxiety with regard to other people, withdrawing from them and seeking to live without them."
      Paul Quay

"The one who masturbates feels as a result deep shame, degradation, or inadequacy."
      Paul Quay

"Habitual masturbators ... are addicted to a narcissistic and selfish pleasure which raises an obstacle to their learning to use sex for its real purposes of forming the family community."
      Benedict M. Ashley

"Masturbation ... a personal flight from reality into the prison of lust."
      John F. Harvey

"Given original sin, most adolescents have to learn self-control by rather painful discipline if they are ever to become mature. ... A personal victory over masturbation thus is an important step in the formation of a mature masculine personality and readiness for the responsibilities of fatherhood."
      Benedict M. Ashley

---

[28] Cf. Jordan Aumann and Conrad Baars, MD. *The Unquiet Heart,* N.Y.: Alba House, 1991.

that he or she is totally unmindful of the meaning of real self-giving love for others. In reality, masturbation indicates a fear of love and an anxiety regarding other people, leading one to withdraw from them. Sadly, one begins to live in a sort of fantasy world that is unfortunately devoid of both the demands and joys that genuine love entails.

It is important to note that while masturbation is an *objectively* disordered act, gravely wrong in itself, still the *subjective* guilt within persons who engage in the act varies. If one is fully aware of the serious nature of masturbation and freely consents to it, he is guilty of **mortal sin**. If, however, the person has only partial awareness of the disordered nature of the act or does not give full consent of his will, he commits a **venial sin**. As with any addiction, if the act has become **compulsive**, the person's will is not actually free and personal responsibility is lessened. Immaturity can also play a part in lessening the degree of one's personal responsibility.

A person suffering from any addiction is not free: free to love, to give and to receive. This is certainly true of the addictive behavior of masturbation. Acquiring and growing in the self-discipline needed to overcome this habit is difficult and often requires that the person receive spiritual help and professional counseling.

We see, once again, how genuine human happiness is deeply related to the right exercise of our capacity to give and receive love.

Pornography

Pornography is a visual representation of human sexuality in a way that removes it from the context that is proper to it. Another way to say this is that pornography places human sexuality in a context that is totally devoid of any consideration of the worth of the person as a whole. In and of itself, sexuality is a beautiful aspect of the human person, who is a being of incomparable worth. A focus which removes sexuality from its proper context, however, and considers it only as an object of entertainment or stimulation, degrades both sexuality itself and the human person.

Saint John Paul clarifies for us the nature of the distortion of human sexuality that pornography presents:

> Pornography is a marked tendency to accentuate the sexual element when reproducing the human body or human love in a work of art, with the object of inducing the reader or viewer to believe that sexual values are the only real values of the person, and that love is nothing more than the experience, individual or shared, of those values alone.[29]

---

[29] Karol Wojtyla, *Love and Responsibility*, p. 192.

NOTES

Mortal sin -- "deadly" sin which removes Sanctifying grace from the person's soul.

Venial sin -- sin which harms the life of grace in the person's soul but does not completely remove it.

Compulsive act -- one which results from a strong and irresistible impulse to perform it.

Pornography -- a visual representation of sexuality which distorts a person's understanding of the nature of sex.

Pornography "constitutes a direct attack on significant relationships because it helps create a mind-set that eventually treats all people as sexual objects. Modern pornography is an education system. It teaches. Its message is: human beings are mere animals; the highest value is immediate pleasure; other people may be used and abused and then discarded. It teaches that sex is divorced from love, commitment, morality, and responsibility, that perversion is to be preferred to normality, that women are fair game for anyone who cares to exploit them."
Nancy L. DeMoss,
The Rebirth of America

Part II -- Chapter III
LOVE WORTHY OF THE HUMAN PERSON

Pornography degrades the true meaning of human sexuality and demeans both the person(s) depicted and the person who views it. Pornography distorts the personal value of those who are depicted pornographically. It causes the viewer to treat the person in his mind as a mere *object* for his sexual enjoyment. In so doing, the viewer also withdraws himself from an encounter with real people in the real world and instead turns to a world of fantasy where he is able merely to use people for his sexual pleasure. The beauty in the sexual expression of self-giving love between spouses is lost. Like masturbation, use of pornography easily becomes addictive and causes deep personal harm.

The disordered act of viewing pornography has bad effects on the person viewing it, on the person's family, and on the society in which the person lives.[30]

Bad effects for the person himself:

- Pornography is addictive. The person easily loses the freedom <u>not</u> to view it.

- Pornography desensitizes a person to the distorted view of another human person, so that he then seeks even more perverse distortions.

- Pornography strongly inclines men who use it to view women as commodities, as mere objects for their sexual pleasure.

- Pornography inclines its regular viewers to have a higher tolerance for abnormal sexuality, sexual aggression, and sexual promiscuity.

Bad effects for the family:

- Pornography distances husbands from their wives, both emotionally and sexually, a situation often leading to infidelity and divorce.

- Pornography is often perceived by both spouses as marital infidelity.

- Pornography leads to a loss of interest in good family relations because the person's interest lies elsewhere, in a fantasy life.

Bad effects for the society:

- Teenagers who view pornography are inclined to feel guilt, loss of self-confidence and sexual uncertainty.

---

[30] Patrick F. Fagan, Ph.D., "The Effects of Pornography on Individuals, Marriage, Family and Community," Family Research Council, 2010.

NOTES

"Pornography, by offering an endless harem of sexual objects, hyperactivates the appetitive system. Porn viewers develop new maps in their brains based on the photos and videos they see. Because it is a use-it-or-lose-it brain, when we develop a map area, we long to keep it activated. Just as our muscles become impatient for exercise if we've been sitting all day, so too do our senses hunger to be stimulated."
— Norman Doidge, Psychiatrist

"A nationally representative survey found that 64% of young people, ages 13-24, actively seek out pornography weekly or more often."
— Barna Group
The Porn Phenomenon
2016

Pornhub reports that in 2016, people watched more than an accumulated 500,000 years of pornography on its site. This is roughly 12 porn videos for every man, woman, and child on planet earth.

"Selfish preoccupation with sex prevents the individual from being open to the truth of reality and from finding satisfaction in the unselfish love for another."
— Aumann & Baars

"Disordered acts have bad effects!"

- Pornography leads to an increase in crime and a decrease in property value in the community that surrounds sexually oriented businesses.

- Pornography harms the relationships of men and women.

- Use of pornography leads to the breakdown of marriage, sexual promiscuity, increase in out-of-wedlock births and sexually transmitted diseases.

The disordered act of viewing pornography cannot lead one to the happiness for which every human person longs. In fact, the exact opposite will happen. Those who become addicted to pornography risk the very *loss* of genuine love; and it is love alone which brings true happiness.

Truth in Dating

From all that we have said thus far about the natural meaning of the sexual act, we can easily conclude to what extent a dating couple may *truthfully* be involved in any sexual activity: Not at all! The reasoning is clear:

> In the sexual act a person physically expresses the total self-giving love which he has for his beloved.
> Two people who are not married have not yet given themselves totally to one another.
> Therefore, they should not engage in the sexual act.

Someone might, however, wonder about the legitimacy of other acts which arouse a person sexually but which are not the sexual act itself, for example, certain kinds of kissing and touching? Are acts such as these ever morally permissible for a dating couple?

In order to answer this question, we need to determine what a person is "saying" with his body through these acts. Naturally speaking, the person who touches or kisses another person in such a way as deliberately to stimulate him or her sexually is in truth saying, "I am preparing to engage in the sexual act with you." This is why we often refer to such acts as sexual *fore*play. They are acts people do to prepare themselves for engaging in sexual intercourse.

NOTES

"Pornography perverts the beauty of intimate love proper to marriage. It regards other persons as objects to be used, manipulated and sold. Use of pornography is a serious sin against chastity and the dignity of the human person. It robs us of sanctifying grace, separates us from the vision of God and the goodness of others, and leaves us spiritually empty. Its use has led to broken marriages and loss of families. It can also lead to sexual violence and abuse."

John F. Harvey, O.S.F.S.,
St. Augustine, Freedom of Will, and Pornography, p. 82

"Caresses and embraces are natural preludes to intercourse ... by means of which the couple suitably prepare themselves physically, emotionally, and spiritually for consummation in intercourse."

Paul Quay

"A couple may not use these symbols of love [acts which sexually arouse] primarily for their own gratification and pleasure -- that would be a still greater lie, using these signs of self-giving simply in order to get for themselves."

Paul Quay

Unmarried couples should not be preparing to engage in the sexual act; thus, they should not be doing acts which arouse each other sexually. Even if they never go further and actually engage in the sexual act, it would still be *untruthful* for them to engage in sexual foreplay. In other words, they would be lying to each other with their bodies if they did these "incomplete" sexual acts.

Sexual foreplay is "incomplete" because it arouses and stimulates, but it does not satisfy. In fact, the thrill it brings a person is rather quickly dulled by repetition. This explains why couples tend to go further once they begin sexual foreplay. It is not that their love has grown; it is simply that they are trying to find new and more exciting ways to express their affection.

The following rule can be used to guide the dating couple: Never deliberately sexually stimulate either yourself or another person by anything you say or do. If such stimulation should accidentally occur, it is important that the couple not to consent to it; and that, in the future, they avoid situations in which this stimulation is likely to happen again.

Remember that the purpose of dating is to get to know the other *person*. A person, as we have seen, is an individual of incomparable worth, not an object. Dating is a wonderful time for two persons to come to know one another in a deeper way, appreciating the qualities that make each other unique and worthy of respect. The couple learns to appreciate and take delight in who each of them *is*, as a person. Deliberate sexual stimulation is always out of place until marriage.

Conclusion

Our bodies communicate a message to other people, especially when we use them sexually. They speak for our souls. The *natural* message we communicate with our human sexuality is a message of total self-giving love. Only when we can "speak" this message truthfully should we let our bodies speak it.
This truthfulness in our body's sexual language is key to forming an authentic *communion of persons*, for only in "speaking" truthfully do we act in accord with our own dignity as human persons as well as safeguard the dignity of those with whom we are relating.

NOTES

"These symbols are themselves exciting and tend to draw one toward still more stimulating action."
Paul Quay

"[W]e have been purchased at a price. Therefore glorify God in your bodies."
1Cor. 6:20

Study Guide Questions:

1. How is masturbation a misuse of our sexual powers?

2. In what sense is masturbation more disordered than fornication?

3. What harm does masturbation do?

4. Why do we distinguish between the <u>objective</u> nature of the act of masturbation and a person's <u>subjective</u> guilt for doing the act?

5. What precisely is the sexual disorder involved in pornography?

6. What harm does pornography cause?

7. Is it morally wrong to kiss passionately the person whom you are dating? Explain your answer.

8. Why is it wrong to engage in sexual foreplay if the couple is sure not to go any further in their activity?

9. Why is it important to emphasize that dating is really a time to get to know the other <u>person</u>? Explain.

CASES IN POINT

#1 -- In 1934, the Motion Picture Producers Association gave guidelines for making pictures: a) the sanctity of marriage and the home should be upheld; b) movies should not infer that low forms of sexual relations are accepted or common; c) excessive and lustful kissing and embracing, suggestive postures and gestures should not be shown; d) profanity, using the Lord's name in vain and other offensive words are forbidden. In the 1960's, these guidelines were abandoned.

- *What purpose do such motion picture guidelines serve?*

- *What do you think are the guidelines for making movies today?*

- *If you could, what guidelines would you like to set in place in order to guide those who produce movies today?*

* * * * *

"Art has a right and a duty, for the sake of realism, to reproduce the human body, and the love of man and woman, as they are in reality, to speak the whole truth about them. The human body is an authentic part of the truth about man, just as its sensual and sexual aspects are an authentic part of the truth about human love. But it would be wrong to let this part obscure the whole -- and this is what happens in art.

Saint John Paul II,
Love and Responsibility

Part II -- Chapter III
LOVE WORTHY OF THE HUMAN PERSON

#2 -- Between 1508-1512, Michelangelo painted frescoes on the ceiling of the Sistine Chapel in Rome. Some of these frescoes included naked figures. Over the centuries, painted loin clothes ("modesty drapes") were added to cover the sexual parts of those naked figures. Between 1980-1994, however, as part of the restoration project of the Sistine Chapel, Saint John Paul called for the removal of these painted loin clothes.

- *From what you know about his Theology of the Body, why do you think Saint John Paul wanted the loin clothes removed?*

- *For Saint John Paul, the problem with pornography is not that it reveals too much of a person but that it reveals too little. Explain.*

- *What is the difference between good art which depicts a naked human body and pornography?*

* * * * *

#3 -- Ted Bundy was executed in Florida in 1989 for murdering more than 23 women. Interviewed the day before he died, Bundy explained how he first encountered soft-core pornography when he was 12 or 13 and soon advanced to the "harder" kind which links violence and sex. Once addicted to it, Bundy kept craving something harder. He explained, "You reach that jumping-off point where you begin to wonder if maybe actually doing it will give you that which is beyond just reading about it or looking at it."
Interview with James Dobson

- *Should society ban pornography for the good of its members?*

* * * * *

#4 -- Helen Alvare, a law professor at the Catholic University of America, notes that women bear some responsibility for their being treated as mere objects for a man's consumption. "Women debase themselves in pursuit of the belief that it will lead to union with a man," she said. "This is not confined to the pornography industry, or even to commercial advertising or films or television. Rather, ordinary women across the continent buy clothing designed to emphasize or expose those parts of their bodies associated with sex. Many women often also debase themselves with their speech, or by exposing themselves to media which gradually desensitizes them to the proposal that women are beautiful, sexualized objects for consumption."
Carrie Gress, "Female Objectification Not All Fault of Men," *Zenit*, 2/8/08

- *What do you think of Alvare's claim that women share some responsibility for the fact that some men treat them as mere sex objects?*

- *In what ways do you think teenagers desensitize themselves to the media's portrayal of women as sexualized objects for consumption?*

NOTES

"Pornography affects the most dangerous sex-offender as well as the normal person, and it interferes with interpersonal relationships and personal moral development in *everyone* who uses it, not only the disturbed and demented...."
John Lofton,
The Washington Times, 2/1/89

"Porn viewers develop tolerances so that they need higher and higher levels of stimulation. Thus, they often move to harder, more deviant pornography."
Patrick A. Trueman,
C.E.O of Morality in Media,
11/18/11

"Marital love is meant to be a total giving of oneself to a lifelong, faithful partner. It is a trusting, selfless giving. By contrast, pornographic sex is selfish, demeaning and mechanical."
Patrick A. Trueman,
C.E.O of Morality in Media,
11/18/11

The Human Person ~ Dignity Beyond Compare

NOTES

#5 -- "Contemporary atheist culture views sex as merely a physical act whose purpose is pleasure The result is that people in modern society experience sex with more and more partners, but with less and less love. In the words from a famous 80's song by Tina Turner, "What's love got to do with it? It's physical, only logical." ...

"So the leaders of our culture -- whether in entertainment, journalism, politics, or technology -- practice a form of sexuality that is completely alien to the concepts of self-sacrificial love, exclusivity, and livelong fidelity. ...

"In Scripture, sex is a physical act with a personal meaning. The meaning is a total gift of self. Even in the Old Testament, a sexual act obligated a man to *marry* the woman he slept with *(Exod. 22:16)*. He had to live up to the meaning of the statement he had made with his body; in other words, he had to care for her, provide for her, protect her, and grant her intimate access to his own body, for the rest of his life. The meaning of the sexual act is not conventional (that is, decided by consent of persons in society). The meaning of the sexual act is inherent in itself. The meaning is, at base, *covenantal*. The sexual act is an attempt to make one's partner a member of one's family. By attempting to conceive a child with another person (because that's what the sexual act is -- an attempt to conceive) you are inherently saying: "I take you as my spouse -- I want to have and raise children with you." ...

"Sex has a spiritual dimension -- it is the uniting of persons, not just bodies."

John Bergsma, *The Sacred Page*, 1/15/2021

♦ Why do you think Dr. Bergsma considers any sexual act outside the context of a life-long, exclusive, covenantal relationship between one man and one woman to be immoral?

♦ Why is this the only appropriate context for the conception and bearing of children?

Point to Consider:

"True lovers have always sensed
how much pain their choice
steadfastly to love any human creature exposes them to.
The Christian discovers the full depth of this connection
in the cross of Christ.
There we see what Love suffers
for the sake of those who are loved....
Let us look long in faith at the crucifix.
There we will see what true love is.
We will see that which united Christ with His Church.
We will learn what it costs, indeed, to be husband or wife;
but at the same time we will gain from Him
the power and strength to pay what is needed."

Paul Quay, <u>The Christian Meaning of Human Sexuality</u>, pp. 83-84

Conclusion

We have come to see that, as human persons, we cannot live without love. This is true of us by our very nature. It was in a specific act of love that each of us came into existence; and it was through the loving care of parents and family that we took our first steps in life and began to grow and develop. From family relationships, we began to enter into other relationships -- especially those with classmates and friends. From receiving love, we learned to return love and give of ourselves. In this way, we came to know ourselves - and to experience the fact that, as human persons, we are by nature beings who are from, with and for others.

Without experiencing love, (that is, both receiving and giving love), we cannot understand ourselves and cannot be fulfilled as persons. We become "closed in on ourselves." When one is genuinely loved by another, he (or she) comes to experience his own worth or goodness. The genuine love of others communicates to us that we are loveable -- that is, we are worthy of love because we are good, not because of what we say or do, etc., but good *in ourselves*, in our very being. Realizing this goodness about ourselves, we are able to go out of ourselves to enjoy the good in others, or even in the world itself. Knowing one's own goodness through the experience of being loved is the key that "unlocks" a person and sets him free to move out beyond himself.

Knowing and loving ourselves enables us to go out of ourselves in love for others, for when we love ourselves, we realize that we have something worthwhile to offer. Loving another even gives meaning to suffering, because suffering can be an expression of love.

Experiencing love (being on the giving end of it) is also key to our happiness, because not until we love someone besides ourselves will we find "more good to love." The will is always looking for more good. In fact, the will is looking for a good that is infinite. Loving another (or others) gives a person something for which to live and to die, especially if the Good is Infinite!

Love, then, is part of our dignity as human persons, a dignity beyond compare. As we mature in our ability to receive and give love, and seek to love generously and responsibly, we come to be more deeply who we are.

NOTES

Appendix A:

AWARD-WINNING ESSAY

by Krista Shaw

It is ironic that I thought I was a slave to other people's ideas and principles before I learned about Theology of the Body, because in reality, I was a slave to myself.

I had been brought up in a steady, very traditional home, and I resented the rules of morality that my family, church, and school held, classing them as old-fashioned, judgmental, and out of touch. Part of the problem was that I was offered no real reason to prove that a life of virtue was the only authentic way to live. Instead, I heard negative reasons to prevent me from doing the opposite, what I felt was fun and normal. When sex was mentioned, it would invariably be hinted at with dark glances and threatening words about getting pregnant and contracting STDs. I was repeatedly lectured on purity and modesty, but I was never told why they were so important for love. Soon I had learned to associate the concept of purity with prudishness, and I assumed that modesty was for people who did not have any fashion sense. The way of life I had been taught seemed boring and strange. Besides, I was sure that the common lifestyle of the world was a quick way to find love and happiness. I so wanted to feel validated by the love of another person, but I did not even understand other people, myself, or love.

I spent my first year of high school rebelling against my parents, feeling insecure about friendships and relationships, and struggling with a sense of the meaninglessness of life. Nothing mattered to me except feeling loved and important, but since neither of these desires was ever met, I had given them up as idealized, impossible daydreams.

At my Catholic High School, The Human Person was a required class my sophomore year. I walked into the classroom with preconceptions about people trying to take away my freedom and narrow-minded teachers "forcing their morality" on me, but I was soon surprised when we began discussing Theology of the Body.

First came the realization that I was settling for less than I deserved and for less than I should have demanded from myself. Theology of the Body taught me to value myself as a part of God's creation, a woman entrusted with so many gifts and responsibilities. I learned that humans are created with the desire for relationships that I had so often experienced. I soon saw that healthy relationship should be seen as an opportunity to give to another person, not a means of making myself feel special. I had previously allowed people to use me in various ways, and I had pretended like their behavior did not hurt me because they told me that they loved me. Now, I knew enough to respect my own dignity and demand the same treatment from others. I also saw that I had ignored Pope John Paul II's personalistic norm in my treatment of other people because I had viewed people as objects, using them to feel good about myself, and not seeing them as subjects who deserve love.

Now that I can see humans as inestimably valuable, I can look at my life and my relationships with different eyes. Suddenly, my life takes on immense meaning because my personhood shows me I was designed for true, fulfilling, self-giving love. Since I know the value of others, I now know that in my relationships, I must try to reflect the love Christ showed on the cross by sacrificing my own wishes for the good of the other person.

Through Theology of the Body, I soon began to understand that my body was not dirty or shameful, but it was actually one of my greatest gifts. I learned that my body and soul are united to form my person, and the Holy Spirit resides inside my body. Rather than thinking that my actions are not associated with who I am, I have begun to see that my actions are my body's way of speaking, and it is just as important to be truthful with what my body says as it is to tell the truth while talking aloud. Because I saw that the language the body speaks is so meaningful and the body itself is a wonderful gift, it was obvious to me that physical affection should also be guarded as a great prize. It is not because sex is terrible or vulgar that unmarried people should avoid engaging in it. On the contrary, it is because sex is so sacred, that it is only appropriate in certain situations. The important gift of one's body must be bestowed upon a worthy recipient, and because the gift is total, it can only be for one person. The language of the body speaks a vow of complete faithfulness and commitment, and therefore, a couple must be married to confirm the promise their bodies are making. It is only in this situation that the union of two people can express true love and bear fruit, because there is no selfishness or deception, there is only truth.

When I finally understood the reasons for the proper context of sex, I could not deny the logic of the Catholic Church. I was no longer subjected to the lies that the world around me advocated, and I was instead freed from the prevalent culture of selfishness and deception. More importantly, I was free from my own false opinions. I was free of the constant anger of rebellion, the pressure of wanting to feel good about myself, and the pain of leading an empty, seemingly pointless life.

Through Theology of the Body, I learned to treat everyone, including myself, as a human person deserves. I understand now that people must be loved because of who they are, not because of what they can do. I also discovered that because my body is such a wonderful creation, it must be saved for one deserving person. If I give myself away too quickly, I know I will be lying with my body, and I see that lying can only hinder relationships, but the truth will fulfill me and give me the chance to share my love.

Now, I am waiting for the man that deserves my total gift of self, but I am not afraid or bored or sad. I can only be happy because I am free from slavery and open to love.

Krista Shaw was awarded a $750 scholarship
for her second place winning essay.
Krista was a 2011 graduate of
Saint John Paul the Great Catholic High School,
Dumfries, Virginia.

Appendix B:

Pope Saint John Paul the Great to the People of the United States of America:

For this reason, America, your deepest identity and truest character as a nation is revealed in the position you take toward the human person. The ultimate test of your greatness is the way you treat every human being, but especially the weakest and most defenseless ones.

The best traditions of your land presume respect for those who cannot defend themselves. If you want equal justice for all and true freedom and lasting peace, then, America, defend life! All the great causes that are yours today will have meaning only to the extent that you guarantee the right to life and protect the human person.

Feeding the poor and welcoming refugees. Reinforcing the social fabric of this nation. Promoting the true advancement of women. Securing the rights of minorities. Pursuing disarmament, while guaranteeing legitimate defense.

All this will succeed only if respect for life and its protection by the law are granted to every human being from conception until natural death.

Every human person -- no matter how vulnerable or helpless, no matter how young or old, no matter how healthy, handicapped or sick, no matter how useful or productive for society -- is a being of inestimable worth created in the image and likeness of God. This is the dignity of America, the reason she exists, the condition for her survival -- yes, the ultimate test of her greatness: to respect every human person, especially the weakest and most defenseless ones, those as yet unborn.

September 19, 1987

Appendix C:

Important Thinkers Referred to in the Text

(in chronological order)

Plato (427-347 B.C.) - Plato, Socrates and Aristotle, form the "triad" of ancient Greek philosophical thought; Plato is commonly associated with his allegory of the cave which is found in his work, *The Republic*.

Aristotle (384-322 B.C.) Philosopher, student of Plato; his philosophical concept of hylomorphism (all material things are comprised of both matter and form) influenced many to come after him, including Saint Thomas Aquinas.

St. Augustine (A.D. 354-430) - Bishop, Doctor of the Church, gifted speaker and prolific writer, including *The Confessions* and *City of God*.

St. Albert the Great (1200-1280) - Dominican bishop, Doctor of the Church, patron of scientists. Teacher of St. Thomas Aquinas. He combined interest and skill in natural science with proficiency in all branches of philosophy and theology.

St. Thomas Aquinas (1225-1274) Dominican priest, philosopher/theologian, best known for his 5 part work, the *Summa Theologiae*, often touted as the gold-standard of theological works.

Edith Stein *(Saint Teresa Benedicta of the Cross)* 1891-1942 - German-Jewish philosopher, convert to Catholicism, Carmelite Nun, died a martyr in Auschwitz, canonized by John Paul II in 1998.

Pope Saint John Paul the Great - (1920-2005) born Karol Wotyla in Poland, elected Pope in 1978 and canonized in 2014. Before and during his vocation to the priesthood, he was a philosopher, teacher, and writer. His pontificate is lovingly remembered by millions for his vigorous defense of life, his affirmation of traditional Catholic teachings, his love for the Gospel and his tireless efforts in promoting the Good News of Jesus Christ around the globe.

Pope Benedict XVI - (1927-   ) born Joseph Ratzinger in Germany, theologian, university professor, and prolific author; elected Pope in 2005, succeeding Saint John Paul the Great.

Glossary

Abortifacient -- a substance or device used to induce abortions.

Abstract - from the Latin *abstrahere*, "to bring forth" or "to draw away;" to separate a substance from its non-essential accidents. The "abstract" concept which is formed by the process is the essence of the thing without any concrete particularities.

Accident - that which is able to exist only in another; it requires a substance in which to inhere.

Accidental change - change in accidental form only; non-essential change because the substance remains the same; change in the manner in which a substance exists.

Accidental form - that which makes a substance exist in a particular manner.

Accidentally ordered causal series - a series of causes that are able to act independently of one another.

Active intellect - that aspect of the human intellect which is always activated and which has the power to abstract the essence of a thing from the completed sense image (the phantasm).

Actuality - having real existence; the opposite of the merely possible.

Adultery -- sexual intercourse between two persons, one of whom is married to someone else.

Angel - a completely immaterial creature.

Angelicum - comes from the title by which St. Thomas Aquinas is often known: Angelic Doctor. It is the name of a University in Rome, the University of St. Thomas Aquinas.

Annulment -- a judgment by the Church that an apparent marriage was in fact never a true marital covenant.

Appetite - from the Latin *appetitus*, "natural desire;" an active tendency within a being towards a goal that is proper to it.

Being - existing; whatever exists; contrasted with nonbeing and with becoming.

Benedictine - the religious order of both men and women following the Rule of St. Benedict of Nursia, which began in the first half of the sixth century. Their Rule of life emphasizes obedience to superiors, the importance of the balance between liturgical prayer and manual labor, and the value of community life. The Benedictine Rule is the foundation for monasticism in the Western Church.

Fickle -- characterized by erratic changeableness or instability.

Final cause -- the end, goal, or purpose of a thing. It answers the question why a thing exists and why the agent (efficient cause) acted.

Finite - from the Latin *finere*, "to limit;" having a limit or end point.

Form - the essence of a thing, the determining principle of a physical thing that makes it to be the kind of thing that it is. Form can be either substantial or accidental.

Fornication - the sexual act between two persons who are not married.

Holy See - term for the central government of the Catholic Church. The word "see" comes from the Latin *sedes*, "chair." The chair was an ancient symbol of authority.

Hylomorphism - the Aristotelian doctrine that all material beings are comprised of both form and matter. In living material beings, the form is called "soul" and the matter is called "body."

Immaterial - from the Latin *immaterialis*; "not matter;" without matter.

Immortal - from the Latin *immortalis*, "not subject to death;" the unending continued existence of life.

Incarnate - taken from the Latin *incarnare*, "to make into flesh;" to be embodied in flesh or to be given a body.

Infinite - from the Latin *infinire*, "not to limit;" unlimited; inexhaustible; endless.

Inherent - existing in someone or something as a permanent and inseparable element, quality, or attribute.

Integrate -- from Latin *integrare* (to restore); to bring together into a whole.

Intellect - from the Latin *intus*, "within" and *legere*, "to read;" the knowing power in human beings which is able to grasp the essences of physical beings.

Intelligible aspects - the aspects of a thing which only the intellect can know.

Internal senses - the common sense, imagination, memory, and cogitative (estimative) sense.

Intra-uterine devices -- foreign bodies introduced into a woman's uterus to prevent implantation of the human embryo.

Intrinsic - from the Latin *intrinsecus*, "inward;" in and of itself, or essentially. It is the opposite of *extrinsic*, meaning external or unessential.

Introspection - from the Latin *intro*, "inwardly," "within," "into" and *specere*, "to look." It refers to the practice of looking into -- giving mental attention to -- one's mental states and functions in an attempt to describe, study, or enjoy them.

Glossary

Irascible appetite - sense appetite whose object is the difficult good or evil which is sensed.

Locomotion - movement from one place to another; a sensitive power of the soul.

Lust -- indulging in disordered sexual desire which treats another person as a mere object.

Magisterium - from the Latin *magister*, "teacher;" the teaching authority of the Catholic Church regarding all matters pertaining to salvation. The Church's bishops in union with the Pope, as successors to the apostles, are charged with the sacred duty of passing on the truth and interpreting faithfully those teachings that come from Sacred Scripture and Sacred Tradition.

Marital act -- the act which is proper to persons who are married: the act of sexual intercourse wherein the two sexually incomplete persons so fully give themselves to each other that they form one sexual organism.

Marriage -- the union of a man and a woman who have publicly consented to share their whole lives in a type of relationship oriented toward the begetting, nurturing, and educating of children together.

Masturbation -- deliberate stimulation of the external sex organs without sexual intercourse so as to produce orgasm.

Material soul - the souls of plants and animals which, although they are immaterial in themselves, are completely dependent upon the matter with which they are united.

Matter - the receptive principle of a physical thing; that out of which a physical being is made. Matter can be either *secondary* or *primary*.

Monogamy -- having only one wife at a time.

Moral - having to do with human activities that are free and that are in conformity to God's will.

Mortal sin -- "deadly" sin which removes Sanctifying grace from the person's soul.

Motion - the reduction of potency to actuality.

Natural law -- man's ability to understand how he ought to act based simply on his own understanding of his human nature.

Nature - the essence of a thing which it has from its beginning; what a thing is.

Novitiate - the period of formation and testing of those desiring to enter a religious community.

Nuptial -- from Latin *nuptialis* (wedding); of or relating to marriage.

Nuptial meaning of the body -- that man's body is a sign of his call and capacity for making a total and irrevocable *gift of self* to another; this is how human spousal love images the spousal love between Christ and the Church.

Object -- from Latin *obicere* (to throw before); something perceptible, especially to the sense of touch or vision.

Objective - (related to object) whatever is determined by the object or based on the object. The term is often used in contrast to the *subjective*, i.e., to what is based on the subject.

Original -- from the Greek word *arche,* which signifies both a temporal beginning and the foundations of a building.

Original nakedness -- the condition of man in which his unclothed body does not cause him to feel sexual shame; man's ability to discern the dignity of the human body, viewing it as an expression of the person.

Original sin - the sin of the first human beings, Adam and Eve, resulting from their choice to disobey God. Original sin is an inherited condition common to all mankind.

Original solitude -- man's foundational openness to God in which he realizes his sonship and his complete partnership with Him.

Original unity -- the original communion of Adam and Eve in the garden in their being created male and female.

Paradigm -- an example serving as a model; pattern.

Passions - from the Latin *pati,* "to undergo." The passions are movements of the sensitive appetite.

Passive intellect - that aspect of the human intellect which waits to be activated by the abstracted nature of the sensed object. It is the knowing power which forms the universal concept.

Percept - the image of the sensed object which is formed by the common sense.

Permanent vegetative state - the condition of a person who has shown -- for over a year's time -- no evident sign of self-awareness or of awareness of the environment, and seems unable to interact with others or to react to specific stimuli.

Person - from the Latin *persona*, "a mask used by actors," a "role;" in theology: a being who is essentially relational; in philosophy: an individual substance of a rational nature.

Personalistic Norm -- the standard by which one should treat every human person: Never use a human person as a mere means to an end.

Phantasm - the completed sense image which is produced by the imagination.

Philosophy - the study of reality, focusing on its ultimate causes. This knowledge can be arrived at through natural reason. Philosophy is literally translated as "love of wisdom."

The Pill -- a chemical contraceptive which uses the hormones estrogen and progesterone to suppress a woman's normal cycle.

Polyandry -- having more than one husband at a time.

Polygamy -- having more than one wife at a time.

Pontifical - the adjectival form of the word "Pontiff," from the Latin *pontem facere*, "to build a bridge." The title "Pontiff" or "Supreme Pontiff" is used in reference to the Pope, the person who is the chief "bridge-builder" on earth between God and man.

Pornography -- a visual representation of sexuality which distorts a person's understanding of the nature of sex.

Potency - the capacity or ability of a thing to be actualized, e.g., a slab of marble has the potency to be a statue. The opposite of *actuality*.

Prime matter - the "matter" which substantial form actualizes; pure potentiality; the principle of receptivity in every physical thing.

Principle - from the Latin *principium*, "beginning;" the source or origin of something; that from which a thing comes into being.

Priory - the houses of monastic orders that are governed by religious superiors who are called priors or prioresses.

Privation - the lack of a good or condition which ought to be present.

Promiscuous -- from the Latin *promiscuus* (mixed up); characterized by indiscriminate mingling or association, especially having sexual relations with a number of partners on a casual basis.

Proper object - the end or goal of a power of a soul; that in reality which the powers of the soul were designed to know.

Psychosexual -- of or relating to the mental, emotional, and behavioral aspects of sexual development.

Psychosomatic - from the Latin *psyche*, "soul," and *soma*, "body;" having to do with the body-soul union.

Rational - from the Latin *ratio*, "reason." It refers to the human way of thinking because our minds move in a step-by-step fashion from understanding one idea to understanding another one, to understanding a third. It is as if we come to knowledge in "piece-meal" fashion. Sometimes the word "rational" is used interchangeably with "intellectual," but strictly speaking they have different meanings.

Rational powers - the intellect and free will.

Reason - the power of reasoning; an activity of the intellect whereby it moves from knowing one truth to knowing another, and from the knowledge of these two, it comes to know a third truth.

Reciprocity -- from Latin *reciprocare* (to move back and forth); a reciprocal relationship, one which involves a mutual give and take of something.

Revelation - the manifestation of the hidden by God, as a result of the personal word and witness of God Himself (via the Prophets, Scripture and Tradition).

Sacred Tradition - From the Latin meaning "handing over." The teachings and practices handed down, whether in oral or written form, separately from but not independent of Sacred Scripture.

Secondary matter - matter which exists because it has already received a substantial form.

Sensitive nature - relating to the five senses -- sight, hearing, taste, touch, smell.

Sense appetites - an active tendency within a being towards an object that the senses present to it. The two sense appetites are call the Concupiscible and the Irascible appetites. The various movements of the sense appetites are called emotions or passions.

Sexual Shame -- the tendency to conceal sufficiently our sexual values from others so that the value of the person is not obscured by them.

Sexual urge -- the basic impulse toward a person of the opposite sex for the purpose of sexual fulfillment.

Shamelessness -- the lack of shame when there is a need for it; at odds with the demands of sexual modesty.

Sin - the voluntary decision to act contrary to God's moral law.

Soul - in Latin *anima*, "living;" the first principle of life; the substantial form of a body which has the potency to be alive; the form of a living physical being.

Spermicides -- substances inserted vaginally prior to intercourse to prevent pregnancy.

Spiritual soul - one which has both an activity and an existence that is free of matter.

Subject -- from Latin *sub* (below) + *jacere* (to throw); the mind or thinking part as distinguished from the object of thought.

Subsequent - occurring or coming later or after; following in order.

Subsistent - able to exist independently or on its own.

Substance - that which is able to exist in and for itself and not in another.

Substantial change - change in substantial form; change in the essence of a thing whereby the substance itself changes.

Substantial form - that which makes a thing exist on its own, as a substance.

Summa Theologiae - literally, "a summary of theology;" an exhaustive five-part work that is St. Thomas Aquinas' great gift to the Church and which is still widely studied and quoted.

Theology - the study of God and things pertaining to the divine, using both faith and reason.

Thomist - one who accepts St. Thomas Aquinas' philosophical outlook.

Trinity - The central doctrine of the Christian Faith, which states that the one God is a communion of three Divine Persons -- Father, Son, and Holy Spirit -- who share one nature. The three Divine Persons are co-equal, co-eternal, and consubstantial, and are to receive the same worship.

Truth - conformity of the mind with reality: I know the truth when what I have in my mind matches objective reality. St. Thomas argues that truth is universal, immutable and can be known by human beings who diligently seek it.

Tubal ligation -- the severing or blocking of a woman's fallopian tubes to disrupt the movement of the egg to the uterus for fertilization.

Universal - from the Latin *unus*, "one," and *vertere*, "to turn;" the idea of the many "turned or combined into one." A universal concept is one which applies to many instances of it in reality.

Unrequited -- not repaid or not given in return.

Vasectomy -- a surgical procedure which severs and seals a man's vas deferens tubes to prevent sperm from entering the seminal stream.

Vegetative activities - reproduction, growth, and nutrition. These activities occur in all living beings, including human beings, and take place without conscious control.

Venial sin -- sin which harms the life of grace in the person's soul but does not completely remove it.

Viaticum - From Latin, meaning "provisions for a journey." The term is used by the Church for giving the Holy Eucharist to those who are about to die. Viaticum as Food for the passage through death to eternal life.

Will - a free and active tendency within a being towards or away from an object that the intellect presents to it. It is also called the *intellectual* or *rational appetite*.

Zygote - the single cell phase of a new human being that is formed through the process of fertilization.

Emonet, Pierre-Marie, O.P. *The Greatest Marvel of Nature, An Introduction to the Philosophy of the Human Person.* New York: The Crossroad Publishing Company, 2000.

Fagan, Patrick F., Ph.D. "The Effects of Pornography on Individuals, Marriage, Family and Community." Family Research Council, December, 2009.

Fasano, Jerome W. (quoted by Gretchen R. Crowe in "Cohabitation: Is it still 'living in sin'?" *Arlington Catholic Herald,* Sept. 9-15, 2010, p. 12.)

Finn, Bishop Robert W. *Blessed Are the Pure in Heart: A Pastoral Letter on the Dignity of the Human Person and the Dangers of Pornography.* New Haven, CT: Knights of Columbus Supreme Council, 2007.

Harvey, John F., O.S.F.S. *The Homosexual Person ~ New Thinking in Pastoral Care.* San Francisco, CA: Ignatius Press, 1987.

Harvey, John F., O.S.F.S. *Homosexuality and the Catholic Church.* West Chester, PA: Ascension Press, 2007.

Harvey, John F., O.S.F.S. "Saint Augustine, Freedom of Will, and Pornography," *Linacre Quarterly,* February, 2010, pp. 81-91.

International Theological Commission, "Communion & Stewardship: Human Persons Created in the Image of God," 2002.

Joubert, J. *Pensees.* Paris: Didier, 1883.

Kasun, Jacqueline R. "Population Questions," International Humanae Vitae Conference, July 27, 1993.

Lawler, Philip F. "The Price of Virtue," *The Catholic World Report,* July, 1997, p. 35.

Lewis, C.S. "Letter to a Mr. Masson (March 6, 1956)," Wade Collection, Wheaton College, Wheaton, Ill.

Lickona, Tom and Judy. "How to Tell Your Children the Truth About Sex," *New Oxford Review,* November 1996, pp. 22-28.

Lowery, Mark. "The Knot that Can't Be Tied," *Envoy,* Premier Issue, pp. 39-43.

Maritain, Jacques. *Creative Intuition in Art and Poetry.* New York, NY: Pantheon Books, 1953.

McInerny, D. Q. *Philosophical Psychology.* Elmhurst, PA: The Alcuin Press, 1999.

Moberly, Elizabeth. "Counselling the Homosexual," in *The Expository Times,* June, 1985.

Mohler, R. Albert, Jr. "Facing the Facts about the Decline of Marriage," *Christian Post,* 9/15/2003.

Morrison, David. *Beyond Gay.* Our Sunday Visitor, 1999.

Mosher, Steven W. "The US Government and the War on Population," *The Catholic World Report,* January 1999. pp. 36-40.

Paul, Pamela. *Pornified: How Pornography Is Transforming Our Lives, Our Relationships, and Our amilies.* Barnes & Noble, 2006.

Pitre, Brant. *Jesus the Bridegroom: The Greatest Love Story Ever Told,* New York: Penguin Random House, 2014.

Pope Benedict XVI, "The Changing Identity of the Individual," an address to members of an interacademic conference in Paris, January 28, 2008.

Pope Benedict XVI, "Address to Catholic Educators of the United States," April 17, 2008.

Pope, Msgr. Charles. "The body God gave us doesn't lie: a meditation on the sexual confusion of our day," Lifesitenews.com. June 4, 2015.

Pope, Msgr. Charles. "The modern age hates anger, but I say we need more of it," *Lifesitenews.com*. April 12, 2006.

Pope Paul VI, *Humanae Vitae*.

Quay, Paul M., S.J., *The Christian Meaning of Human Sexuality*, San Francisco: Ignatius Press, 1985.

Ratzinger, Joseph Cardinal. (Pope Benedict XVI) "Concerning the Notion of Person in Theology," *Communio* 17 (Fall, 1990), pp. 439-454.

Ratzinger, Joseph Cardinal. (Pope Benedict XVI) God and the World ~ A Conversation with Peter Seewald, San Francisco: Ignatius Press, 2002.

Scalia, Paul. "Same-sex attractions: Part II - The Church's pastoral response," *Arlington Catholic Herald*, October 13, 2010.

Schneible, Ann. "Multipurpose Theology of the Body. ~ Janet Smith Speaks of Digging Deeper Into John Paul II's Contribution." November 1, 2011. www.zenit.org/article-33848?!=english

Sheed, Frank. *Theology and Sanity*. New York: Sheed & Ward, Inc., 1964.

Smith, Janet. "Children: the Supreme Gift of Marriage."

Smith, Janet. "Humanae Vitae: A Generation Later." http://www.goodmorals.org/smith6.htm.

Smith, Wesley J. "Nihilism as Compassion," *Catholic World Report,* April, 2010, pp. 26-29.

Sri, Edward. *Men, Women and the Mystery of Love: Practical Insights from John Paul II's* Love and Responsibility. Cincinnati, Ohio: Servant Books, 2007.

Trueman, Patrick A. "The pornographic pandemic -- we are awash in porn," www.lifesitenews.com, Nov. 18, 2011.

Van den Aardweg, Gerard J. M., Ph.D. "On the Psychogenesis of Homosexuality," *The Linacre Quarterly,* Volume 78, Number 3. August, 2011, pp. 330-354.

Vann, Gerald, O.P. *The Son's Course*. London: Collins Clear-Type Press, 1959.

West, Christopher. *The Love that Satisfies*, West Chester, PA: Ascension Press, 2007.

Wilhelmsen, Frederick D. *Man's Knowledge of Reality: An Introduction to Thomistic Epistemology.* New York: Preserving Christian Publications, Inc., 1990.

Wojtyla, Karol. *Love & Responsibility.* New York: Farrar, Straus and Giroux, Inc., 1981.

Wills, Susan E. "Nicholas Kristof and Toddlers: When You Really Need a Fact Checker, The Witherspoon Institute, Nov. 9, 2011.

Whitehead, N.E., Ph.D., "Latest Twin Study Confirms Genetic Contribution to SSA is Minor," www.narth.com.